NINE

HILLS

TO

NAMBONKAHA

———

HENRY

HOLT

AND

COMPANY

—————

NEW YORK

NINE

HILLS

TO

NAMBONKAHA

———

*Two Years in the Heart
of an African Village*

———

SARAH

ERDMAN

Henry Holt and Company, LLC
Publishers since 1866
115 West 18th Street
New York, New York 10011

Henry Holt® is a registered trademark of
Henry Holt and Company, LLC.

Library of Congress Cataloging-in-Publication Data
Erdman, Sarah.
    Nine hills to Nambonkaha : two years in the heart of an African village /
Sarah Erdman.—
    1st ed.
      p. c.m.
    ISBN: 0-8050-7381-7.
    1. Nambonkaha (Côte d'Ivoire)—Social life and customs.   2. Erdman, Sarah.
3. Peace Corps (U.S.)—Côte d'Ivoire—Nambonkaha—Biography.   I. Title.
DT545.9.N36E73 2003
966.68—dc21   2003044955

FIRST EDITION 2003

Designed by Fritz Metsch

Printed in the United States of America

1   3   5   7   9   10   8   6   4   2

FOR

MY PARENTS

AND FOR

BILLY DIDIEGO—

radiant, good, and gold
around the edges

*The world will freely offer
itself to you to be unmasked,
it has no choice, it will roll
in ecstasy at your feet.*

—KAFKA

CONTENTS

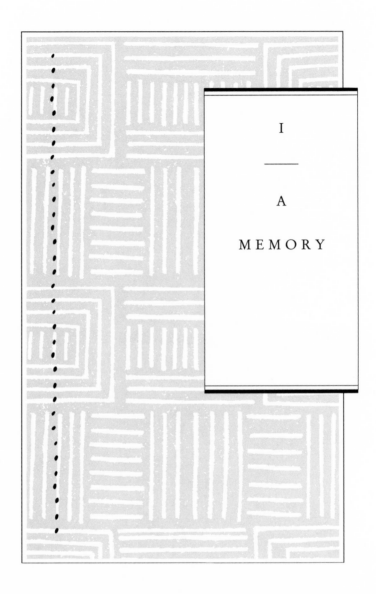

I

—

A

MEMORY

A single lantern filled the room with flickering light, throwing Fanta's shadow toward the door. The glow bronzed her tight cheekbone, her deflated breast, her moving stomach. There was not a cushion in sight, not a sheet, not a bar of soap, not a bucket of water. There was just the hard mud floor to support this woman struggling through labor. I could only think of the blinding fluorescence of the American delivery ward: the blankets, pink or blue, the menu of painkillers, doctors in white coats, white gloves, the hard white hospital light. How much different it was here in the hushed, dark tension of the hut.

From the start of my two years as a health worker in rural Côte d'Ivoire, I'd known that trust would be vital to my work. But that meant a certain degree of assimilation, which is not always easy—especially for an educated Western woman living in a tiny, traditional, West African village on the cusp of change.

The early days were rife with small talk and polite misunderstandings. I wanted so much to get past it all, to connect on a deeper level with the people I was supposed to be helping. The waiting was hard. But that night, about two months after I arrived in the village of Nambonkaha, it became apparent that the villagers were just as eager to bring me into the fold.

I was tinkering with dusty cans of food, trying to summon the creativity to make dinner, when a breathless man appeared at the screen door.

"Come!" he said, his eyes wild. "My wife's stomach hurts."

"What's wrong? Is she throwing up?"

"No!" he cried. "A baby is coming out!"

I knew nothing about childbirth. "Why have you come for me?" I asked, steadying the rising panic in my voice. I'd been dispelling myths of my medical expertise ever since I'd arrived. He answered, in his tattered French, "My wife—she said to find you." Suddenly my ignorance just seemed an excuse: the fear on his face persuaded me. I strapped on my headlamp, grabbed my *Birthing for Midwives* manual, and followed him into the night.

The man led me to a courtyard not far from my own, then pointed to a dimly lit doorway. *"Pei ba,"* he told me in Niarafolo, the local language. They're there. And then he was swallowed into the shadows. Low voices came from inside the hut—creaking, scratchy ones—and my pulse slowed as I listened. Tonight this birth would not depend on me. The elders were there. For centuries, the village has relied on its grandmothers, its *vieilles*, to deliver its babies. One of the old women, a friend who sold salt at the village market, beckoned me from the doorway. "Come look," she said.

My neighbor Fanta sat naked on the dirt floor. She seemed so calm despite all the women pacing around her. The salt seller stood straight, arms akimbo, a presence far greater than her four and a half feet warranted. Her jaw rotated in slow circles around a cheekful of snuff. I could tell right away she knew I had not seen this before. The other old women scrambled to find me a stool, urged me to sit. I couldn't yet speak Niarafolo well enough to say much. I had learned many phrases, but none applied to childbirth. We communicated with hands and eyebrows.

Crouched on the stool, I opened my book to find the right page, but there were hundreds of pages about childbirth, and Fanta's labor wouldn't slow for me to catch up. Pain crumpled her face in waves. I had only known Fanta as a pregnant woman, but that night, as the baby shifted downward, her scrawniness was suddenly apparent. A shoulder jutted out grotesquely above her hip and I realized I could trace the baby's progress through her thin flesh. I riffled through the pages of my trusty manual, but instead of answers, I found a whole catalog of causes for panic. The salt seller rasped orders to the others, chomping vigorously on her tobacco, shaking her head.

One woman grabbed Fanta's belly from behind and rocked it vigorously, as if she could shake out the baby. Suddenly there was blood pooling on the floor. So much blood! Fanta's teeth flashed in a grimace, and then she clamped her lips together. She seemed so strong, but I was scared—this might be the end of Fanta, and I, the ostensibly trained one, was a helpless spectator. My teeth carved up the inside of my lip; I watched anxiously, feeling useless. The bloody prelude gave way to a pale patch of skull, visible just under the bright pink scar where Fanta had been circumcised.

The swollen head emerged slowly, and then the neck—noosed with a blue umbilical cord. I turned back to my book, trying frantically to find this particular complication. After the tense and sluggish delivery of the head, the rest of the baby slid right out, flopping against a cloth on the ground. I was used to scenes of babies smacked and screaming seconds out of the womb. This one lay still, translucent and whiter than me. The hut filled with our breathing. The salt seller poured water on his chest in a thin stream to check his reflexes. Nothing. Fanta lay on her back, staring at the ceiling.

Without speaking, the women simultaneously picked up the rusted tin basins they'd been sitting on and started hammering them with spoons and fists. The metallic din smashed our dark silence; it suffocated the room with noise. The sound was violent, unbearable—it seemed to explode in my head. But the women banged on, louder and louder, as if the world's noisiness were reason enough for the baby to stay.

The child's chest barely moved. I flipped through the manual, squinting against the clatter, embarrassed not to have found any answers.

And then, amid all the ruckus, the tiny thing gurgled and flickered a hand. That's all it took. The old women's voices returned, their faces crinkled into smiles.

I had just watched a miracle, but the others didn't seem to

notice. Fanta didn't look flushed with excitement, didn't reach out her hands to hold him first. The atmosphere turned curiously businesslike. The vieilles cut the cord with a razor blade, sprinkled some dust on it to stanch the bleeding, and stuck him in a basin of dark red bark water. Fanta crouched over, the placenta slipped out, and she slid it directly into a clay pot. According to tradition, she alone must bury it in a secret place outside the courtyard. She would also be expected to laugh and sing as she buried it, or the child would be sickly. If a sorcerer got hold of the placenta, he or she would have complete power over the baby's mortality.

An old woman scooped the tiny boy out of the water and tossed him in the air three times, muttering prayers as he fell back into her hands. Then the child was wrapped up and passed straight to me for inspection. I tried to hand him to Fanta to start nursing, but all the women shook their heads. *"Yirma wo ba."* She doesn't have milk, only water, they said sadly, as if she were defective. Strange that they regarded this normal delay in milk production as the result of something Fanta's body had done wrong. How could I explain the virtues of colostrum in Niarafolo? I said, "The water is good!" They cocked their heads, smiling quizzically, and kept passing the baby.

The salt seller held him for just a second, then handed him off. *"Allons partir,"* she ordered gruffly, and so we left. But some boundary had been crossed: they had let me in. I trailed the salt seller's small, strong figure walking briskly under a bowl of glittery stars.

People ask me now, "What was Africa like?" I tell them that the place I came to know is laughing yet troubled, strong yet crippled, and dancing. Africa was like nothing I had known before, until I knew it better. But to really explain it, I have to start from the beginning.

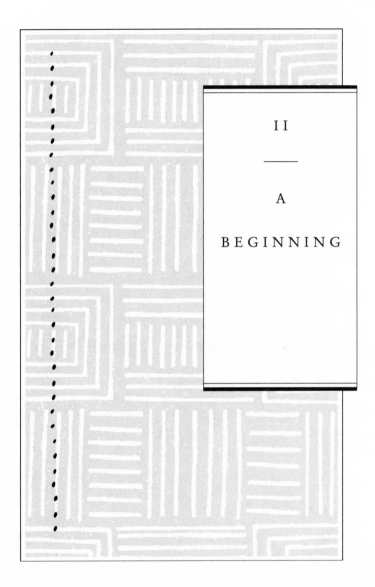

II

—

A

BEGINNING

Shadows slide across the table, shrouding my dinner in darkness. Something resembling a tiny shark is floating in my sauce, but I can barely see it. The girls, the mothers, the children are clustered in the dust of the courtyard below, eating on low stools. But I am white, and something of a trophy just now. My place is on the balcony, seated at a rickety table covered with flowered plastic, overlooking the family. The girls and mothers below eat fast, lips smacking between words. Lachaud's jaw moves in slow, powerful circles. He sits next to me, silent, a bit fierce. This morning, he was the one sent to greet me at the welcoming ceremony, when my fellow Peace Corps trainees and I sat sweating and dazed amid throngs of grinning Africans. Later he brought me into this courtyard to introduce the rest of the family that will be mine for three months while I learn to be a health worker in rural West Africa. Lachaud, it turns out, doesn't live here. Still, he seems to have a kind of authority.

He says nothing for minutes, and then, *"Il faut manger!"* You must eat! I look down. The dull bulb on the wall sheds light on Lachaud's plate, but mine is drenched in darkness in the shape of my own head and shoulders. I know it's *foutou* on my plate—they pounded boiled plantains all afternoon. Mama No. 2 sat low next to the mortar, thudding rough paste into shiny globes.

I stab my fork at the lump of black submerged in the bowl of okra sauce. The head surfaces, its eyes blank and white, its teeth still gnashing its tail. I want to be good, to slurp up this meal with gusto and ask Mama No. 2 for seconds. *That* might make my strangeness less glaring. *"Il faut manger,"* repeats Lachaud, glowering faintly. My fork trawls the murky sauce, and I swallow what emerges with my eyes shut.

Two tall girls appear in the darkness below and call out a greeting. Lachaud's teenage sisters are twins with long thin braids, identically smooth, strong faces, and the same mischievous eyes. They scamper up the stairs and hover behind me. Sandrine glances at the remnants of the monster in the sauce, but it is Sylvie who grabs my shoulder and relieves my culinary torture. "Come!" she says. "Let's go for a walk." I abandon that fish in a flash.

There is one paved street in the village of Abenké, a pocked ribbon of asphalt that splits the community down the middle. But the earth on either side of Abenké's street has washed away, and the village around it seems to be sinking. Orange light pools under streetlamps that run the length of the village; the intervals are dark. I walk up and down the road, a moving centerpiece in an assembly of so-called siblings. Fingers wander in my hair, brush my shoulders, my elbows, my hands. My teenage "sisters," Sopi and Rosine, lead the way, laughing a little too loudly. Around our little nucleus swirls a kinetic pack of children in rags. We pass boys collected by a stereo whining reggae, a tailor spinning out stitches by lamplight.

A voice calls out my name. *"C'est Lachaud,"* says one of the twins. Saturday night and he's pacing the street, too. My entourage goes orange under a streetlight, then falls black a few steps on; orange, and then black again. We pass Lachaud for the second time a few minutes later. I say, *"Ça va bien, Lachaud?"* even though I asked just minutes before. Everyone has told me to never skip a greeting. His smile has loosened. Somewhere down these black alleys there must be a moonshine maker.

When I finally head home near ten, reeling from the whirling crowds of staring, dusty children, I feel flattened by so much strangeness. We pass Lachaud on the way. He's bleary-eyed and slumped against a wall, wearing only white shorts.

I wake up the next morning in my turquoise-painted room to the whispers of a silhouetted head against my window. I know it's Sopi. She is fifteen maybe, an imp, a joker. Stubby braids sprout all over her head, and her face balances on a wide, unfaltering smile. I love her already. "She's still asleep!" Sopi croaks. She coughs and clears her throat, then finds some reason to yell to her sister far across the courtyard. It works. I'm up and laughing already, and it seems some of the foreignness has rubbed off with sleep and daylight.

My giant duffel bag has erupted across the room. It occurs to me that there is too much stuff—dozens of batteries, flashlights, cassettes, books, pens, herbal medicines. I brought tennis shoes, two pairs of sandals, and Birkenstocks, when clearly all anyone wears is flip-flops. Although I've stocked up on amenities, maybe all I really need is in me.

My parents are in the Foreign Service; I grew up on the move. Being a foreigner does not faze me. Coping with cultural differences is something I've done since childhood. Before leaving the States in January of 1998, I pored through every book I could find about Côte d'Ivoire and learned that the country has sixty-four ethnicities, strong animistic traditions, and the most political stability in West Africa. I came confidently. I thought I was prepared. But already I am humbled and astonished by what I've found.

My room is on the lower floor of a worn-down two-story house, built by the father of my host family—the *vieux*—during his heyday. A long, narrow balcony looks out at the fields and the courtyard below. The dark staircase between the floors has nearly catapulted me into the courtyard several times already; the steps are drastically uneven, as if each one has been collected from a different flight. The house speaks softly of former success: the large, vacant salon gathers dust. The bedrooms, except for mine and the vieux's, remain sealed behind doors that don't quite fit their frames. Life happens outside. The women and children sleep on plastic mats to escape the heat. Cooking takes place on low fires in the courtyard. Washing—of dishes, clothes, and babies—is done in basins in the dirt.

I come out into the sunlight to the smiles and clucks of all the courtyard women, whom Sopi immediately introduces as either sisters or mothers. I'm stymied. "All the same family?" She giggles and nods. Is she *trying* to trick me? Sopi's older sister Hélène grabs my bucket, new and pink in this dusty courtyard, and hops up on the well platform to pull water for my bath. She wears a *pagne,* or sarong, of faded dark red; her shoulders sweep out of it, smooth and rippling with fine strength. Hélène may be nineteen, but it seems to depend on whom you ask. She has given her flashing eyes and her dimples to a three-year-old daughter, Eloise, who hides behind her mother's knees in my presence.

I step up on the well beside Hélène. Already it is clear that I am considered weak and somehow superior to manual labor—misconceptions to be dashed before long, I hope. The last thing I want is for them to serve me, though it almost seems they want to. When I take the rope and fill the bucket, slashing my shirt with wet dirt in the process, the whole courtyard erupts in laughter. Rule No. 1 becomes quickly apparent: Laugh first.

The N'Guessans' latrine becomes, within hours, my favorite spot, the only place outside where I'm confident of my solitude. The bathing section is made of baked clay, draped with vines and roofed far above by the edges of a giant mango tree. It is lovely purely by accident. Hélène says I must bathe twice a day, and I wouldn't dream of arguing with her. My first bucket bath is like skinny-dipping—splashed cold water in the sun's slow burn, the smell of wet clay. I dry off in minutes just standing there. At night it must be even better, when the water is warmed over the fire, the air is soft, and the ceiling is a million shimmering stars.

While I'm dawdling in the latrine, the twins show up, boisterous already. I emerge in my Western garb and they rush up, a bundle of rioting colors in their arms. "You have to try on these!" they pant. "*Comme une femme africaine!*" In all the excitement, we leave my own clothes on. Over my pants goes a narrow skirt that binds my knees and reduces my walking to the mince of a geisha. A bodice fits snugly over my shirt and leaves my shoulders swimming. The neckline is low and lined with ruffles; the short sleeves are entities of their own: giant wads of padding puff out level with my ears. The girls pull out a long warped mirror, and I note in my reflection that my outfit is made from the *"cellulaire"* fabric that seems all the rage: mud-green background patterned with giant orange cell phones, symbols of modernity just out of reach.

The sun is racing to the top of the sky. February is the onset of the hot season. I am wearing two whole outfits and nearly suffocating when they bring out the pièce de résistance: a thick, black velvet cloth traced with sparkling gold designs. "This goes around your waist," says Sandrine, who, when asked what purpose it serves, can't think of a good one. With an everyday pagne, you can tie on a baby or bundle up your purchases at the market. But this one is too nice for all that. The girls step back and grin into their fists. I am wearing a *complet*, a three-piece pagne, the traditional costume of West African women. They're mighty pleased with their handiwork.

I'm their doll. They sit me down in front of an onion omelette glittering with oil and watch me try to swallow it. Then they decide to walk me across the village to the sacred pond. My steps are tiny, my face flushed with the heat.

They say there are twelve thousand people in this village, but I can't figure out where they all are. Abenké is only six parallel roads and a few cross streets, bounded by an elementary school on each end. The sacred pond is beyond the south school, Rosine says. We pass a handful of upper-class houses along the main road. They are one-story and drab, but you can see their tiled floors and paved courtyards through cement lattice walls. We pass an empty baby-blue villa with a glass annex that boasts a black-and-white-checkered floor and pizza parlor furniture. That, says Sandrine, is the house of a gendarme, a member of the national police force, but he's never there. There are less auspicious courtyards along the way: paint streaks off walls, cement crumbles, roofs rust. But this is a village of coffee growers in a region favored by the government, and despite the round bellies and the rags, I'm not overwhelmed by poverty when walking its streets.

The sacred pond is down the road a couple hundred feet. It's man-made, scintillating under the sun. Why is it sacred? The children waffle at the question, look sideways. "Um, you can't eat the fish." "Can you swim in it?" I ask, tempted to fling myself in, clothes and all, to escape the sun. Sopi scrunches up her nose at the dark water lapping at the banks. "Why would you want to?" On the way back I nearly faint from the heat. Pieces of the costume come off every several yards.

Papa, the vieux, sits in his armchair, eating alone in his old pagne toga. Quiet but omniscient, he seems to materialize in forgotten corners with wisdom on his tongue. His coffee and cacao fields still produce thousands of kilos a year, worked by hand in week-long shifts by all of these girls, Lachaud, and, once in a while, a visiting son. The glory days are finished, though. Coffee prices plummeted in 1994, with the devaluation of the CFA franc, a West African currency tied to the French franc. The evidence of his misfortune is in the courtyard: two concrete shells that would have been houses for the children have been left derelict since the money ran out. On Sundays the vieux puts on a brown suit and a bowler hat, pulls out a smudged pair of plastic glasses that he only uses to see God, and shepherds his family to church. Otherwise, he mans his chair as if it might get lonely without him.

Mama No. 1 sits under the mango tree hacking the skin off manioc root with a machete. Mama No. 2 trundles in and out of the cement brick shell that serves as a kitchen. I've settled into a wood-slat chair in the middle of the courtyard to scribble a letter home. And everyone under thirty is within my arm's length. Hélène hunkers down to paint my toenails an obnoxious shade of red, then attacks my left hand. The right she ignores—according to a Muslim tradition that's trickled into their Christian habits, it must be left clean for eating. Sopi and Rosine are recalling all the words of English they ever knew. (*Good mohhhhhning, class!*) They thread their hands through my ash-blond hair, exclaiming at how many colors there are.

I decide to clear up the family situation once and for all. After a week of confusion I've realized that maybe their definition of "sibling" is different than mine. Is Sandrine your sister, *même père, même mère?* How many children does Papa have, anyway? Why aren't there any boys? Hélène speaks French with softened edges, and I listen hard to understand. She whispers names and counts her fingers and then announces, "Papa has seventeen children." She points across the courtyard with the scarlet polish brush. "There are two wives, my Mama and the second woman. There are one . . . two . . . three . . . four boys, but they are at university. Or else they're already married." And the rest? Lachaud? The twins? She shrugs. Cousins somehow, but who really cares? I'm the only one concerned with determining exact relation. "They're my father's family," she says, and turns to my fingernails again.

One night, after rice cooked in red oil and chunks of gristled mystery meat, Sopi and Rosine come up to the terrace to give me a grapefruit. I gush and grin over it—it's so blissfully familiar! Sopi slouches across from me, Rosine sits up straight. They are only half sisters, and which is eldest depends on the day you ask them. They pipe out names of brothers and sisters and have trouble getting all the way to seventeen. They mention Valérie, their big sister studying commerce in the city, and Hugo, learning about computers in Adzopé. "There's Eric, who's in school too." Rosine looks down at her uncounted fingers. "Ohhhh, and then Albert, who died when a plane ran out of gas and fell out of the sky." She shudders a bit. *"Moi, j'ai peur d'avion."* Sopi says she's afraid of airplanes too.

"What else are you afraid of?" I ask. They lean back in their chairs and laugh a little, eyes on the ceiling, as if that's where they've hidden their fears. "Are you afraid of AIDS?" The word falls through the night like shattering glass. In Abidjan, they say over 10 percent of the population and 50 percent of the prostitutes are HIV positive—one of the highest rates in West Africa. This village is two hours from the city, but it's close enough to be implicated early in an epidemic. AIDS education is already an integral part of my Peace Corps training classes. We've been given wooden phalluses so we can demonstrate how to put on a condom, and books with detailed educational cartoons. But outside of my first training classes, I have not even heard the virus mentioned. It's so much easier to talk about hygiene or malaria. AIDS seems untouchable. I have to start *somewhere*. If I don't, who will?

At the mention of the disease, Sopi claps her hands and hoots; Rosine rocks forward, laughing, and hits the table with her palm. I remain serious. "It's a very bad disease, you know. A lot of people in Côte d'Ivoire are dying from it." I don't know how far to go. They are in their early teens but still wear the checked pinafores of elementary school. They seem so young, yet they're only a year or two away from the game and the boys and the time when life gets complicated. Sopi looks at Rosine for reinforcement, sticks out her chin, and announces, *"Si un homme m'approche, je refuse!"* The last word rings out in her boyish voice. Still, I'm loath to let the topic go. Maybe they are too young to grapple with an issue that's so vast and terrifying. Perhaps there are no adults, no role models who will concede that this is a reality to fear. Or maybe the girls have seen more than they care to admit.

This must be dying season. Several weeks after my arrival, Sopi's oldest sister, Valérie, comes up from school in Abidjan for a neighbor's funeral. She wears jeans and a T-shirt in this courtyard of pagne-clad women. She is quick to befriend me and wants to talk, but there is something sad about her eyes. Valérie says there were ten deaths in the village in the past week. "Many are young people, stolen before their time," she tells me, her voice wavering from bitter to despondent. My inclination is to ask how they died. Maybe I want to hear that it was AIDS, just to confirm my preconceptions. But my hints garner nothing. Even though the village morgue is packed and four corpses lie in morgues in nearby towns, the deaths are clearly not a subject for discussion.

In addition to the recent deaths, the returns from the cacao and coffee harvests have just come in, and all of last season's funerals can finally be funded. Villagers vie for time and space to hold funerals. The village is largely Christian, with a vibrant animist undertone. Valérie tells me that the burial tradition dictates that the deceased be laid to rest on a pile of expensive pagnes. "If they can, they decorate the body with lots of jewelry—rings and bracelets and anything gold. So the dead person looks rich and beautiful. Everyone comes to wail and honor him and donate a little money for the funeral." At four o'clock, there's a procession to the cemetery, and the body is given a Christian burial.

Glitzy relatives show up from Abidjan for the important funerals, a strange reminder that a metropolis lies less than two hundred kilometers to the south. The distance seems unbridgeable. Abenké still coddles tradition: its women rarely wear pants, its people run to the *fetisheur*, the witch doctor, before they consider hiking up the hill to the modern infirmary. The village has a daily market and a dozen "boutiques"—dingy huts with merchandise and merchants caged behind walls of chicken wire, where you can buy soap and pens and palm oil.

Abidjan seems surreal and un-African in comparison. There are racy cars, women in short skirts, streets lined with ethnic restaurants, supermarkets with everything from Panasonic televisions to teriyaki sauce. Because it's cosmopolitan, all relatives hailing from the city can claim worldliness too, even if they are mere barbers or checkout clerks. They breeze into the village with studied airs; the women move in clouds of cheap perfume, wincing at the dust. They dress in the newest West African fashions and high heels and don't go anywhere without vinyl pocketbooks clutched under their arms, while their village sisters wear Dr. Scholl's rip-offs and tie up money in the corners of their pagnes.

Nearly every day since I've arrived, some corner of the village has stayed up all night to honor a death. Reedy music blares from loudspeakers till dawn. Stereos here are purchased at the outdoor market and include tape chewing and unpredictable bursts of speed among their standard features. Cassettes are mostly bootlegs, with jackets featuring badly photocopied pictures and misspelled words. The sound is equally creative: voices warble and slide off-key, accompanied by wheezing feedback. The music itself comes mostly from Zaire. It's a raucous mix of sirens, arcade sound effects, shouting, and jangling, tinny synthesizers. We don't sleep well.

Hélène shaves her head. Her hair, previously straightened and combed back in a wild mass, had nearly reached her shoulders. When I ask her why she did it, she mutters something like "It was time." She's ashamed of her French and tries to keep her explanations to a minimum. Later I realize that she has gone bald to identify her mourning; she walks about with a fragile air for a day or two. *Son ami* is all they say when I ask whom she's lost.

Then one evening she brings out a new three-piece pagne, smiling. There are different ranks of pagne cloth—the cheapest, the "my husband has no job" pagne, is generally tie-dyed and used for the fields and housework. "Fancy" is the lowest-quality wax print. It fades fast and impresses no one. The aristocrat of pagnes, Côte d'Ivoire wax, is heavy, shiny, stiff. Fifty dollars' worth will make a complet. Hélène's new pagne is the expensive kind, dark red and black—the mourning colors for the Atié, the local ethnicity that originally came from Ghana. She puts it on and prances around as if it's her wedding dress, admiring herself. There's a funeral tonight, Sopi says. And funerals are all about being *sapé*—snazzily dressed. She and Rosine tear through their pile of clothes, looking for just the right thing.

Papa calls out from a shadowy corner as we leave for the funeral. He seems tired out, and Rosine has told me he has diabetes. He administers a daily enema of crushed hot chili peppers—the cure-all for any intestinal woe for everyone from infants to elders. In other societies, this information might be something to hide, but Papa can't be bothered with embarrassment. Every morning, Sopi mashes the peppers on a grinding stone, fills a rubber bulb, and Papa disappears into the latrine. From his chair, he calls out orders, resolves disputes, fixes problems, unsolicited. Tonight he rasps, "*Les filles*, there's school tomorrow! Come back early!" He doesn't want his daughters out gallivanting with drunk men, but he seems a little protective of me as well.

Maybe I'm expecting some mysterious ritual, an ancient dance.

Instead, my first funeral in Abenké is like a frat party: people yelling over loud music, running their eyes over members of the opposite sex, dancing in self-conscious spurts. Gourds of palm wine are passed around. Circles form around a few sloppy drunks. It's like rings in a circus—the drunks play fools, the audiences howl and slap each other on the back. My sisters and most of the women stick to cups of water. This is, for all intents and purposes, a meat market. The specter of AIDS seems to hover over the crowd, but I wonder if anyone else senses it. I leave not disgusted exactly, just disappointed and desperate to escape the screaming Atari whine of the music.

Valérie sits across from me one night after dinner and talks of racism. It's the first challenging conversation I've had with an Ivorian. It starts when I laugh at how neighbors and small children who don't even speak French scream out my name as I pass by, only weeks after my arrival. She says, *"Mais tu es blanche."* She's right, for certain. I have been here only weeks, but it's already apparent that people defer to me. "What's it like in America?" she asks. "There are blacks there, right? How do you get along?" I tell her it used to be horrible, that black people were treated very badly in America. I mention slavery, expecting to have hit some nail on its head. She just listens. I tell her it's better now, but it's still not good.

Valérie leans on the table and combs her fingers through her hair. "We die all the time here. Africans just keep dying." Finally she raises her sad eyes to mine. "Why am I black and you white?" she asks. There's a frantic note in her voice. I mumble something about both being the same in the end but she just shakes her head.

Sopi has a game that makes me laugh. She asks me for some word in English, then turns to her sister. "Emilie, do you know the word for *manger* in English? *Mais tu ne connais pas!*" She feigns shock and horror at her older sister's ignorance, then squares her shoulders. "Me, I know! *C'est* eeeeet!"

She is my little sister, devoted with boundless energy to being my clown and my tutor. All my sisters have been diligent about teaching me how to run a courtyard. Rosine showed me how to boil hibiscus leaves to make a sweet tea called *bisap*. Emilie taught me to splash water on the pestle to keep the *foutou* from sticking to it. Hélène has explained why green eggplants are better than orange ones, and told me how to pick palm nuts at the market. Sopi's main duty is laundry, and she's set on making me her apprentice. I insist at first that I'll wash my own stuff. A small conference of observers peers over my shoulder as I gently wallow a shirt in soapy water. See? I can do it. They rattle off a commentary in Atié, and finally Sopi, hands on her hips, interrupts my progress. She sighs, then declares dramatically, "Let me show you how to do it, because *that* is not the way." All of a sudden my shirt is subject to a fast and rhythmic thrashing. I'm certain it will emerge in tatters. Instead, it ends up the cleanest it's been in its life.

The family has taken to consulting me about meals ever since something I ingested at their table landed me in the Peace Corps infirmary in a nearby town for several days. For three days I was caged like a leper in a black mosquito net, downing nothing but Gatorade, losing my guts every way possible, and bawling at the thought of home.

The N'Guessans must have thought they'd killed me. Hélène took over cooking for me, and ever since, dinners have been composed of macaroni on top of rice and other curious concoctions she imagines might be closer to home cooking. One night I declare that I will make salad for the family, although raw vegetables seem revolutionary in this courtyard. While the lettuce soaks in a basin of bleached water, we discuss what other growing things we like to eat. Sopi jumps up, sprints into the house, and emerges with a giant pineapple. An unfamiliar woman appears at the same time, calls out her greetings and, as if it were her reason for coming, takes charge of the pineapple without a word. In her hands, the skin winds off in a long spiral. She hacks the fruit into enormous chunks and puts them on a plate in front of me. "No, no! We should *all* eat it!" I insist. But they won't have any of it;

they suck their teeth and shake their heads. The argument is over when they suck their teeth—this much I've learned.

So I devour it. And then, to my exasperation, the others pick up the skin to gnaw on the inside. Later, we eat our salad sitting in a cluster in the courtyard. In the courtyard! Caught up in the novelty of *me* making the salad, they have forgotten my table setting upstairs. Only when we've finished do they glance up at the balcony and slap their hands to their mouths. "Eh! We forgot!" But I'm grinning. Just for a few seconds, we've all been tricked into thinking I'm just another sister.

Sopi pulls out the *awaleh* board, a piece of wood with twelve smooth scoops in two rows. She runs her hand over it, dropping polished cacao seeds into each hollow. In the beginning, I watched the game played three times without a word of explanation and then was challenged by the reigning champion, Papa. I have caught on somewhat: it's a game of strategy and counting, where you try to clear all your hollows of the seeds by filling up your opponent's side. But my cautious stabs at strategy leave me with the seeds every time. Sopi and I play in the dim light of the moon and the bulb outside my room across the courtyard. The air is clear and warm; it vibrates and ripples with my sisters' chatter.

Facing me is the tiny bum of my favorite child, Hélène's daughter, Eloise. I sit in the courtyard writing a letter. Only Mama No. 1 is around, and she's busy at the fire boiling plantains. Elo is on treacherous ground.

When her mother is near, Eloise traipses around the courtyard, a dark sprite with a laugh like a waterfall. Her hair, twisted into long strands and tied together at the ends, looks like a fragile birdcage sitting askew atop her head. Even after many weeks, she is still scared to death of me, yet she flirts, catching my eye, then scampering away and giggling furiously. She calls me Meeess Sarah, as if we lived in antebellum Georgia, and sings it out boldly. I call back Meeess Elo and she thinks that's pretty funny, but she still can't decide if I'm a big monster or a remarkably pale toy. It's all right when there are aunts and grandmothers around to save her from the white peril, but today there's no safe haven and she's nervous again. She buries her head in a wooden chair across from me, not quite sure she wants to sell me her soul, but definitely too intrigued by her own bravery to leave.

When I walk through the village, the sight of me sets naked toddlers along the road to jumping and chanting, *Boufouet! Boufouet!* (White! White!) Eloise and her mother walk back from the market with me in the afternoon. As we pass jumping kids, Eloise takes on a funny swagger—fast, with her shoulders swinging forward. Her chin is thrust in the air as if to say, Hah! She's *my* white lady! But as soon as Hélène ducks into a friend's courtyard and instructs Elo to follow me home, all confidence is lost. She looks up at me for one second in stubborn fear, then sprints home, elbows pumping, her yellowed lacy dress fluttering. She is off so fast she leaves both shoes in the dirt behind her. I pick up one tiny flip-flop and then the other, completely charmed.

My training classes run from morning to evening. We're taught how to analyze a community, how to motivate a village, how to teach people who have never been to school, how to achieve sustainable development. Our trainers give us piles of books about health work, informal education, preventive child care, and well construction, but they never assign pages to read. Instead, we are expected to develop small-scale projects in Abenké on our own. We conduct classes about hygiene and breast-feeding for fifty villagers, survey the population about the underuse of the clinic, and put together a billboard advertising vaccination day. There are also daily French classes, though I have eight years of courses and six months in France behind me. And finally, there are cross-cultural classes, which delve into gender roles and the importance of respecting tradition, teach us never to offer or accept anything with our left hand, and remind us to always, *always,* follow village protocol.

As I'm taking a break after French class one day, two figures emerge from a blur of schoolgirls, all brown legs and blue-and-white checks, and run up to me on the street. Sopi and Rosine join me under an acacia tree for a few minutes before school calls again. When I ask them what they want to do after this year, they're quick to affirm their interest in continuing education. They list their sisters who didn't make it, who have ended up with kids and no husbands and no skills. "Look at Emilie," Rosine says. "She didn't get to go to school at all and now she's just waiting around for some man to choose her for a wife. And Hélène too." Sopi perches forward on the bench, says earnestly in her raspy voice: "We're the youngest daughters and we're the last chance. We *have* to get through school."

One afternoon in late March, their older brother Eric comes home from secondary school in Adzopé to recuperate from an illness. He sits day after day in the courtyard, drinking glasses of a muddy liquid in which leaves float. I, of course, eye him for signs of lost weight and frequent trips to the bathroom, still on the naive search for an AIDS case to bring the crisis home. He is fighting off malaria, it turns out. When he saunters onto the balcony, where his sisters are studying one afternoon, the girls pull the books closer to their faces. His weak voice turns teasing. He pulls his sisters' textbooks across the table and flips through the pages. "Hah! I remember all this stuff! It's so easy."

Eric has glittery eyes and smooth skin. When he asks his sisters questions from the book, he rolls his *r*'s luxuriantly, and his hands carve the air gracefully as he speaks. *What is the capital of France? What is the population of Côte d'Ivoire?* The girls crumble; they attempt answers, fail miserably, and then resort to sucking their teeth at his injustice and clucking with excuses. It's funny, but it's depressing too—they don't know the answers, and maybe the teaching system will never allow them to learn. How can they possibly hope to get to university?

This is beautiful. My sisters drift around me, they comb each other's hair and play with my fingers. Our square of dim light under the terrace stays dry in the hushed straight rain. Eloise sleeps wildly next to Mama No. 1 on a striped mat, limbs flying everywhere. My sisters tell stories, compare their French skills, animated and laughing. They fold at the waist, lean into each other, throw their heads back, clap their hands. Their voices rise and fall with the rain's soft static. Their flat strong noses, straight necks, smooth brown arms shine in the wet night. Thunder cracks violently, but it's like an accent to our joy. We are protected, together.

Sopi has thrown her arm around my shoulder. I am leaving soon, and none of us wants to think about it. I bring out my journal to read what I wrote the first day I met them. Hah! I was so scared of the sauce! And you tried to teach me to dance, remember? Elo writhes and tosses. Maybe she's just been faking sleep—when I read what I wrote about her, her eyes flash up at me. She squiggles against her sleeping grandmother every time she catches my eye.

"Oh *Dieu!*" shouts Sopi in her deep voice. "*Quand tu pars, on va tous tomber malade.*" When you leave, we will all fall sick.

I ask for foutou and peanut sauce on my last night and nearly lick my plate clean. The Mamas and Hélène watch wide-eyed, and then triumph washes across their faces. Papa has on his suit, his bowler hat, his glasses. We're playing one last game of *awaleh*, one last game of cards. He has splurged tonight, for my sake: bought a round of orange Fantas and a kilo of popcorn. Rosine is busy popping it over the fire, sprinkling it with salt and sweet powdered milk, and packing it into long plastic bags for my trip north. I am ready to be a health worker, to try my hand at changing behavior, my trainers say. Infant mortality is high due to dehydration, malaria, parasites, malnutrition, unclean water sources, and poor hygiene. Polio stubbornly refuses to be eradicated, outbreaks of meningitis happen yearly, and a particularly hideous parasite called guinea worm still troubles certain regions. Preventive care is not a priority; most people wait till they get sick before thinking about staying healthy. And traditional populations are still skeptical of modern medicine.

My destination is Nambonkaha, a tiny Muslim village deep in the northern savanna, with one infirmary and one nurse. I have been told that many women in the north are circumcised, that there aren't many maternity clinics there, and that women die more often in childbirth. The north is poorer, less developed, more illiterate, more conservative, more isolated. And AIDS, while less prevalent than in the south, is slowly infiltrating. I have been trained for this. But it's daunting.

Sopi says, "You know, you won't be happy up north where you're going. It's really, really hot. And how will you live *all* alone? Who will cook for you or do your laundry?"

Rosine looks up from her line of lumpy bags, "You'll live in a hut. You won't have any light. They don't have electricity up there, you know?"

Sopi sucks her teeth. "Plus the women there can't even cook well."

The moon is shining, and lightning blasts all over the sky. The wind sifts through the mango trees, and my lovely sisters laugh at the night. They're linked in a circle, teaching Emilie's nine-month-old how to dance only two days after she's learned to walk. She's picking it up fast, bouncing up and down with her knees, a self-conscious smile widening as she sees she's the star of the show. Eloise runs to me, grabs my hands, and thrusts her hips from side to side, squealing at the great discovery that I'm not *that* scary. Her eyes twinkle up at me. She spent nine weeks traipsing across the courtyard to hide from me and has finally decided she loves me the week I'm leaving. My sisters stand, smooth shoulders rising out of pagnes, black bodies fading into the night, voices bubbling into music. Hélène sways forward and sings the first bars of a song I've heard on the radio, and soon the four of us are scratching out steps on the uneven terrain, dancing with the wind and lightning. So sweet this night.

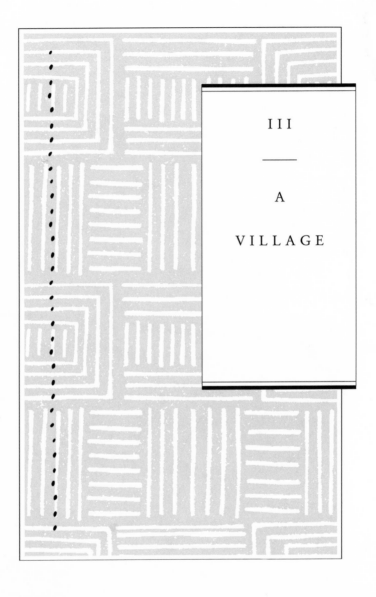

III

—

A

VILLAGE

I
———

Savanna

The chief of Nambonkaha sits on a bench under a mango tree next to a candy-red tractor. He wears a faded gray robe called a *boubou* and a tattered cap with a pompom atop. I sit facing him, in the middle of a tight cluster of men. "Protocol," says the government nurse, Sidibé, who comes from a town a few hours south and has lived in Nambonkaha four years. "The amount of people accompanying you shows how important you are." He speaks slowly in well-educated French, then bursts into a grin. I am anxious, and already Sidibé seems to understand.

This morning my taxi took the paved road north from the town of Ferkessédougou and hurtled over nine hills before Nambonkaha came into view. The road that runs by the village is a thoroughfare, though it is barely two lanes wide and is cracked and empty save for ramshackle trucks and men on bicycles. Starting as an expressway in Abidjan, it cuts through the lush forests of the south, then narrows and becomes cluttered with flatbed trucks stacked with mammoth tree trunks. Six hundred kilometers north, it passes beyond the village of Nambonkaha (pr. Nambong-Kaa), into the barren semidesert Sahel of Burkina Faso and Mali, the southern fringe of the Sahara. Between jungle and desert, where Nambonkaha lies, the savanna undulates. Baobab trees lord prehistorically over low woodlands. The horizon is wide, and villages seem sparse and forgotten among the trees.

My journey north from Abenké took two days. I traveled first in a tiny van piled high with mattresses, then in a bush taxi, or *badjan*, towering with bags of avocados and porch furniture, and finally in a crumpled orange cab, held together by twine. As we approached the village, dark faces peered from stacks of firewood along the pavement. The cab driver said, "See, the village is still very traditional. Only five hundred people. No water except from pumps. No electricity. You're not really coming here to live, are you?" But then Sidibé's entire family tumbled out the wooden gate of his courtyard to greet me, and I felt better.

Rural healthcare in Côte d'Ivoire is a national program. Sidibé, with a high school diploma and three years of nursing school under his belt, is its representative in the village. His house is a comfortable concrete affair, painted yellow on the outside and mint green smudged with handprints on the inside. His four children and two wards will sleep on the salon floor to make room for me until my own house is ready.

My introduction to the chief is begun by a short, compact man called the president. "What is he president of?" I ask Sidibé. "The school parents' association," he tells me "And the budget committee for the clinic. But he can't read." The president mutters monotonously in the local dialect. It sounds like he's telling the chief what he had for breakfast. When he stops, a tall man called the mayor picks it up. "It's a joke," Sidibé whispers before I can ask. "There's really no mayor here. He's just the leader of the village youth. He can't read either." When an older man speaks up, Sidibé says that in Senoufo tradition, the message passes through four or five interpreters before the eldest and most important says it directly to the chief.

The Senoufo, the major tribe in the north-central region of Côte d'Ivoire, are known for their animism, their diligence, and their dedication to tradition. Niarafolo, the ethnicity (and language) in this village, is a subdivision of the Senoufo. Sidibé laughs a little high when I ask about sorcery. "No, this is a Muslim village," he says. "You don't have to worry about that." He is not Senoufo but Dioula, a tribe that spreads from Mali throughout the north of Côte d'Ivoire. Aside from French, Dioula is the most widely spoken language in the country.

Almost all the villagers speak enough of it that Sidibé hasn't bothered to learn Niarafolo. I can converse easily in French with the mayor, the president, and Sidibé. But the women, the girls, and the elders of the village, including the chief, I'm told, speak only the local dialects.

The chief's left eye has a whitish cast; his right is lively. Both watch the ground. Strange words tumble from his mouth. Then his message trickles back to me, losing some of its vital parts as it passes from Niarafolo into Dioula and then into French. Sidibé looks me straight in the eye and extends the chief's welcome. The whole affair takes thirty minutes at least. It's subdued, formal—a letdown. It almost seems like I've surprised everyone by coming. No foreigner, let alone a white person, has stayed here since the French colonists passed through. The chief, the mayor—everyone except Sidibé, really—seem to have no idea what I am doing here.

I'm beginning to think I don't either. Nambonkaha is still and silent. And hot as hell. Whereas Abenké's heat was heavy and lazy, this heat sucks at my skin, burns into the top of my head. I have traded succulent jungle for savanna stubble, rich red earth for bloodless dust. Nambonkaha is open, baking, and brown. My sisters, maybe, were right. Abenké all of a sudden seems like Beverly Hills. There are no tiled floors here, no two-story houses, no cement courtyards. This is a village of mud huts and thatch, with a few narrow cement houses interspersed. It looks as if someone shook the huts like dice and let them scatter.

The small pack of somewhat self-important men show me to what will be my new home: two tiny rooms at the end of a long concrete house. It's arranged like a motel—as are most concrete houses here. Each set of two rooms has one door to the outside and is otherwise cut off from the rest of the house. "Who else lives here?" I ask my escorts. As he fiddles with an old key, the president tells me that an old man who lives in the outlying farming settlements, or *campements,* comes in once in a while and stays in the rooms on the other end of the house. The door creaks open.

Gray cement floors, gray cement walls, two little windows shaded with rusty metal slats, a tin roof with no ceiling, and nothing inside but a collection of flies. It smells stale. *Two years.* I'm going to live in this place for two years.

Sidibé's wife, Abi, has made a trip into Ferkessédougou, nick-named Ferké, a half hour away by bush taxi, to stock up on foods she imagines they serve in America. She trudges up to her porch to meet me as we return from my house. As soon as I'm seated, she places in front of me a plate of salad and a bowl of fried plantains, a traditional snack called *alloco.* Then she disappears into the house to raid the pile of fruit on the floor in the corner. This is a welcome surprise. After months of mashed roots and ambiguous sauces in the modern south, I am eating fresh salad and pineapple for lunch in the bush.

Abi is taller than most of the men, including her husband, very dark and solid. Her face is large and oval, but all her features seem to crowd toward the middle. Laughter rises quickly from her gut. There is something earthy about her—maybe it's her thick, strong arms or her stalwart poise. Her walk is languid, yet her eyes move fast, swooping up details and omissions.

The men banter with her, hoping to tease some alloco out of her pot. But she just teases them back. As the nurse's wife, Abi wields more power than the average village woman. She doesn't have to subscribe to village laws and appears straightforward and daring. With me, though, she is deferential. She seems nervous about my judgment, wants to show that she is "civilized" too.

Abi and the men chatter, but not to me. Their French is fast and cluttered with local words. I can't make the effort to join the banter just now. Too much is foreign; too much is missing. I'm all alone surrounded by people. I finish my food and shut myself in my room, curl up on the thin foam mattress, and sleep a long time. Once I'm awake, I don't get up. My siesta stretches late into the afternoon.

And then Sidibé batters at my door, saying, Get your camera, and all of a sudden I'm sitting next to the chief in the breezeway of the village clinic in front of a moving wall of staring children and smiling, curious adults. Where did they all come from? Twenty old women gyrate and hop toward me, leading a troupe of musicians in long blue robes and feathered helmets. The musicians are sweating like mad, hefting gigantic instruments called *balafons,* like xylophones, made of wooden planks and hollowed calabashes. Others smack calabash drums so fast their bare hands blur. The sound resonates on the walls, fills up my ears. Women shake and fold in front of me, a quarrel of ruffles and stripes and colors. They drop down at my feet, and the chief shows me that touching their shoulder means I accept their honor. Some have babies tied on their backs with a pagne. From the front, you can only see miniature feet bouncing on their hips. The breezeway turns hot with so many bodies. I'm overwhelmed, but I'm okay, laughing again, heart beating again, wide-eyed again. I can't really say anything, can't really think much at all.

At the chief's house a different band awaits—one from the campements, dressed in red jumpsuits with tassels and helmets of straw and mirrors. Mangos dangle around us like a thousand marionettes shaking and bouncing off the heads of the twisting musicians. An old woman dances before me—the oldest woman in the village, Sidibé tells me. She wears a tattered turquoise sweatshirt that says, "Washington, D.C." Hey. That's where I come from.

The young women come out to dance, one by one, two by two, then finally in a great circle, all of them moving quickly, closely, simultaneously. Halfway through the ceremony, the mayor calls through the cacophony and whips up near silence. He wants to present my gift to the chief. (I was told long before I came to Africa that no upstanding visitor arrives without a gift.) I have brought an inlaid box, thinking that, if nothing else, he could keep his money or his valuables in it.

The mayor holds it out and turns for all to see. The crowd murmurs and nods. He tips it, unlatches it, and maybe everyone's holding their breath or maybe it's just my imagination, but all that falls out is the glare of red felt. Did they expect bills and coins? I'll never know. The crowd under the mango tree engulfs me in long and loud laughter.

The chief ordains that we dance for a week to honor my arrival. He gives me a local name, Guissongui, which means "the dreams of the enemies will not be realized." I am told that Niar-afolo names are highly contextual; the idea behind mine is that neighboring villages might get jealous of Nambonkaha's good luck in getting an American and put a curse on us. My name is their amulet, their protection.

Night falls with a thud on the dancing crowd. There is no canned light here; there are no power lines. Abenké had coldish drinks, streetlights, televisions, and fans. Nambonkaha has darkness that cradles the round glow of lanterns.

The second night the music comes to me. It finds me eating french fries and salad on Sidibé's porch. The darkness thrums when the crowd is still far, and within minutes the courtyard is throbbing with dancers. I sit on the terrace with the elders while hundreds of youths and women dance hard and fast. The fire shines in bursts behind silhouettes of spry bodies and children's heads leaping and ebbing in unison like a herd of gazelles. This night I feel it in my gut. That old cliché moment of catharsis has arrived: *I am in Africa.* The drummers catapult across the circles of dancers—crazy feathered, glittered helmets flashing in the pitch night. This could be any century. In the middle of the dust and the flying legs, one toddler, a tiny squat shadow from where I sit, bobs back and forth, arms and legs moving to his own earnest rhythm.

I win a coopful of chickens over the first few days, gifts from the chief and some of the elders. I entertain vague thoughts of raising them until they show up sautéed, alongside my fries. The dancing ordinance, it turns out, is a symbolic one only. After the first two nights the villagers call it quits, content to postpone the rest of the week's mandate till the next funeral.

Abi steadies a bowl on her head and loads her arms with plates. It's our signal that dinner is ready. Sidibé and I eat indoors—they must assume I think it's more civilized—but the stiffness is sloughing off bit by bit. My recent request for rice stunned Abi. You *like* rice? she asked. Well, why have I been frying you potatoes all this time? Since she's realized I'm content with whatever the kids are eating, my Western plates have gradually disappeared.

Sidibé's house is a countrywide standard designed for government employees, or *fonctionnaires:* two bedrooms, an inside bathing room, and a large salon. The layout varies, but fonctionnaire interior decor is consistent. The most up-and-coming villagers might have a bed, a few wooden chairs, and a small table indoors. Everyone else has a couple chairs for visitors, a scattering of stools in the courtyard, and plastic mats to sleep on. That's about it. Fonctionnaires are the bourgeoisie of the village. Furnishings are part of their distinction. They have a dining table that serves as kitchen counter, desk, or garage, a gas stove that's turned on a handful of times a year, and beds—or at least mattresses in all the bedrooms, though some hold four kids at a time.

The hub of the fonctionnaire house is the salon, and all are variations of the same theme: a few chairs and couches face the television. The couches are made of painted wood and foam cushions upholstered in cheap velour that invariably resembles a Jackson Pollock in the rain. Some "entertainment centers" I encountered in Abenké were dark, heavy hutches with plenty of space for the all-important knickknacks, a stereo, a television, and various framed photographs of loved ones looking dour. Sidibé's setup is a humble particleboard desk, with cabinets for his tape collection and his Koran. The desktop has room enough for a tiny black-and-white TV—which on good days brings state-run news, rippling madly and covered in snow—and the car battery that runs it. On the wall above the desk hang fuzzy, faded pictures of his parents and Abi. Old calendars curl on the other walls. Each has a beautiful modern woman grinning about her product: Défrissant hair relaxer, skin-lightening cream, and Eclador palm oil. This is one of few modern households that is not graced by the pudgy mug of the current president, Henri Bédié, nor that of the Vieux, the old beloved president Houphouët-Boigny.

Tonight Abi serves us bushrat in eggplant sauce. In order to avoid unpleasant encounters with unidentified floating objects, I have told her that I don't like meat that much. (The amount of meat in your sauce hinges on your sex, your age, your prestige, and how much the cook likes you.) Tonight, my dictate comes in handy: I pull the head of the bushrat from my sauce, a bit startled. Sidibé savors my squeamishness. He grins mischievously when I pass it to him. "Ahhhh! *La tête!* My favorite part. Look, there are its little teeth! And now"—*crrrrack*—"I'll eat the brain." He sticks up a finger of mush for approval. "Mmmmm, *mais c'est doux!* Now I'll be smarter!" I am learning quickly that he loves to shock. If he's testing me, it's not working. I refuse to squirm at his tricks. Instead, I laugh. Because it *is* so funny, this dynamic—two people from opposite worlds brandishing their differences just to get past them.

"Americans think we live in trees, don't they?" Sidibé asks. "When you came over, were your friends worried you'd start living in trees, too? Did they think you might get eaten by a lion?" I say that I'm sure there are Americans who still think all Africans wear loincloths. I tell him some people know a lot about Africa, but others don't understand that it's made up of many countries and tribes. Yet he brings up the old stereotypes jokingly whenever a new facet of life in Africa comes up. "Well, that's because we run around naked like monkeys," he'll say, and I can't figure out if he is bitter or just joking. He resents our Western misconceptions, but even more he dislikes fellow Africans who shun tradition, wear suits and ties instead of boubous and complets, and eat so-called Western food. "*Je suis un africain!*" he says, slapping his chest. "Don't give me hors d'oeuvres, don't give me sandwiches or croissants or pineapple sliced into pieces just big enough for your mouth. Give me a big bowl of rice and sauce and let me at it with my hands!"

He is an African with his mind open. He spends his working hours wearing his white nurse's coat over a tailored pagne shirt. Five times a day he dons a flowing boubou and a skullcap and kneels on a synthetic Oriental prayer rug next to the desk in the salon. He rattles off prayers in Arabic and presses his forehead to the neon-colored mosque on the rug. After work, he changes into a T-shirt and shorts, makes tea, and settles back to listen to music. He is a middle-class educated African but, at the same time, a respecter of tradition. He is progressive—not seduced or dazzled by Western culture, as so many of his compatriots are, but interested, nonetheless, in what it has to offer.

Sidibé dunks his hands in a bowl of water to clean off the remnants of bushrat brain, grabs his flashlight, and stands abruptly. "I'm so glad you're here!" he says. "You can explain what Bob Marley is saying!" He opens the cabinet under the television and pulls out boxes of old tapes.

Then he lugs one of his stereos onto the porch; he keeps a collection of them, since each has a sickness of some sort. He rotates them like invalids—too much action and one might expire completely. A tape is slipped in, and Sidibé stretches back in his chair, grinning, his hands behind his head, before the music starts. He wants to know all about "Redemption Song." "'Emancipate yourself from mental slavery?' I think I understand the words," he says, "but what does it *mean?*" Later, he sings a few bars of "Waiting in Vain." It sounds as if he's crammed all the words together and sliced them up in the wrong places.

I click through his box of tapes, finding African musicians I've never heard of, old Phil Collins, Rod Stewart with a long earring before his "Some Guys Have All the Luck" days. But I also discover Van Morrison, a Rolling Stones bootleg, Peter Tosh, Dire Straits, Pink Floyd, Tracy Chapman, Sting. His mixed tapes flit from Donna Summer to Joe Cocker to Bonnie Raitt.

The villagers have little exposure to popular Ivorian music, and Western music is an unknown entity. Badjans veer up to the village plastered with photos of Madonna with streaked hair and lace bandannas. Youths in Ferké parade around with Tupac glaring from their T-shirts. Yet all this amounts to is snazzy decoration. Ask whom the faces belong to, and most people shrug their shoulders. Even educated Abidjanais with an ear to the West can list only Céline Dion and a few French singers when asked about Western music. But Sidibé has done his research about music, and everything else too, it seems. This box of motley tapes is just the beginning.

Excitement runs just under Sidibé's skin. It shows up as mischief in his eyes when he challenges me. It springs into his eyebrows when he's learning and opens his whole face when he's amused. Tonight he hums with good energy. He says, "I'm going to teach you all about African music." He flips in a new tape. "Hear that twang like a guitar? It's traditional, a calabash with some strings. It's called a *ngoni.* They have them here, but this is typical Senegalese music." He plays Malian, Nigerian, Zairean, and Ivorian music and points out how some are based on fluid, nasal call and response, others on reggae beats and political words, others on whining sound effects and shouts. He tells me stories of the artists, of Fela Kuti from Nigeria, who had over twenty wives, ran for president, and died of AIDS last year, and Alpha Blondy, who supported Houphouët and believes that Africa's worst enemies are Africans. And then Bob is back, and Sidibé settles down, content, and sings "Steer it up" to the sky.

Abi brings out a pot of *bisap,* that sweet hibiscus drink that puts soda to shame. She figured out early how much I love it and whips it up on the sly to surprise me with it at dinner. She has her seven-month-old tied to her back. The other five children have been cleaning the dishes and studying their schoolbooks by lamplight. Sidibé's son Tidiane places my glass and four bowls in a neat line in the dust in front of me. I pour theirs first and we all drink it together—smiling a little into our cups. Sidibé reaches into a bag at his feet and pulls out a loaf of fresh-baked sweet bread made by the school director's wife. Still warm. He chews a piece pensively. "It's a good thing you've come," he says. "Before now all we knew of Americans was Mike Tyson and the Baptists down the road. One is a cannibal. The other thinks we're cannibals." Then he turns to me and says, "So far, I think we get along pretty well, don't you?"

Sidibé handles his patients with a gruff sense of humor: no woman feels compromised when he pokes a syringe of antibiotics in her hip, no man feels challenged when Sidibé speaks of his wife's pregnant body. He brushes over awkwardness by making them laugh. And, besides medicine, people come to Sidibé for good conversation and the harmony of his courtyard: there are no wives bickering, no *vieilles* (old women) giving orders, no babies screaming. Instead, there is Abi, who cooks for her husband as a good wife should, but who listens and muses and adds spice and insight to conversations. She is not like their wives— she doesn't subscribe to their rituals, doesn't belong to their cooperatives. She has only a few good friends among the women, but the village men are intrigued by her.

Sidibé speaks intelligently of politics, whether in the village or in the country, and the villagers want to hear what he has to say. Not many in the village think outside the boundaries of northern Côte d'Ivoire. Not the mayor, and not the president, who are both illiterate planters. Not the elementary school director, whom I will witness pointing to the Philippines on a map of the world and explaining to his students that this area, the Balkans, saw the start of World War I when Ferdinand was shot off his horse.

Sidibé listens to the radio every day—French BBC, he says, since the state-run news is so warped. He is always in the know, but he is, as they say, *sans façon,* humble. The villagers rely on him as a mouthpiece for everything outside of Nambonkaha. He asks me about American current events. *Guissongui, did you hear that a boy shot a bunch of students at a school in America? Vraiment, ton pays-là. . . .* When he realizes I have lived in the Middle East, the questions stampede. *Does it really go all the way back to Isaac and Ishmael? Who was there first? Is any side right? How can it ever end?* He talks to me about religion. He has read the Koran and the Bible, prays five times a day but is adamant about *understanding* Islam and not just going along with it. Tolerance, he insists, is the key to life. He wants to know more about Judaism; we discuss Buddha. He has come to the conclusion that all faiths merely describe different ways to love the same God. He has principles—totems, he calls them—of his own. He refuses to hit. He won't kill anything bigger than a mouse. Women, as life givers, are traditionally not allowed to slaughter the chicken or the goat for dinner. That much of meal preparation is the husband's duty. At Sidibé's house, however, the animal gets passed over the wall to their Burkinabe neighbor for its execution: Sidibé won't do it.

Sidibé's totems alone distinguish him from most other men, but it's his relationship with his wife that clinches the contrast. Abi and Sidibé eat together, from the same bowl. She sits on a stool close to his long bamboo chair; they talk in low voices, look each other in the eye, and share their food. This is unheard of in a village where the sexes separate to eat, to pray, to mourn, even to work the fields, where the only thing men and women share is the bed—on some nights. There is mutual respect between Sidibé and Abi, and dependence on both sides. This makes Sidibé in some ways one of the most modern men I've met so far in Africa. But in this traditional village, it is something he tries to hide.

The mayor and the president come by Sidibé's courtyard almost daily. The president is short and supercilious. He walks around pompously in a gold chain and a boubou, thrusting out his chest and standing askance with his arms tightly folded, as if to show that he must keep the lid on his bursting masculinity. The mayor is lanky and laid-back. His face falls naturally into a grin; his eyes dance as if life is just hilarious.

Both are successful planters, owing to a dozen hectares of cotton that they reap each year. Their small concrete houses are packed with rarely used furniture. The president's salon is plastered in yellow wallpaper with a sketched pitcher and fruit motif, beamed here from some seventies' suburban kitchen. Photographs dot the wall—some of relatives, many of a friend who immigrated to Italy. Not a good friend, incidentally, but he moved to *Italy!*

For each of their wives—each has three—they've built a mud hut, and the nights of the week are divvied up so that all get the same number of conjugal visits. Both men have a bevy of small children, whose names they invariably forget. They come to Sidibé's with stories of girlfriends in the city, with scandalous anecdotes and frank discussions of problems with their wives.

Polygamy shows that you're a man, demonstrates that you've got some money, and allows you to pass on your name, but it's not all golden according to *Monsieur le Maire.* "I can't have a decent conversation with one of them," he says of his wives one night, "or the other two will get mad. And I can't have one with all of them because they argue too much." He speaks in rapid-fire, staccato French, peppered with Dioula. I'm concentrating hard to understand when suddenly Sidibé turns to me.

"Would you ever marry a man with another wife?" he asks. It catches me off guard. I'm still trying to figure out how I feel about polygamy, having arrived with the sentiment that it was the downfall of Africa. When he turns the focus on me, I blurt out, "No!" and add that I won't marry unless it's for love. They're surprised by my certainty.

Abi and Sidibé have four children, and here they plan to stop. He has been a nurse for nine years and earns about two hundred dollars a month if the check comes. Nurses haven't gotten a raise in eighteen years, he says, despite the devaluation of the CFA. Nonetheless, Sidibé is considered one of the major breadwinners in his extended family and is obliged to help out the others. His oldest brother, a mechanic in Sidibé's native village to the south, has a fickle income. All he is adept at producing is children. His two wives trade off pregnancies, and the child count hovers around eighteen. Spreading the wealth and supporting family is an African institution, and Sidibé's generosity is only driven further by the Muslim tenet of charity. He sends a bag of rice to his brother's family monthly, forwards money for his nieces' and nephews' education, and takes care of a shifting cast of his brother's children. Sidibé seems to have done everything right: his relationship with his wife is healthy and balanced, he's kept his own family to a manageable size, and yet he reaps no benefit from his wise decisions. It's as if he's striding forward with his weight on the foot in the modern world while the other is mired down in old-fashioned obligations.

Tonight the sky is crazy pink and bright. The Saharan wind called the harmattan drifts down in November, they say, and lingers till March, dusting the sky, sucking color from the sun, and killing the ground with thirst. Tonight April is battling the dust, and vividness reigns in the savanna skies. The clouds put on a fire-work show, but then the deep grays roll to the foreground and the wind starts to career around the village. And then comes rain, smacking, gutsy, wet, cold rain. The first since my arrival.

As soon as the wind picks up, whole courtyards are set to running. They grab their boiling pots, collect chairs, laundry, and children and run inside. Once everything is safely in, they look for reasons to go outside again. Sometimes the artifice breaks down completely: they take advantage of the water they don't have to pump and strip down and shower in the streams pouring off the roof. Rain is living, breathing happiness. Mad happiness.

Abi trundles up the terrace steps with the last armful of drying dishes as the drops start. She slams the front door shut, panting and laughing. The eight of us stand in the salon a little breathless, beaming at each other with silly grins. There's one long pause in the action as rain thunders on the roof. Then the older kids glance at one another surreptitiously, and the four of them slip out the door. Adjaratou is the eldest daughter at eleven. She's got Sidibé's lively eyes, and her smile lights up her face. Kharidja is one of Sidibé's older brother's brood. She has lived with the family since toddlerhood. She's eleven, too, but she plays the wisecracking, mischievous sister to angelic Adjaratou. Seven-year-old Tidiane is a skeptic, already toying with idea of being a man. He saunters around with his chest puffed up. But his high-pitched laugh spoils the effect. Tenen comes from the village where Sidibé worked before Nambonkaha. She helped out with the children and the washing there, and has become an adopted daughter. Now she is fifteen, bashful and giggly, with a faint stutter.

The rain floods the cement floor of the open porch. The kids strip down to their skivvies, throw their lithe little bodies on the floor, and slide on the smooth surface, back and forth on their backs, on their stomachs, gliding, squealing, limbs flickering into form in the lightning. Rain slaps the roof and thunder growls, echoing across the savanna. Amid the roar their laughter rings out. Tenen peels off her clothes too, giggling uncontrollably as she stands with a bar of soap under a stream of water gushing off the roof.

Little Aicha, four years old, is still nervous about the thunder thing. She drapes a white cloth over her head and wraps herself up against the cold. Standing against my legs like a tiny ghost, she refuses to let go of her fears and plunge onto the slick floor with the others.

Sidibé leans out the door, shaking his head, his face drawn up in a wistful grin. *"Si j'étais enfant..."* If only I were a child, he says, and the wind billows up and floats his words away.

2

Stranger

I have painted the porous, crumbling concrete of my house. Two plastic mats serve as my couch and my bed. Abi helped me pick out a lantern at the market in Ferké so I may survive past dusk. A kerosene stove sits on the floor in the corner, and there is a line of edibles along the wall. (Eating suddenly seems a chore. There's nothing quick to prepare except mutant Quaker oats from the United Arab Emirates, so I have oatmeal for breakfast, oatmeal for lunch.) I have ordered a desk and a table from a carpenter in Ferké and have moved, finally, into my humble home, out on my own after weeks at Sidibé's and months with the N'Guessans in Abenké. My new privacy is like letting out a long-held breath.

The owner of my house is an old man with a mustache named Goutoumaya who is said to have fought with the French during World War II. He carries a musket everywhere, as if he's expecting invading armies or a miraculous influx of game. He calls me *"ma femme"* and asks what I've prepared for him. He's joking, of course, but I only became certain after I told him I eat only raw vegetables and oatmeal.

Young men have built a woven hay wall around a square of dirt outside my door. All of a sudden a regular patch of village is my own courtyard. Through the red metal slats that screech open, my bedroom window looks out behind my house on the winding path that serves as a main north-south axis. Across it lies a courtyard with two small mud huts and sons that come in all sizes. My front window looks out at the leaves of a mango tree and its dangling fruit. If I walk out the door and look left over the top of the hay wall, I can see an old woman sitting under another mango tree. To the right, fifty feet away, is my latrine and shower: a cement box divided by a wall, with a hole on one side and a drain on the other, and then a wide expanse of nothing before the next courtyard begins.

The burning glare of a few weeks ago has let up; the downpour broke the harmattan spell, and the village almost sparkles. The dust has impossibly given way to green fuzz, and color changes everything. "Look!" I exclaim to Sidibé's niece Kharidja. "There's grass! The village is bright!" She sucks her teeth. "Grass is no good, Guissongui. It's dirty. Bad things like snakes and scorpions hide in it! As soon as it grows a little more, we'll dig it out." She speaks as if reassuring me.

As soon as I have a courtyard, I have children. Big-bellied and small, lean and strong, tall and tiny, covered in dust or in talcum powder, dressed, naked, undressing, crying, yelling, laughing, dancing, fighting. Within hours of my move my courtyard has became the local hangout. From dawn until late night there are up to twenty kids of all ages within the fifteen square feet of my enclosure. Before my bags are unpacked, they've sequestered my pack of cards and are deep into a hardball game of *huit américain*—a flavor of crazy eights that everyone assumes I should know since I'm *American* and everything. Everyone not playing stands inches from my screen door, watching me.

This first night, however, they leave an hour or so after I finish dinner to dance at a marriage in the president's courtyard a few meters away. Generator-powered fluorescent lights have been rigged up nearby, and the white glow outside my back window throws a diagonal shaft of light across my bedroom wall. Shadows stream down it, bobbing, heads thrown back; I can see their noses, their mouths moving, sliding across my wall. My first night alone after all these months, and I'm surrounded by noisy ghosts.

I step outside. Voices cackle and sing from all directions, flashlight beams skitter across the night. "*Guissongui! Changwoanan!*" Good evening, they call. I can't tell what corner of the night they come from, much less who calls, but I call back anyway to reassert myself.

One evening the president of the women, Kinafou, invites me to learn how to make millet cakes. I miss our date by accident, and trek across the village with a translator to apologize the next day. Kinafou is in her forties, maybe, and is the most powerful woman in the village. Her twisted teeth poke out so that she can barely get her lips around them, and carved lines radiate from her mouth, vestiges of the old ritual of scarification, in which babies' faces were cut to denote familial allegiance. She's feisty and berates me in Niarafolo for not coming sooner. I pound some corn as penance and demand "pardon," laughing, though not sure she's joking. To demand "pardon" is paramount in West African social custom. That one word, if muttered with the right gravity, will get you off any hook.

Kinafou's eyes are light and soft. She looks at me directly—most women here don't—and it seems as though I've known her for years. There's amusement in her face and perception, but most important there's an assurance there that she is not swayed by any difference in our skin. She's summing me up without pandering, fully confident in herself as an African woman and unwilling to fall into the inferiority trap. As I leave, she piles food in my arms: a stack of greasy millet fritters, four mangoes, and a gigantic bowl of *kabato*.

Plantain trees are scarce up north, and the *foutou banane* I ate in the south is a rare treat. The diet here is based on *kabato*—a bland mix of corn flour and water that requires, for each meal, hours of pounding and sifting corn till dried kernels become fine flour. Down south, women sit by their mortars and pound with a dull thud. Here the action is aerobic. Girls stand with the pestle high over their head and slam it into the mortar, jumping a little to offset the shock on their arms. It makes a hollow *tok tok* sound that rings out across the whole village. I wake up to it in the morning, the whole village *tokking;* sometimes it goes on till I close my book late at night.

Cooking kabato takes all morning. It goes through several stages of consistency: buttermilk, porridge, then pudding, until it reaches a flanlike state. It takes the shape of its container, and some digging is required to pull loose a jiggling hunk. It's a joy to cut, like tofu, but eating it is no treat. It tastes like pasty nothing and leaves your stomach empty not long after you've cleaned your plate. Kabato with sauce—okra, eggplant, leaf, peanut—is breakfast, lunch, and dinner for the villagers. I can eat it, but I don't enjoy it much. I'd rather have plain old oatmeal with brown sugar. Kinafou's bowl of kabato is only cause for consternation, it doesn't melt or burn or dissolve—there's really no way to get rid of it.

The kids mostly just stand in droves at my screen, jostling for a good position, but a few have decided to show their appreciation of my arrival, or at least to buy credit for when they want something from me later. A tiny one named Moussa sprints to my courtyard daily with his arms bristling with mangoes. He's one of the assorted pack of boys from the courtyard behind me. He speaks a bit of French somehow, despite the fact that no one else his size seems to. Every day, I take the fruit from him with a big show of thanks and put them in a basin. Within a few days there is a towering pile. Most are squashed and bruised— Moussa's mango-collecting methods involve a giant stick and a long drop.

The best housewarming present by far comes from the butcher. On the way back from a walk, I pass his rickety stand, perched on a hill next to the paved road to Burkina Faso, and stop in to greet him. Lumps of raw meat line his crooked table; cow heads stare disconcertingly at the sky. The butcher hails from Mali, an ex-nomad of the Fulani, or Peul, tribe who's come to rest in Nambonkaha. He grins and says in curlicue French that he'd like to offer me some *"pattes de boeuf."* I assume my own translation can't be right—he must mean some kind of pâté. But the next thing I know he's selecting cow legs as if they were pool cues. He thrusts four at me—all knee to hoof, still covered with fine black and white hair. Sidibé's son Tidiane bounces beside me, clearly thrilled at my acquisition. He grabs them, shouting, "I'll carry them home!" and tucks them under his arms. He runs back to Sidibé's house with me at his heels and throws them on the ground next to the fire. They land in pairs, calling to mind a cow running so fast she left her body behind. Abi grills them up, but when they're finally cooked to a furry gristle and passed around to be gnawed in all their two-foot glory, I am already home with my oatmeal.

I came here with three months of training under my belt. I was packed off to this village with only a collection of health-education books and a head full of vague ideas. I wanted no direction, no preconceived mission, and that's what I've gotten. I am here to see what I can make starting from scratch, and the tiny village of Nambonkaha is my ready canvas. But where do you start when health is vast and elusive at the same time? How do you strike a balance between old and new? How do you promote behavior change so that people have more control over the state of their bodies but stop at the threshold where important traditions get destroyed? And how can you presume to change anything at all as an outsider with a two-year contract? The infirmary runs well, thanks to Sidibé's diligence. There's no role for me there. Vaccination campaigns seem well attended, but they last only a few days at a time. The clinic budget committee seems surprisingly uncorrupt. So what is my calling?

I start a list of education techniques I can try, and it grows off the page. The items are mostly games, considering that my obvious audience comprises the kids in my courtyard. I could emphasize hygiene with a kid wash. Or make up a card game based on good and bad health practices. We could do a puppet show about the importance of washing hands. But these are trifles. Such fleeting amusements will never change habits; they'll be remembered more for their fun than the lesson. I could start a carrot cooperative: instead of just nutrient-empty eggplants and hot peppers, women could provide themselves with a great source of vitamin A. Except how do you introduce a completely new food into an ingrained and unchanging diet? All my training has convinced me that no development is worthwhile unless the idea comes from the community. I survey the villagers about the needs of Nambonkaha. But they seem happy enough to boil up bark for sickness. They are not clamoring for any specific changes. And I have no idea where to start. Despite my blossoming knack for patience, my acceptance of this slower pace, and my general happiness, I am American in the end. Maybe time *is* money. I have only two years. A blot of guilt starts small and spreads as the weeks tick on.

A month and a half into my stay, I am washing dishes on the stoop when a crew of village men and Sidibé filter through my courtyard opening. Something leaden sinks to my gut. My conscience writes the script before the conversation starts. I imagine it will start out with Why exactly are you here and aren't you supposed to be working? And maybe it will end up with some unbearable demand: Please just build us a new school or bring us a water tower. How do you explain to people who have never left the village that it takes some time to figure out life this far away from home? They take their places dotted around the courtyard, hands behind their backs. I square my shoulders for the barrage of questions.

The chief's face is stern as he speaks. He talks for a few minutes, but all I understand is my name, Guissongui, which keeps bobbing up amid the foreign words. The message trickles down through a few listeners before it gets to me, diluted from flowery Niarafolo to prayer-filled Dioula to plain old French. "The elders would like to offer you a gift," Sidibé says. A rice sack rustles, and a large pitcher of guinea fowl eggs appears. I'm so relieved and abashed that I thrust out my left hand to receive my gift. I might as well have spat on it. The left hand has rigidly prescribed responsibilities (toilet paper has yet to catch on in rural West Africa). Extending it is a great insult. Sidibé grabs the pitcher from me and hands it back to the chief. He clears his throat at me, then crosses his arms, "This time do it correctly."

The chief presents the eggs again, bowing slightly at the waist. This time I accept them with my right hand. Thirty guinea fowl eggs. What's a girl to do? I shake their hands, all of them, and send my message of thanks back up the chain to the chief. Guinea fowl eggs are small and hard and mostly bright orange yolk. I learn how to cook crème caramel in old oatmeal tins and feed my courtyard regulars the biggest dose of protein they've had in weeks.

The next day, the chief and his retinue return. The troop of long boubous and prayer caps converges at my courtyard entrance, and this time I'm sure it's trouble. The chief takes the floor, his voice solemn and low. He's brought the presidents of each campement. Each one speaks before they get to the point. "Normally," says the chief through all his translators, "we give a visitor enough corn or enough yams to last for many months. But you're American and we don't know what you eat, so we can't offer food." He pulls out a stack of bills. "So please accept what we've collected from each campement." In a superlative act of irony, they've pooled together seven thousand CFA (about twelve dollars, enough to last at least two weeks), so that I may eat.

I have five flashlights, and each performs its own trick. I have a raincoat with zippers and net material so I never get too hot in a downpour. I have a shelf crammed with books and a shortwave that speaks Arabic, Japanese, Dutch, and Russian. They have mud huts with maybe a few chairs and faded pages of old magazines fastened to the wall. I ride my twenty-one-speed Peace Corps-issue bike to Ferké not to save a dollar on transport, but for the luxury of exercise. They ride in from their settlements on cranky old mopeds or bikes with a single cog because it's the only option. And *they* give *me* charity. I just stare at it—near tears. To refuse their offer would be pure insult. So I do the rounds again, shaking hands with all the men in boubous, saying over and over, "*An y ché*," Thank you. There are a few sides to my gratitude: my stipend has gone toward the screening, painting, and basic furnishing of my two rooms, and I have all of three thousand CFA (about five dollars) to my name till my next deposit comes in a month. They have saved me from certain—if brief—destitution.

．　　．　　．

Every afternoon as the sun sinks into the trees, egrets glide golden across the sky. They converge from all directions into rippling arrows and head west, toward the sun. I want to know how they get back east to start all over again. Maybe they fill the sky before dawn, maybe they trickle back into the bush throughout the night. Whenever I see them, they are heading west.

My designated translator, Dramane, explained during my first weeks here that the birds fly nightly to a breeding ground not far from the village. There's a pond down the road a ways, he said, and a wooden bridge. This was before the first rains. Life in general seemed thirsty. I said, "I'd love to see a pond." Dramane seems a dainty man, but only around me. He is my age, an inch or two taller than me. His head is small and dark, and his nose swoops low over his mouth. With others he speaks normally, but he addresses me in an irritating falsetto, as if I'd shatter if his voice had a bass note.

"It's quite far—are you sure you can walk all the way?" he asked. I swallowed sarcasm and explained that people walk for fun in America. I coaxed Abi to come too, hoping she'd dilute his silly antics. We ambled for half a mile along a dirt road, between the dead remnants of a cotton field and short, crisped savanna trees. Then a wide expanse of burned weeds opened up to our right. "That," said Dramane, "is an egret breeding ground." But it was silent and charred and there was not a bird in sight, so I was a little skeptical. We walked on a few meters. Dramane stopped suddenly and planted his feet. "Here's the pond!" he declared, an octave too high. We were standing in a sand hollow; the ground around us was brown and thirsting.

"*Where's* the pond?" I asked, assuming it had all been a joke or my French skills were really floundering.

"Right here!" He looked around. "Only it hasn't rained yet." He pointed out a log bridge nestled in the trees. It started across from the egret nesting ground, a makeshift boardwalk of twisted branches lashed with wire and strips of bark. As the terrain fell away, the bridge continued through the trees, twenty feet above the ground at its highest point. "It was ancestors who built it," Dramane said, pursing his lips. "They came one night and the next morning it was complete. No one saw them at work." Dramane explained that during the rainy season the whole area fills with water.

I wobbled across the bridge behind him. "If you live in the campements," he continued, "and you need to go to the market or the mosque or the clinic, you have to cross the bridge because the water is too deep for walking. At the peak of rains, sitting on the highest part of the bridge, you can dangle your feet in the water."

On the other side of the dry pond stood a tall tree with a carpet of chicken feathers at its base. "This is where they do their adoration," Abi whispered, with her eyes theatrically wide. "What do you mean, adoration?" I asked, but she'd tell me no more. Dramane cleared his throat and said, "The annual sacrifice to the ancestors. This is where they do it, because this is where a lot of the important ancestors live."

Beyond the bridge lay the campements where Nambonkaha began. "Several families from a village just outside of Ferké migrated in search of new land to till," said Dramane. "They walked north, led by a man named Nambon—that means Stranger. They crossed a stream, and filtered into the bush. Eventually each family created its own settlement, or campement, and all fell under Nambon's authority." What year was it? "No one knows," he said. "They didn't follow the Western calendar so much back then. But no one alive now was alive then." When the French colonists began to build a major route to Burkina Faso and Mali, they tapped into the local population. They hired young men to coax their brethren out of the fields. Once roped in, the laborers were virtually roped up, forced to work long hours in the hot sun.

Nambon put up a fight, attempting to organize his people to resist the "recruiters." But his efforts fell short, and he was taken away and never heard from again. Legend has it he was killed by the colonists. They say Nambon derived his strength from the stream, that through its water he communicated with the ancestors. Our patriarch spends occasional nights on his own in the bush, striking deals with the spirits, soliciting the help of ghosts. Since the stream is still the key to communication with Nambon and the rest of the other world, the annual sacrifice is held on its banks. *Kaha* is the Niarafolo word for village. Nambonkaha is the village of Nambon. The Village of Stranger.

Early in June, I take a walk to the ancestors' bridge on my own. Leaves have sprouted since the rain came; grasses push out of the dust. The dead stalks of last year's cotton have been hacked down, and in the fields on either side of the path, villagers chop at the soil. At the breeding ground, the trees bloom with squawking egrets. The "pond" Dramane swore by is now a thin rush of water cutting through the sand hollow. I climb the bridge and stand at the center under a canopy of leaves, watching egret feathers ripple down the stream.

Far ahead, on the road back to the village, a dark figure appears in the half light, wearing a ragged cloak and walking with his head bowed. I look away for a moment and then he is gone, dissolved into the low trees. He is one of a small cast of *fous,* or crazy people, a token part of every village. He sleeps in the wilderness and appears occasionally to weed huge patches of the village. He kneels at intervals in his work, reverently holding up a leaf and nibbling it as if it were sacred. There is also a babbling *fou* who used to chop wood for Abi, till one day he left his pile of branches on the train tracks and the train from Burkina Faso shrieked at the village for hours.

After two months in the village, I've become fairly familiar with Nambonkaha's fous. Some were apparent right from the start, like the young woman I first saw dancing under a mango tree wearing nothing but a tattered pair of underwear with the back torn out. Breasts have about as much sex appeal as elbows in the village. Once a woman has her first child, it doesn't matter if she goes shirtless in her courtyard. But below the waist is off-limits across the board, even in the presence of other women. That crazy girl danced on nearly naked as tittering children peered around corners.

Other fous seem sane most days and burst out unpredictably. One who has an obsession with property owns nothing but makes the rounds of the village, accusing others of wrongfully squatting in his house. "Who gave you that house?" he growled at me last week, his finger pointing rigidly at my door. "Don't you know it's *mine?* I didn't even have time to paint it and then they stole it from me!" I nodded gravely and ran to Sidibé, who said that the fou shows up at the clinic occasionally to try to evict him.

The fous have a few things in common. They each have their particular fixation, and for the most part, they've adapted it to some task in the village. The angry landlord keeps empty houses in order. The tall one scrapes down grasses so people can keep their courtyards "clean." Also, notably, nearly all of them speak good French in a village where most older men and younger women do not.

The houseless landlord depends on Kinafou, the president of the women, for food but pumps his own water and does his own chores. The dancing girl gets water, too. And despite the fact that during seizures she occasionally throws herself into the cooking fire, she also prepares meals for herself and her aunt every day. She speaks in a high-pitched voice and sounds nearly normal until you pay attention to her words. "*Ça va bien, Djeta?*" I call to her as I pass. "*On est là,*" she says, We're here. And then she always adds, "We haven't died yet."

People here seem so resilient, so hardy, I wonder how much they can take before they break. I'm sure there are labels, syndromes and sicknesses that a Western psychologist could pin on the fous. But here there is just *folie,* craziness, a blanket term for those whose life scars are inside.

Returning from the bridge, I gather my buckets left earlier at Abi's gate and fill them up at the pump outside the clinic. Abi cries out to me from across the courtyard, "Guiss, stay for dinner— we're having braised fish and *attiéké.*" This, she knows, is the perfect bait. Manioc, or cassava, is a flavorless, nutritionally empty root that Africans have contrived a hundred ways of preparing. Attiéké is the winning combination, the silver lining, manioc's redemption. The root is pressed by hand through a screen till it looks like couscous, then fermented. It tastes sour and, by itself, it's likely to lodge in your throat. But it's served with grilled fish and tomatoes, cucumbers, and onions, covered with vinaigrette and hot pepper sauce. You ball up a handful of attiéké, drag it through the dressing, pull off some fish, and eat it off your fingers. It's fresh, tangy; I could eat it for every meal.

Abi is scaling fish, scattering translucent flakes in the dust. I pull up a stool next to her. "Where are you coming from?" she asks. When I tell her, she looks up from her fish, her eyes wide. "You went across the bridge?" Her voice is low. She narrows her eyes. "Did you remember to sacrifice chickens first?" Sacrifice *what?* "You remember the chicken feathers at the adoration ground? Every time you cross the bridge, you have to give the chief two chickens to sacrifice." Ai! How did that escape my translator? "What do I do?" I ask, trying not to panic. She shrugs. "I guess you can go to the chief and ask pardon." I am perhaps paranoid about offending this culture. I can laugh it off when I pick up food with my ignoble left hand instead of my right or when I skip a certain step in the protocol. But I'm terrified of unknowingly transgressing some sacred law and alienating the community for good.

When the mayor shows up in Sidibé's courtyard at night, it seems like a good time to confess my sins. "I forgot to sacrifice a chicken today for crossing the bridge," I say. The mayor sits up in his seat. "What are you talking about?" I tell them about Abi's reprimand, expecting to render them serious. They burst out laughing. "Abi *had* you!" Sidibé smacks his thigh. Abi mumbles something from the darkness of her pots and then lets out a peal of deep laughter. The mayor cackles with his head in his hands. "You don't have to do anything to cross the bridge—it's a public road."

"But what about the feathers?"

"That's something different," he says. "That has nothing to do with the bridge." Abi laughs on. Vengefully? Derisively? What is that sound in her voice? She laughs a lot—a deep, earthshaking belly laugh that sometimes has an edge in it. Abi can be mean: she bellows, wags her hand, and her kids scatter because she's not afraid to hit.

I chastise Abi for leading me astray. Then I laugh too—it

seems my best defense. If I'm sensitive about this, it will set a bad precedent. It's a practical joke, that's all. Maybe it is funny around the edges, but I'm scratching out my path, I'm trying hard to understand this place. She's mocking my efforts and my ignorance. Abi will let out a stream of insults to someone's face and then follow them up with a long laugh as if to dismiss all she has said. "I like to have fun," she has told me many times. But this isn't fun. She might be testing me to see how far I can be pushed. I could handle that. Or else it's more serious. I have this nagging sense that she could be jealous of my friendship with her husband. Abi has cooked so many meals for me, has offered to wash my clothes; she nursed me back to health when I had dysentery in my first weeks. Yet I have to stack up the sandbags so her barbs about my clothes, my weight, my French don't hurt. She is my closest female friend here, but I don't know if I can trust her.

Angélique instructs in a singsong voice she must have learned years ago at school. Each phrase is prefaced with a transitional word and a long pause. *"D'abord... tu prends la farine."* She is directing me as I mix a batch of the sweet bread that has made her famous in Nambonkaha.

The lesson is tightly controlled. Angélique holds up each ingredient: the flour, the yeast, the sugar, the vat of neon-orange, unrefrigerated "margarine" with a year-long shelf life. She explains how much to put in, but then takes each ingredient from me to adjust the quantity. After all, her measurements are in her eyes; there are no tablespoons here. When Angélique makes bread, she mixes and kneads twenty pounds' worth of dough in a huge basin. Then she rolls it into a few hundred firm little balls, sticks them—in groups of two or four or five—into tomato sauce cans of all sizes, and shovels them into a round oven made of dried manure. She's going on ten months pregnant with her sixth child. My apprenticeship, I thought, might give her a break. Instead, it seems to be complicating matters. I crouch over the basin, the muscles in my arms bursting as I knead the mass. Drops of sweat plunk into the dough; I am breathing hard and covered in sticky stuff to the elbows. Angélique looks at me struggling and says, That's probably enough. Though she does it with a full-grown baby tucked in her belly, she is graceful and composed. I have come out flushed and panting.

Angélique's husband, the wall-eyed school director, is polite when he speaks to me but seems severe with his family. In the fonctionnaire system, civil servants working in a village often come from an entirely different section of the country. Sometimes this fosters an important bridge between ethnic groups and helps debunk stereotypes. Sometimes it means strained relations between village and fonctionnaire. In Nambonkaha, aside from the two junior teachers, all government families come from the north. Angélique and her husband hail from a village just on the other side of Ferké. Their ethnic group, like the Niarafolo, is a subdivision of the larger Senoufo tribe. They can communicate with the villagers in the local language, and over their five years in the village they've garnered respect and trust in the community.

Angélique is one of the very few women her age who has been to school. Abi made it to second grade and then dropped out, but Angélique tells me proudly, "Me, I know how to read. I went to school. I was a good student." She graduated from sixth grade nearly twenty years ago, when it was still uncommon for girls to be educated. Now she seems tired out by life—maybe it's the baby who refuses to appear after all these months. Maybe it's the pounding, the sweeping, the washing, the cooking that don't diminish despite the burden she's carrying. She holds the distinction of being the only Christian woman in the village. Despite her friends, I think it makes her lonely. She beams at me when she finds out I was born Christian too, says maybe we can pray together. I don't say I never pray.

I sit at an old wooden table, rolling dough balls that look soft and flabby next to Angélique's. She is patient, shows me over and over, but moves fast. There's something in her fingers, in the pressure of her palms that I can't mimic. She smiles at my frustration and pinches off more dough. I taper my efforts: no use sabotaging the whole batch. But it's addictive, this work. I tell her I'll come back for the next round at dawn.

The sun rises on Angélique and me balling up sweet bread to the waking beat of pestle and mortar. She has spared me torture by kneading the dough late last night. Now a hundred little spheres—hers perfect, mine a little slack—are stuffed in tomato cans and covered with a pagne. While the loaves rise, we cross the village to visit the wife of Monsieur Coulibaly, the government agriculture agent—both also Senoufo fonctionnaires. Madame Coulibaly is otherwise known by the nickname Sidibé has given her: Femme Claire, or Light Woman. Next to Abi and Angélique's deep black, her skin looks like mahogany.

Femme Claire has large hands, like a man's. Her voice is husky, and she laughs a lot. I follow her back to Angélique's courtyard. A wide patch of her back shows above her scooped collar. Her skin in the morning light glows like embers. Like Angélique and Abi, Femme Claire is in her mid-thirties, but unlike the others she has kept a young figure. She has no children of her own. Sterility in Africa, I've been told, is a source of great shame. Yet relatives seem happy to share their families. Femme Claire has raised a niece and nephew on loan from her sister, and no one seems to shun her. On occasion, she borrows her husband's moped and rides into town. It's becoming a standard mode of transportation for city women, but it's still a giant leap for womankind in the village. Even Angélique and Abi wouldn't dream of it. Angélique says, *"Cette femme, elle est comme garçon."*

Angélique disappears into the small cement room that serves as her pantry and emerges balancing two calabashes full of cloudy brown liquid. Baking bread makes Angélique popular, but *chapalo,* millet beer, is her ticket to success. Her house is the closest thing to a *maquis*—a traditional outdoor eating and drinking establishment—that Nambonkaha has to offer. It is distant enough from the mosque's air of disapproval that villagers may imbibe without too much shame.

Angélique hands the gourds to Femme Claire and me. I swirl the beer around, and white clouds of sediment bulge up from the bottom. I take a sip. It's spicy with hot peppers, fizzy, a shade citrus. I'm sold. This is like an initiation—I feel as if I've crossed some barrier. It's barely eighty-thirty in the morning and I'm sipping chapalo somewhat surreptitiously in this Muslim village. Angélique is Christian, so there's no sin there. And Femme Claire is too—this morning at least. We sit with our gourdfuls, clandestine in our nipping, waiting for the bread to cook.

And then other women start to appear. Some sneak around the corner, others stride right up. The chapalo drinkers, it appears, are mainly old widows. A woman who grins as if she's been tippling since dawn hobbles up to fill a calabash. An old withered woman with swollen ankles and no toes arrives with an empty jug. Islam comes off like a coat in hot weather. They'll put it back on again—just after this bowl is drained.

Angélique drags out a basin and a rice sack full of peanuts. I grab a handful and start popping open shells, pinging nuts into the basin. Then I nonchalantly ask how they met their husbands. Femme Claire throws her face to the sky and lets out a sharp laugh. Angélique looks at the ground, shaking her head. There are traces of bitterness in the twists of their mouths, and it occurs to me to take back the question. Finally Angélique says, "My husband wanted to be a priest. He traveled far south and went to divinity school for two years." But apparently he couldn't quite cut it. He became a teacher instead, then came back to the village to find a wife. And he found her. *"C'est ça qui est là."* There it is. They live in a government house with enough furniture, enough beds for their children. They eat well. She's not independent, but she is a breadwinner in her own right. Her sweet bread and chapalo earnings are enough to keep the business going and to allow her to buy vegetables at the market. Occasionally she runs out of money to buy flour, since she also has to pay for the family's pots and pans. But sometimes her husband will give her a loan.

Femme Claire's story is shorter. When she speaks French, she cobbles together subjects and verbs that don't quite match. *"C'était pas mon affaire,"* she says. It wasn't even my business. "My papa said I must marry Monsieur Coulibaly. So I did." End of story. Her husband is a decent, benevolent man who makes a good living as an agriculturalist. They work together on vast experimental gardens. Still, the decision was her parents', not hers.

I later ask Abi about her marriage, and a smile plays on her mouth when she speaks of meeting Sidibé. "He was nice, he paid visits to my courtyard a lot, but *vraiment*, I was not interested," she says happily. "I went to Abidjan and I liked my good life there!" Then on a visit home she saw Sidibé and—*pof!*—she was pregnant. She claps. "*C'est fini.*" Unlike the other women, she's happy to tell the story. I've come across Abi and Sidibé sitting at a table on their porch drinking black coffee and chatting, a scene that I sometimes forget is near revolutionary. First of all, no one ever drinks their coffee black here. Second, no man in the village drinks anything sitting across from his wife, having an earnest conversation.

3

Mba'a

I don't have to shoo children away in order to open my door anymore. The indiscriminant masses have tapered down to a collection of regulars. Though I'm still a spectator sport, I've found activities to distract them from my screen. Colored pencils and scrap paper have distinguished the artists; my discarded training papers come back covered with odd, squarish human figures. The pack of cards I sacrificed to the children has become, in a matter of weeks, a frayed and dwindling pile that no longer fits in the box.

Many of the regulars are the boys next door. Mandou is the oldest at about fourteen, Daouda is maybe ten, and Moussa the mango collector, fiveish. Somehow they speak patchwork French despite the fact that their parents have withheld any form of education and don't know more than a dozen words of it themselves. Mandou is frank and funny, a leader and clown. His trademark is high-drama speeches declaiming life's joys and injustices. We get along famously.

Usually, blackness permeates the village by seven and life retreats behind closed doors soon after the evening meal. But tonight the moon is full, and it's like someone left the hall light on. The village reappears after dusk like a black-and-white photograph—all silvers and shades of gray. Most nights, without my trusty headlamp, I trip over rocks and trample on cow pies and scorpions on any journey outdoors. But there are no hazards tonight. I leave my headlamp on the shelf and step out into the fresh, bright night. Young men swagger by in pairs, women chatter and pound corn in the courtyard across the way. No one can resist coming out to play. The silver sound of little girls singing ripples in from across the village. It bobs and babbles—I can tell by the cadence that they are dancing fast.

All this astronomical interference with bedtime also means that the children playing cards in my courtyard could very well play until dawn. It's a game of *huit américain*, made giddier by moonlight. Mandou, the ringleader, flings down a jack with a flourish and crackling laughter—jacks skip the next player. He rearranges his hand, a thick mess of cards pointing every which way, and looks up at me. "Guiss, do you know that the sacrifice is tomorrow?" The question seems jarring amid all this glee. The sacrifice? Abi and Dramane have teased me with tidbits of information, but I have no idea what it really entails.

"What's it for?" I ask Mandou. He straightens his back. His explanations are charmingly outlandish and always end in a harangue about his poor French skills. "They shoot guns. The old man," he says, referring to the village patriarch (the chief of all chiefs, a spry bearded fellow in his seventies who bikes to and from his settlement in the fields several times a week), "takes a chicken. Because everybody who wants to brings a chicken. Because if you had bad luck this year or you need good luck for something you started, you have to kill a chicken for the people in the water. . . . Ah, *mais, vraiment,* I can't explain it right."

After noon the next day, a series of musket shots shakes the village. Dramane drops by just in time to lead me down toward the ancestors' bridge. With all the excitement, he seems to have forgotten his dainty airs; his voice is masculine, his steps sure. And he's explaining everything. The gunshots signal the departure of the patriarch for the stream. Why sacrifice? I ask him.

"Say you planted a new kind of crop or just got married," he explains, "or maybe you've just sent your son away to secondary school in the city. You bring a chicken to offer to the genies—the spirits—in the creek to ensure your success." The patriarch and the elders bring chickens for the big-ticket demands: abundant crops for the villagers, enough rain during planting season, freedom from blights of pests or disease. In a nutshell, the sacrifice is a petition to the ancestors to look after their village, indemnity in case Allah's will does not come through.

The balafon band arrives on bicycle, their giant instruments tied upside down onto bike racks, gourds vulnerable like bare bellies. The villagers hop across the stones in the creek—it's wider now than when I last saw it three weeks ago, and brown with dust it's licked off the savanna. The spectators separate by social group. The kids veer left to perch on a giant log. The women collect in a grove a few feet up the hill. The men take their places on fallen trees around the sacrifice spot, a clearing carpeted with feathers. I suppose I belong with the women, but Dramane and an elder call me over. My gender, apparently, is of no issue. They want me front and center for the sacrifice.

When the music hushes, the patriarch, speaking Niarafolo, introduces the first chicken: a white hen, the most coveted kind of poultry around. With his eyes lowered, he indicates the hen's owner and details his wishes. After a stream of blessings and solicitations, the patriarch hands the hen to another elder, who pulls back her head and, in one swift move, slits her throat. The children inch forward. Everyone else cranes in to watch the flopping death dance. If the bird finally dies on its back, it portends a good year; death on its stomach is a bad omen. This particular hen brazenly gives up the ghost on her side. The patriarch reaches for the next bird.

When the deed is done (apparently only a few villagers can expect good years), little boys pluck and singe the chickens over a small fire and offer them to the elders. Young women walk down to the water, swinging babies of all sizes off their backs and giving them baptisms in the creek. They believe the water swims with ancestors and good fortune, a whole flowing bath of traditional protection. What I see is mud and egret droppings. But I can only wince—to decry the dangers of parasites and germs would only highlight my alien status. I have to find a way to work *within* their belief system. Meanwhile, the older women uncover a giant vat of home-brewed millet beer. My good Muslim villagers pass around calabashes and toss back a few dozen liters of the stuff before wandering home.

This is the granddaddy of all village sacrifices. Anyone who has a serious favor to ask of the spirits participates in the occasion. But the villagers feel a need for a spiritual insurance policy, and follow-up sacrifices continue regularly throughout the planting season. These tend to be quiet, private affairs.

Islam in West Africa is a brittle shell. Inside lurks living, breathing animism. Animism has a thousand facets; it touches every aspect of life. It is baffling and huge. And yet it's so foreign to the Western mind that one forgets to take it into account. It is a given, entrenched in the African belief system, understood tacitly and rarely addressed with candor. A stranger forgets that it's the answer to every question, the culprit behind every illness, every misfortune, every death. The villagers give lip service to the will of Allah while silently petitioning the spirits.

I have a volley of questions, and Dramane seems like the best target. I realize while speaking to him that, unlike so many others, he doesn't just tell me what I want to hear. About sorcery, he is candid and unapologetic. Although relatively educated and Muslim, he believes in it wholeheartedly. And so when we get back to my courtyard, I bombard him. "Everyone talks about genies and spirits and ancestors and sorcerors. What exactly are they? Are they all the same thing?" He chuckles at the sky, sees that he's in for the long haul, and asks for some water. "Genies," he says, folding himself onto a stool I've brought out, "are powerful spirits that dictate how your environment responds to you. A lot of them live in trees, some in water. If you please them, they will look after you, keep your soil fertile or bring enough rain. But if you refuse them or defy them, they will lash out, causing drought or crop failure. Sometimes they take their own sacrifices by killing people.

"Ancestors are genies," he continues, "You often please the genies in the name of an ancestor, but not all genies are ancestors. With today's sacrifice, we were honoring the spirit of Nambon, the village founder, who exists in the water of the stream." I'm a little lost, but I keep listening. If I were a devout something or other, this might seem ludicrous. But I'm not, and if I want to understand the villagers at all, I have to try to understand this.

"Sorcery is different," Dramane notes. "If genies and ancestors belong to the spirit world, sorcery happens among the living. Sorcery takes place in the village on a day-to-day basis. Certain villagers are witches." Dramane glances at me quickly to gauge my reaction. I urge him on. "They meet regularly in a secret place to curse other individuals and to decide whom to sacrifice."

" 'Whom'?" I interrupt. "You mean chickens, don't you?"

He pauses, pats his fingertips together in front of his nose. "Every witch has to sacrifice someone in his own family once in a while. They choose a child, sometimes the smartest or the most beautiful, and eat its soul—not really *eat* it, of course; it's just a manner of speaking. And then within days or weeks the child dies." I'm trying to be fair here, but this new dimension is making it hard. Either this is preposterous or really scary. Sacrificed chickens suddenly seem like child's play.

"Sometimes they base their selection on revenge," Dramane continues. "For instance, if a son has become successful in the city but rarely sends money or food back home, they might choose him. Witches guarantee their own survival by participating and paying dues—in the form of family members. If they choose their smartest niece or handsomest son, none of the other witches can fault them for being soft."

Clearly it's all an attempt to justify their fatalism, to compensate for their lack of control over mortality, to deal with deaths caused by rampant disease and not enough protein. Right? It's so much easier to blame some evil force than to berate a mother for allowing severe dehydration to set in before bringing her child to the infirmary. It *must* be a world made real only by belief. Why would a community with enough problems already *try* to hurt itself? And, how, *how* could a father agree to sacrifice his favorite son?

Dramane says simply: "Some people are just evil."

Later I will hear of incidents where witchcraft takes a mundane turn: sorcerers sometimes have a Plan B. Just in case the figurative eating of souls and abstract curses don't work, morning gruel might be laced with rat poison.

How can you tell who is a witch? I ask. "Ohh." Dramane cocks his head. "If a daughter brings her baby over to her mother's house when her mother is sick and the baby dies, then you know the mother is a sorcerer." He thinks some more. "If a man predicts something bad and it happens, he's probably a witch, too." But how can you be sure? How do you know you're not excommunicating someone who's perfectly innocent? "Just because someone's a witch doesn't mean we cut them off from the community. For the most part, everyone gets treated the same, because no one does know for sure, and, in the end, no one wants to make a witch angry."

"Isn't there a force of good?" I ask. "Isn't there anyone more powerful than the sorcerers?" Dramane tells me there are *féticheurs,* witch doctors, who offer cures for curses and heal sicknesses by attacking the witching culprit instead of the disease. Dramane can think of only one in the area. "He's in a far settlement, but he visits different villages and summons the sorcerers. He sits in the chief's courtyard and yells out their names. When their identities are revealed to the community, their power shrinks."

Nambonkaha, he says, has a handful of seers, or "charlatans." They can consult spirits to determine if someone is being targeted by witches or define the cause of certain troubles, but they have no real power against sorcery. "Féticheurs are the most powerful. They can detach the sorcerer from the victim."

"Why aren't there more here, then?" I ask.

His answer rings with irony. "It's a Muslim village, Guiss."

As much as my Western sensibilities urge me to toss the whole idea, it seeps into my perception and erodes my impression of simple harmony in the village. I feel myself looking closer at these friendly people, wondering which ones are involved in the evil club.

·   ·   ·

Time in West Africa is not a linear measurement. It can be free-flowing or motionless, but it is never a constant. Time in Africa is personalized, divided and defined on an individual basis. Villagers are ambivalent about it. Some watch for time in the sun; others *want* to be faithful to the hours—it's the modern thing to do, right?—but find that no two clocks think alike. Some imagine that they *own* time. Tardiness is a luxury that comes with power: the higher your rung on the ladder, the longer you can keep people waiting. *Ponctualité* is in the dictionary, but no one seems to know what it means. Estimated time of arrival tends to get as specific as "today." Hurrying is what a kid does when he's late for school and knows he'll get a wallop. Most everyone else figures life *will* wait around, so there's no bother rushing about. And with any show of impatience, an educated African is happy to throw an old American axiom in your face: *Time eees mohney!*

In the village, time is especially elastic. Witness the greeting custom: if you pass within a twenty-foot radius of someone in the street, you must go through the whole gamut of often redundant questions: *Ça va? Ça va bien? Et la femme? Ça va chez elle? Et les enfants? Tu te portes bien? Et le travail? Bon.* You'd think the repertoire would end there, but there's usually a closing round of reaffirmations: *Donc, ça va chez toi?* Often both sides fire off questions at once, so that each person is asking and answering in the same breath. You stare at the ground or just past each other's heads. Eye contact is not part of the ritual.

Once all the bases are covered, fields and kids and wives have all been asked after, you explain where you're off to, tell your friend to pass on your greeting to the family, say good-bye, and utter a few blessings. Walking the eighth of a mile to the market sometimes takes an hour.

A few villagers wear watches that haven't budged in months. Ask the time and they look earnestly at the still hands and make educated guesses. My neighbor's watch has a large silver face and a leather strap. At all hours it swears it's eleven twenty-five, but whenever I ask him for the time, he comes up with something different. Several have battery-run cuckoo clocks hung in their houses. Few have actually adjusted the hands; they just like it when the clocks lapse into frantic cawing twenty-four times a day. The chief's clock hangs askance on a dark wall in his empty salon, its batteries eternally ailing. One day at twilight as I meet with him and an elder, it lets out twelve dying wails. The chief doesn't blink. He can't tell time anyway.

The Niarafolo boil down the day to basics: there is morning, there is *midi*, there is night. Day in Niarafolo is *chang*, or sun. Night is *changwo:* no sun. I ask the kids when they'll be back from the fields and they hold out an arm, hand flat, and point to a spot on the sun's axis. The villagers wake up before the sun and go to sleep early (except when the full moon shines). They have their own routines: the women sweep at dawn, fetch water and chop wood just after sunrise, pound and cook corn till the meal's ready; the men wake up and head to the fields as soon as they've eaten. The only thing that runs on a real schedule other than the school gong, kept strictly to the hour by the school director, is the imam's call to prayer; and that, too, depends on the sun.

The whole structure of days is negotiable. The Senoufo week is only six days long, each day named after a local market. The first day of the week depends on which village you're in. Nambonkaha's market day is called Nafuochangué. The next day is Malouochangué; another village's week hinges on that day. The two systems work together like cogs: one goes ever forward, the other ever backward. The Senoufo week is in a constant state of shrugging back from the Western calendar. Tradition and the market dictate that the Senoufo week must be followed. But there is too much modern influence in the village—and Nambonkaha is too close to the town—to abandon the Western calendar. The big market in Ferké is always on Thursdays, so Thursday retains its identity. Mosque day is always Friday. There's no school on Wednesdays and weekends, so those days need to be remembered. The two designs tend to cohabitate agreeably, and in the end they fall in line. There are roughly four weeks to a moon and out of concession, twelve moons to a year. But not many are counting.

Beating under all of it, under the two-faced days and the ignored hours, there is a pulse that says, *"only today matters."*

Villagers override it in some ways: a few take their money to post office savings accounts in Ferké, plan for schooling children, or stock up their granaries to last the year. But it is an ancient and pervasive pulse, fed by the uncertainties of life and death and the unpredictable shadow of sorcery. There is little thought of cause or consequence, little faith that their own actions can determine the future. In Niarafolo, "yesterday" and "tomorrow" share the same word: *mba'a*. They do not dwell on the past, but the future goes equally unnoticed. Today is all that counts. And that dictates much about how they live their lives. I will spend my money today just in case I'm not around tomorrow. I will plant the same land over and over because it gives me a harvest now. I will chop wood to sell every morning and night, because there are plenty of trees in the bush, even though we have to walk farther and farther to get to them. I will have unprotected sex because today I am healthy.

Abi usually goes to the market around ten. She doesn't look at the clock; she just knows when to go. She leaves the house with a full basin and two bowls stacked on top of her head. She is among the first there, under the tall mango trees in a corner of the village abandoned all other days. Most women sit on the ground. Abi's spot at the market is big enough for a ramshackle table and a wooden chair.

Most of her goods have been bought at bulk rate in Ferké. She might make a few pennies on each item. She sells a mismatched collection of talcum-powder containers, each already opened. Bottles of nail polish in dark metallic blue or blinding pink have also been opened, their particular shades visible in experimental patches on Abi's own nails. There's a jar of mothballs to make your clothes smell fresh; a stack of steel-wool sponges to rub the carbon off your pots; bare razor blades for hair cutting and shaving; plastic string for braiding; henna for dyeing feet and palms on holidays; tiny metal pods of Tiger Balm for stiff muscles; matchboxes, mirrors, glitter for teenage girls' faces; blunted-down lipsticks in hideous shades. Near the edge of the table, she scatters her best-selling item, her backup, since vanity is a luxury for most of these women: Maggi flavoring cubes of all different persuasions—shrimp, onion, tomato, chicken, bushrat. They are the heart and soul of Ivorian cooking, the only source of spice other than dried hot pepper and bay leaves. The magic little blocks of MSG are a cheap substitute for any ingredient.

The strangers always arrive at the market first. A few women come in from Ferké with items you can't get in the village. One stocks coolers with bisap, sweetened yogurt, cold water—all treats for this village, where tepid pump water is the going refreshment. She also brings a giant bowl of attiéké and a basket of frozen fish to fry. Merchants ride in on bikes laden with painted enameled plates and bowls or balancing tall stacks of pagne cloth on their handlebars and bike racks. In late morning, villagers stream in from the campements: the men on bicycle or moped, the women on foot, having spent their mornings pounding corn and fetching water. And finally, near noon, the village women filter in and take their spots under trees and under thatch, sitting on low stools and overturned basins. They flatten empty rice sacks in the dirt and lay out the fruits of their gardens, their fields, their crafts.

City markets are cobbled shanties of weather-beaten wooden beams and corrugated iron. The women sell produce and take breaks between clients for naptime, stretching out on narrow benches or plastic mats and dozing off. Waking them is fair game; there is nothing sacred about sleep in Africa, as I have quickly learned. Men sell cheap prefabricated outfits—shiny sports shirts emblazoned with strange names like Jordan and Ewing, and used clothes collected as "donations" by charities in the West. The price of vegetables and rice is more or less set, though a little haggling is always part of the routine. Generally, I have to bargain twice as much to knock off the tax added for my being white and therefore rich. But the price of clothing and material is up for serious contention for anyone.

Men make kissing noises to get your attention. They call out the merits of their selection: *"Très bonne qualité! Moins cher, moins cher!"* They ask how many shirts you want exactly, maybe five or six? If you show the least bit of interest, you can expect to have them follow you through the market with urgent pleas—they refuse to believe that you can overcome the temptation.

The village market is more like a neighborhood garage sale, with greetings and gossip instead of hawking and yelling. People come with empty buckets to fill with food and supplies. But it's largely a social event. Business acumen is not a priority—most women sell the same things, and they rush to give *cadeaux:* there is a bonus attached to every purchase.

At the height of the market, the Peul women appear in single file, walking gracefully with tremendous gourds of milk on their heads. Nomads and cattle herders, they come from the Sahel regions of Mali, Burkina Faso, and Niger. Some have set up dwellings in the bush; others materialize in the village, looking for a place to live for a spell. They might stay a few weeks or a few months, but their disappearance is always abrupt and their destination always unspecified. Their blood is African blended with Arabic; they do not look like the villagers, and with a few exceptions, they do not mix with them. The Peuls are usually light-skinned and straight-nosed, tall and slender among the short, wiry, dark-skinned villagers. The men have gaunt faces and long, bright scarves twisted into turbans around their heads. They wear only boubous, always in deep shades of blue. Village men won't be caught dead in a blue boubou.

Peul women wear high-waisted dresses trimmed with eyelet, and closed plastic shoes instead of flip-flops. They rarely wear scarves as the village women do: instead, their heads are their showcases. They leave them bare to display their wealth. Amber beads, colored glass, and silver coins are woven into their hair, some pieces dangling in front of their ears, others covering their scalps like a precious helmet. Lips and eyebrows are dyed purple; a few noses are pierced through the middle with gold rings; ears are full of holes, yarn, and beads. Their necks are wound all at once with chokers and long leather amulets and necklaces of huge clinking beads.

Despite a hint of animosity between the Peuls and the Niarafolo, they are mostly symbiotic. Peuls need villagers to supply their vegetables and grains, their mosque and health facilities. Villagers need Peuls to herd their cows, and to provide meat and milk. The untrustworthiness of the Peuls, however, seems a given in the village: they are West Africa's gypsies. But tensions are usually kept in check.

I can never just zip by the village market to pick up tomatoes or a bar of soap. I have to go expecting I might not be back for hours, even if I don't need much. Because I'm the token *touba-bou,* or white person, my market forays take up most of the day. Before I start shopping, I tuck my basket under Abi's table and visit every corner of the market, shaking hands, asking after families. I pass little heaps of dried mushrooms collected in the bush, dried okra slices, groups of lobed tomatoes, some smushed and smelling like sweet rot. There are bunches of leaves to pound into sauce, bitter green eggplants smaller than my fist, piles of tinselly fish dust for flavoring, pads of homemade shea butter used to fry millet cakes or rub into dry skin. Towering above all the miniature collections are fresh hot peppers, tall pyramids of brilliant red and green and yellow, shining like Christmas.

The women perch behind the flattened rice sacks on which they've arranged their goods. They ask me how my house is, how my health is, how my husband and children are. The normal response to all of the above is "They're there," even if you're sick, widowed, and barren. But in my ventures into Niarafolo, I've recently learned to tell the truth. When they ask, I shake my head and suck my teeth and say, "I don't have a husband" or "I don't have any kids." Their faces crinkle into grins, they hoot and laugh and slap each other on the back. One routinely grabs her breasts, shakes them, and says, "Why don't you want kids? You're ready to have them." Another grabs my breasts. Week after week, the ritual never seems to lose steam.

Aside from vowing celibacy, I use my marketplace rounds to rehearse any other Niarafolo phrases I've picked up during the week. I can say basic things regarding washing, eating, going, and buying, but my vocabulary is slim and my grammar nonexistent. The villagers seem flattered that I want to learn their language, but there doesn't seem to be *one* tutor who can help me regularly:

I have between two and two hundred who tell me contradictory things all the time. I've only recently discovered that *ki mi den* means "I don't like it"—not to be confused with *kuh me den,* which means, "I like it." The former phrase I've espoused, apparently incorrectly, from the get-go. Market women stuff little gifts into my basket every week, and I've been diligent about insulting them every time. When they've offered me a gift chicken or extra onions or a free bowl of porridge, I've smiled big and said, "Thank you! I don't like it!" Somehow this blunder has morphed into a success—chalk it up on the Reasons to Laugh at Guissongui list. I figure that as long as I'm laughing too, they must be laughing *with* me.

So I move past chattering women, clasping hands, asserting my singleness, and eventually buying sugar and soap and matches and leaves to make leaf sauce. If I don't have the correct change, they'll just expect me to come back later and pay up. That's what everyone else does. And for everything I buy, these women in flip-flops who have rarely left the village, who save up their market earnings for months to buy a new outfit for Ramadan, fill my basket with extra handfuls. I wander home each week as the sun slips west, with several things I've paid for, as well as bowls of peanuts, heaps of hot peppers, spare rolls of sweet bread, bags of millet fritters, bunches of miniature bananas, all piled into my basket by grinning women who dismiss my protests with a wave of the hand.

Gray water swirls in the washing basin, my last pair of socks tossed into the rinsing bucket. Women walk by the courtyard occasionally and call out, "*Fochanganan,* Guissongui!" Good day! "Are you washing your clothes?" The obvious is fair game in village conversation. Dramane appears between my drying clothes in his camouflage vest and sweatpants. He watches me twisting my socks for a minute and then sits on a stool under my mango tree and takes off his woven plastic hat. When I ask him how he is, he smiles weakly and sighs. He has a story to tell me.

It begins when he was at secondary school in Korhogo, the

largest town in the north, some three hours from the village. He was always a good student, he says. He got through *troisième*, tenth grade, with no trouble, but then he failed the exam. He repeated the year, studied very hard, and failed again. When he came back to the village, the city still ran in his veins. "I wanted to spend a year at home and then get back to Korhogo to get a job, maybe in a bank, maybe in commerce."

But his father dismissed a dozen years of schooling and ordered him to stay in the village. "He wouldn't let me leave," says Dramane. "He wanted me to stay and work in the fields. I'm the eldest of two sons, and the rest are daughters. He thought I should stay and support him. And to make sure I wouldn't leave, he announced that he had chosen a wife for me. It was like he beat me twice. Arranged marriages don't happen that much anymore." Dramane says he had dreamed of a modern family, one wife and a few kids. But both families agreed to the arranged marriage. Dramane found himself destined to be united to one of the poorest families in the village. His sixteen-year-old fiancée, Senata—Mandou and Moussa's only sister—had a reputation for being difficult.

"I didn't sleep that whole night." He fiddles with his hat. "I thought and I thought, and in the morning I worked up all my courage and said, 'Papa, I have decided I can't marry Senata.'" It was a plea for mercy and acceptance of change. His father listened silently but said, "The choice is not yours."

Dramane says he's considered a bit of a lackey by the villagers. Everyone had expected him to go far, to become a professional— a cadre—to be successful in the city. Now, when they ask what he wants to do, he says, "I don't know, whatever comes."

"I feel like I'm not in control of my own life," he says. "I'm like a fish being knocked around by waves, just to and fro, hitting rocks, hitting the sand, no control, no will." Dramane pauses and then, conspiracy glimmering in his eyes, adds: "But I've formed a new plan—a strategy."

This rainy season the chief made him the manager of the village tractor, which is hired out to large-scale farmers to pay it off. Dramane has been gone a few days every week since the planting season started, working at these farms. He considers it his only legitimate means out of the village, and he's working like crazy to keep the projects coming. "My father can't say no to my trips because the chief delegated the job to me, and it has evolved as my duty in the village," he says. Dramane thinks of the job as an opportunity to get exposure to other possibilities outside the village and as a way to ease himself out of everyday commitments to his father.

"And," he says, "since Senata is not my choice, we will be engaged, but I'll postpone the marriage as long as possible, and I will have other wives who I alone choose. Maybe I'll have another uneducated village wife as well, and then one who has been to school and can speak French. Just like the mayor has." I am a bit dismayed. But who am I to slash at his hopes with a dose of Western moralizing? The irony is that my opinions about polygamy are slowly transforming. Despite my initial certainty that it was a chauvinistic evil, I am learning not to write it off so fast. Polygamy has a few untrumpeted benefits: to some extent it reins in the spread of AIDS. One would have to be blind to assume that a man becomes faithful just because he has two wives waiting for him at home instead of one. But the need for prostitutes is, one hopes, somewhat reduced.

More certainly, polygamy has a built-in family-planning aspect in many African cultures. Many ethnicities believe that after a woman gives birth, having sex or getting pregnant again will poison her milk. Therefore she waits till the child can walk before having sex again. Meanwhile, the husband doesn't have to go outside the courtyard to find other women. And considering the paltry state of romantic love in the village and the incredible workload for the average wife, often polygamy is a breath of relief for a wife—her chores are cut in half. Granted, women are given little voice in choosing their cowives. But it's a system that has worked for centuries. The women aren't humiliated by it; they expect it.

While I'm considering Dramane's plan, Mandou pokes his head through my line of clothes and speaks to him. Dramane stands and stretches. "Guiss," he says, "they say there's a snake in the grass behind your house." I jump up immediately and follow them. My fascination with snakes stems from the fact that I've never seen one alive.

Mandou's mother, Massieta, stands with her thin mouth set and her arms on her hips. Dramane seems to stand a little straighter in front of her. I wonder if she knows he wanted to reject her daughter. All eyes are on a wide patch of grass just behind my bedroom window. When I arrived, the spot was stubbly dirt. With the rains, the grasses now reach nearly two feet. Dramane pokes around with a long stick, then parts the weeds and reveals a skinny green tail. With a tail so thin, it must be harmless. "Dramane," I say, "please don't kill it. It's such a little thing, it won't hurt us."

He smiles and throws a rock into the grass. A tremendous reptile hurls out of the weeds, tongue flailing. I jump back. That little tail was just the tip of the lizard. The savanna is littered with pink-headed chameleons and geckos, routinely hunted, grilled, and eaten by gangs of young boys. But this monster is over two feet long.

I expect Dramane to leap after it with a machete—that thing would make dinner for a family—but instead we watch it slither back into the grasses. "If that had been in the fields," he says, "I would have killed it in a minute. But a lizard that big in the village is probably no lizard at all." What do you mean? I ask. "Genies and sorcerers can take the form of a wild animal to spy on the village. If that was a genie and I had hurt it, it could have killed me or my whole family."

Senata stands under a mango tree with her hands on her hips and challenge in her face. She breathes an unimpressed laugh and then swivels on her foot and walks into her hut. Dramane doesn't even notice her.

4

Ali

Mariam the Burkinabe is the wife of Nambonkaha's fisherman. She has thick eyebrows and spaces between her teeth. Her eyes admit that she's always falling short and she just hopes no one else notices. She has two children, and her belly is full with the next one. Mariam's three-year-old daughter has a big square head and, somehow, a chubby body. I don't know how old her son, Ali, is—he might be four; he might be seven. To look at him, you might think Nambonkaha was in the throes of a devastating famine. He is dying of starvation in a village where everyone has something to eat.

Ali is top-heavy. His head is too large, and though he can steady it, it's unwieldy. His belly is round and taut. He usually wears nothing but an old sweatshirt that hangs just past his stomach. It covers scrawny arms and jutting ribs, so from the waist up he looks nearly healthy—except for the tightness around his jaw. But the shirt gives way to a wrinkled bottom and spindly legs. He can barely walk on those toothpick legs. He can't crawl. To move, he scoots across the dirt on his bottom. When I pick him up, his slack skin moves with my hands, as if I've just pulled it right off his bones.

Ali sits mostly. Like a rag doll. He can balance on his bottom if he keeps his legs tucked in next to him. Otherwise he'd fall over backward. This is how I always see him, sitting like a sorry pile of little boy in the dirt. Yet Ali grins. His smile is wide and full of little teeth—incongrous, given his tiny, brittle body. This is how he looks at the world, with his face emanating blank trust, total confidence.

Ali's mother says he's two, maybe three, but it's part of her cover-up. Illness is expected in infants, and the sudden death of babies is rarely a surprise. Having a sickly child die slowly at home, however, is more shameful—there's always the question of how much the mother could have done. Perhaps Mariam believes that if she shaves years off Ali's age, his wasting will seem less mortifying. Whenever I pass her courtyard I stop in for a greeting and pick Ali up. He is never on his mother's back or in her arms. Ali is not only nutrient starved, he's also starving for attention. I try to hold him near Mariam to encourage her to notice him. I say, "Mariam, *please* take him to the clinic. Or at least bring him to my house. I can teach you to make porridge that will help him grow." But she just lets out a strangled chuckle and looks away. "Eh, Guissongui . . ."

One day I cooked a pot of enriched millet gruel and brought it straight to Ali. I arrived in Mariam's courtyard, all patronizing words and self-righteous smiles—the great American come to save the starving child. Mariam crumbled in the corner, too humiliated to speak. Ali gazed up at me with his inert grin when I sat in front of him with the gruel. And then he pressed his lips together, still grinning, and watched me coo and coax in vain. He kept his eyes on my face, never looking at the food, and then scooted on his bottom to his mother. It was as if he were in on the dying scheme, as if he, too, were choosing not to change his fate. I left Mariam with the gruel and walked home, humbled.

Children like Ali are just expected to die. And they seem to know it. They are born old, fleshless like their great-grandparents, with the same air of waiting for death about them. It is possible that Ali's pitiable state is the upshot of his mother's negligence. Angélique says that he has never grown because his sister was conceived while he was still breast-feeding. "If a woman with a baby gets pregnant," she says, "her milk turns poisonous, so she has to stop nursing." Quitting breast milk cold turkey is traumatizing—it's conceivable that the child would fail to thrive. But starvation? I wonder if mothers just presume that these milk-deprived older children will be weak and let nature take its course without interfering. Or maybe it has nothing to do with Mariam. Maybe some hideous disease is eating away at Ali's insides and only expensive lab tests and visits to doctors in the city could save him.

In the end, it doesn't matter what's killing Ali. Whatever the reason, a child that sick is begrudgingly considered better off dead. The prevalent philosophy about children seems to be "You win some, you lose some." Women bear ten kids so that five might survive. When a child starts out healthy and then gets sick, they'll often make trips to the clinic and to Ferké to get him the right medicines. But if he's just weak from the get-go, if he never really grows or is sick all the time, he's considered by many to be stuck in the clutches of sorcery or chosen by Allah to return to the earth. Little is done to help him survive.

The day I humiliated Mariam the Burkinabe, I could not yet fathom how far fatalism reached in the village society. I didn't realize that she had already given up hope for Ali, that he was too fragile and vacant to survive the rigors of village life. I wanted to show her with my gift of gruel that she could turn around the health of her child. Instead, my tactlessness only intensified her shame. When Mariam sees me now, she usually bends her eyes to the ground. I shake her hand and greet her in Dioula; I want to make up for my thoughtlessness. She just looks away. But somehow, when her womb starts to clench and heave with her third child, Mariam sends for me.

When I arrive it has been night a few hours. Mariam's husband, the fisherman, sits with a few friends on a mat on the stoop outside. He's stuffing mint leaves into a tiny, gurgling teapot. Mariam and her husband rent a mud hut in an old blind man's courtyard. But she's delivering in a room in the blind man's house—a concrete room like mine, covered in ocher-colored stucco. The room is bare but for a few baskets of pagnes and tomatoes stacked in a corner. The walls are studded with lobed hornets' nests; the cement floor is spotless.

Kinafou and Salimata, another Burkinabe woman, sit on miniature stools against the wall, waiting for the action to begin.
Mariam stands smiling thinly, as she wraps a faded pagne around
herself and tucks it in under her arm. I pull out my midwiving
book to study up. Ali sits idly off to the side, legs crooked under
him, a glassy-eyed smile stretched across his face, white crust
under his nose. He lolls his head back to rest on his neck and
watches us as if we were a boring television show. His chubby
sister prances in and scurries back out again, full of giggles and
energy, as if to spite the brother whose milk she sucked away.

The lamp in the center of the room casts Mariam's shadow
upon the wall. She paces, urging on labor, hands on her hips. She
walks toward the lamp and her legs grow colossal, stretch up the
concrete, and bend onto the ceiling. Then she turns, and her
shadow shrinks to meet her at the wall. A hand holding a tray
of shot glasses shoots through the curtain in the doorway. Salimata passes the glasses around; we drink our gulp of tea and scoot
the tray back out the door to the men. In the hushed night, the
men mutter outside; inside, voices ring soft against bare walls.

I can time the contractions by looking at her face—they twist
up her mouth and squeeze her eyes tight. They are still quite far
apart. She's anxious—keeps taking off her pagne in preparation
and then putting it back on when the pain subsides. My book
tells me all about pressure points that can stimulate labor. I rub
spots just above her ankles and on her wrists. I tell Mariam to
pull her nipples. She snorts at that, doesn't see why something
so ridiculous could have any consequence inside her body. So I
bite back all my Western prudery and do it for her. Mariam
laughs; her eyebrows shoot up. I consider pointing out positions
that encourage labor, but Kinafou's ready to get down to business. She has eyed my amateur techniques with curiosity, but her
expertise is generations old.

She sits on the floor, back straight, legs out in front of her,
arms long, strong, and loose. She summons naked Mariam to sit
in the same position facing her, with their legs crossing at the
knees. Mariam is exhausted already. She stretches her arms
around Kinafou's neck and lets her head droop in the space

between their bodies. For a minute, the weight of baby and pain is lifted off her shoulders and her back, and settled on Kinafou's neck. One woman wears a pagne and a scarf tied to her head. Another wears nothing but a strand of beads slung around her hips. One's belly is slack and retired; the other's is hot and moving. On the wall, their shadow is a sturdy, unmoving circle. The embrace is poignant, sweet—grandmother to mother, old woman to young, linked in the ancient and purest element of womanness.

Mariam the Burkinabe has misjudged her labor, but we don't find that out until more rounds of mint tea are passed in from the expectant men outside. First we take shifts waiting wide-eyed for the pain and the magic, or half-sleeping on plastic mats. Kinafou hands me a stool to use for a pillow and lies next to me, swatting at mosquitos with her scarf. Mariam takes turns padding quietly around the room in bare feet and crouching in the corner with her eyes shut and her eyebrows buckled. Ali sleeps curled on the same spot of bare cement he's been on since I arrived.

When gray light seeps in through the doorway, Kinafou looks hard at Mariam, slouched against the wall, and tells me, *"Te wa kpa man."* Go home. The baby isn't ready yet.

The fisherman himself comes at nightfall to beckon me back to Mariam. She has been in labor over twenty-four hours, but little has changed from the night before. There are a few more vieilles attending with Kinafou, and the men making tea have given up and left the premises. Ali is further toward the back of the room, still sitting.

Mariam is a complicated case. She is no longer pacing, and she looks cold and pale against the pagne that serves as a delivery table. Her contractions come strong, but nothing happens. There are rushes of blood, swallowed cries. This labor is too long for a third child. With the help of my midwiving book, I conjure up several drastic life-threatening scenarios and try to figure out which one applies tonight.

Abi appears outside the door, eyes wide with concern. She won't step inside, doesn't want to interfere, though she likely knows far more about this than I do. "What do you think the problem is?" she asks. "Is it grave?" I explain that Mariam's been pushing for a day but nothing's coming out or even visible, and there's been a lot of blood. "Eh, Allah!" she gasps anxiously and runs off to tell Sidibé.

The vieilles try indigenous techniques. Kinafou fills a calabash with dried corn. She fits it against Mariam's stomach and rocks her back and forth, the corn shaking with a sound like maracas against her tight belly. Another vieille finds a clay pot with its side missing and puts burning cotton inside. Mariam squats over it, as if to smoke out the baby. My book says that the fumes of certain burning herbs might help turn a breech baby. Maybe the vieilles know different attributes—I have felt this baby's head through Mariam's skin, and it is not upside down.

Mariam tenses and shudders. A tear squeezes out of her eye and slides to the floor. It is pitch-dark outside, and the air is cool. There is no car here, no phone, no sink, no bright light. We are one village under the stars, and we are all alone. But the vieilles are working hard, crouched around this struggling woman. One sits behind her, supporting her head and torso, holding her hands. Blood saturates a pagne and pools on the floor.

Then there are loud footsteps on the stoop outside and Sidibé bursts in with a chill gust of air. His flashlight beam veers to her swollen, bleeding vagina and then scampers off. He barks orders, trying to cover up his embarrassment at seeing this naked vulnerable woman on the floor. I can hear in his voice that he's nervous, too, that he's out of his element, and doesn't want to risk being responsible for a woman dying of women's ailments. He is stifling taboos and his own discomfort by stepping into this intimate scene as Village Health Authority. "Vieilles," he commands, "clean her up. She's going to Ferké!"

Evacuation sounds like a rapid solution. But, in truth, it entails Mariam's husband hitchhiking to Ferké, then finding a taxi driver willing to make the late-night round-trip trek to the village and back again with a bleeding woman in his backseat. Sidibé jabs the beam of his flashlight at everyone in the room. Then at me. "Guiss," he yells. "*Vas chez toi!*" I can't be annoyed, exactly— he's far off his territory, and it must be so awkward. But his voice is too harsh—it cuts violently into our cohesion. He's dismissing our hours of attendance, but worse than that, blustery modernity is about to defeat wise tradition in one blow.

Sidibé strides out as quickly as he came. When the dust settles and the cackling at this intrusion quiets, we all realize that there is no time for Ferké. A circle of skull has come into view. All fall into their places and focus again on Mariam. Contractions ripple through her body. The head pushes forward. The pink scar where Mariam was circumcised stretches till it shines and then splits down the middle. The head squeezes out, face pointing upward. Mariam's baby is in backwards; the face should be turned to the floor. The head emerges huge and purple and hideous at first. Then it's knocked into proportion as one shoulder appears and the rest slops out behind. The little girl cries fast, before the stream of water even hits her slick chest. Mariam the Burkinabe lies back limp in the arms of a vieille, her eyes shut and her head turned to the side.

The vieilles complete the procedure as if it's a dance they've rehearsed. Each picks up a chore simultaneously, and evidence of the long toil disappears. They thank *me*, saying, *An y che, Guissongui,* but *they* are the ones with amniotic fluid on their hands, they are the ones snipping the cord and washing the child and throwing dust to soak up the puddles of blood on the floor. It is past midnight when we leave. I strap on my headlamp and make a beeline for bed. The vieilles walk into the blackness on bare feet that know the ruts and rocks on the path home.

I stop by Angélique's courtyard the next morning to see if she has any sweet bread for sale. She slings her own new baby on her back and accompanies me back through the village. When I tell her of Mariam's difficult delivery, she says, *"Cette femme-là, elle a des problèmes."* It turns out there's a story behind Mariam's troubles. "One day her husband was really sick," Angélique says in a low voice. "She didn't want to bring him food. She was too lazy to prepare meals for him, or take care of him. So in revenge, he wouldn't take care of her either. The truth is, Mariam has *always* had a hard time giving birth. This one was no different. But her husband was angry at her, so he wouldn't take her into Ferké when the labor began."

Angélique turns on the path to Femme Claire's house. I head to the scene of last night's trauma. Mariam looks good, younger than before. She is smiling, eating, happy to see me. "I'm going to bring her to the clinic as soon as her cord falls off!" she blurts as soon as I've sat down. In the village, a baby must be hidden until the umbilical cord falls off—they say if a widow sees him before this, he will die. Mariam's French is basic but clear. I'm tickled by her enthusiasm and tell her how she can go about getting vaccinations. But maybe it's too easy. Is she complying with my wishes out of gratitude? Or does she feel like this is a chance to start fresh with a healthy child, a chance to prove she's a good mother? Mariam spoons up porridge like a little girl. Her eyes are sparkly and her body relaxed. Her new baby lies on a pagne at her side. I ask if she will please try to breast-feed even though milk won't come out. She clanks down the bowl and picks up the girl. The baby sputters at her nipple, won't open her mouth. "Keep trying," I say. "She just has to learn it."

Sunlight falls through the doorway and shines on the curve of Mariam's cheek and the stretch marks on her breast. She fiddles with her nipple, draws it back and forth across the infant's mouth till finally it opens, just barely, and starts suckling. Ali has been sitting in a heap of bones, with his head too big. He scoots across the floor on his wrinkled, naked bottom and comes to a stop just by his mother's foot. The bowl of porridge is inches away, but he doesn't even look at it. He just looks up with his strange benevolent eyes at his mother giving milk to her baby, and swings the corners of his mouth into a wide grin.

5

Grasp

Every night, a few kids stand at my door and watch me eat dinner. Maybe I should feel guilty about devouring full plates in front of kids who have to compete with all their siblings at the dinner bowl. But my house is hot: by necessity I keep the door open. And my house is tiny: by necessity my kitchen (read: table) is in the front room, my vegetables and eggs are in bowls on the table. During the first few weeks, kids would stand at the door and plead for the food on my table. Guilt and irritation nearly drove me insane.

As the months have passed, the audience has developed from a pack of begging urchins to a cluster of culinary critics. Watching me has become less about the food and more about what I am doing to it. First of all, *why* on earth is she cooking inside and not in the courtyard when it's so hot? Eh! Allah! She's eating tomatoes *raw!* Dusty packs of spaghetti sold in the market are customarily used by the villagers in place of meat when there isn't enough money. I'm the only one for miles who eats spaghetti for the sake of spaghetti. The kids launch into an excited babble whenever it appears on my plate and can't wait to watch me twist it around my fork.

Mandou's younger brother Daouda is not waiting for food; he has too much pride for that. He blends in with the night outside my door, reclining on his elbow, face to the screen. He sits alone, since the packs of other kids took off for dinner and sleep. He watches me quietly. I've made too much spaghetti tonight, so I hand him a bowl of it with a fork. He grips the fork in his fist and peers into the bowl. For ten minutes, he tries to tame the noodles with the awkward utensil, chuckling softly. Then he looks up with a triumphant smile.

Kids are the lowest rung in the well-entrenched "petit system" that rules West Africa. Basically, anyone younger or less important than you will double as your errand boy or girl without a complaint. It's a system ripe for exploitation. I began my days doing everything myself, but I've quickly realized that little trips to our boutique (a ramshackle hut with ancient-looking cans cordoned off by chicken wire) are done far more efficiently by small children. I still insist on doing my own chores, yet when I'm out of matches or need kerosene for my lantern, I hand the errand off to the first kid in my courtyard and have whatever I need within minutes. There's a certain beauty to the system: kids respect their elders wholeheartedly and often consider it an honor to serve them. They actually *argue* over who gets to go buy my batteries.

Children graduate to petit status around age four. In a sudden transformation, a little girl stops being a dolled-up baby and becomes a baby-sitter, water pumper, dishwasher. The same goes for boys, though they're more likely to be summoned to the fields or sent to fetch something. Parental affection is all but curtailed. Kids are taught to consider themselves inferior until they grow up and can lord over a new flock of petits. Their pride is trampled upon so they don't become too uppity, and they grow up without confidence. Rarely do they receive stimulation or positive reinforcement from parents or elders. At school, hitting and humiliating are considering motivational tools, and later, in adulthood, workplace hierarchy dictates that there is always someone to serve. As the individual is only a cog in the machine of community, conformity seems everyone's best option. The selfishness of rejecting an expected role would alienate a person from the rest of the community. And alienation is the worst curse of all.

I am doing everything I can to foster a little self-respect in my small friends. Daouda doesn't go to school, but he has bright eyes and a quick, questioning mind. He watches me reading nightly, listens to babbling English on BBC, and asks what they are saying. We flip through free *Newsweeks* that arrive in my mailbox and talk about the pictures and the stories. Tonight I take the bowl from him and sit down beside the screen.

"Daouda, do you want to learn how to read?" I ask. It feels like the climactic scene in some feel-good TV movie. I have not a lick of teaching experience. French is not my native tongue, and how do you explain reading when half the letters are silent and the rest make ten different noises each? At the same time, how could lessons possibly hurt? Daouda clears his throat and says, "*Oui.*" Real low. I can barely hear him.

I make alphabet flashcards with drawings of familiar things. A: *arachide* (peanut), *agouti* (bushrat). B: *ballon* (soccer ball), *balafon*. I pull out my *Newsweeks* and use them to identify letters. I open my dusty travel Scrabble board, arrange the letters, teach vowels versus consonants. I offer Daouda a pen, then trace lines on the back of scrap paper so he can practice writing. He's a fast learner. Despite his lack of previous experience, Daouda's letters are neat. He can rattle off the alphabet in a few days, can recognize all the letters in a few weeks, and begins to put together words at the end of the month. Kids collect at the screen to watch us—apparently my visual aids make this more interesting than school lessons. I'd like to invite more in, but the house is too small and my materials too minimal to begin a full-fledged class.

And then I notice Oumar, another courtyard regular, a beautiful boy with troubled knees, standing nightly by the screen, watching intently and whispering the letters to himself. He is around eleven years old and struggling through third grade, constantly plagued with episodes of swollen joints that force him to miss school. I open the door and ask if he wants to come in.

Oumar's father is a small, frail man who sits under a thatched roof day after day. In the past, he set up his antique foot-pump sewing machine there and made his living as a tailor. But recently he says that using that machine makes him sick. He suffers from migraines that appear to be brought on by the act of sewing.

According to village logic, this type of symptom is indicative of only one disease: sorcery. His machine is cursed, Oumar's father says, and he has no choice but to retire it for good.

Oumar's eyes are clear and long-lashed. He has high cheekbones and straight teeth. His voice sounds like a handful of coins dropping; it ripples and clangs and smooths. He laughs a great giggle: a rising set of *heh heh hehs* that makes me laugh to hear it. He beams at the prospect of being part of the "alphabet" lessons, as Daouda calls them, and gets straight to work. In three years of school, he has learned to attach sentences to pictures, memorize rhyme schemes, and write nice letters that he can't recognize. He has to catch up to Daouda.

Moussa, the mango collector, is a little too small to be useful in the fields. He's supposed to be at school, but his parents can't afford the uniform, and, anyway, he prefers to chase lizards. So he spends much of his time in my courtyard, singing balafon songs with gusto in front of my door, playing cards, drawing, and musing about life.

I've offered to teach him the alphabet, as well—during the day, when Oumar is at school and Daouda is in the fields. But he says he wants to know how to write first; he's more interested in drawing endless curls and squiggles than reciting abstract letters. Once in a while, though, he turns to a friend and earnestly, patiently, tries to teach him, saying, "a-b-c-d-e-f-g-h-p-q-r-y-z" over and over again till his friend gets it right.

Then Mandou joins the group and we cram onto my plastic mat, wedged between my kitchen table and my bicycle. Mandou adds some distracting energy to our little literacy party. Older than the other two, he is boisterous and dramatic and gets frustrated with himself easily. But he really wants to learn to spell his name. I insist on making him understand the alphabet, refusing to let him get away with just learning to trace the lines of the letters. They grin and roll their eyes and forget their *q*'s and write *g*'s that float and *f*'s that have fallen flat. I try to explain that the line is like the ground: *g*'s are buried up to their necks, as are *p*'s. But they are hesitant to go outside the lines.

Moussa flits in and out of the shadows outside my screen. After a few weeks, he gets a little jealous of our foursome, but still insists that the alphabet is useless. Instead he stands outside my door and repeats every word I say, mocking my very intonation as if he were teaching his own class outside. If he were any other kid, I'd have sent him scrambling, but I'm a sucker for Moussa, so tiny, running in giddy circles, yelling "a-e-i-o-u" in his gravelly voice.

My lovely boys. They loll and strut, hoot and sleep outside my screen. They're proud and poor, ignorant and eloquent. Today Daouda wears a baseball cap pulled low to his nose. He takes it off to help me dig up my new garden and reveals an eye swollen out of all proportion to his head. He looks like a Picasso portrait. All the health-worker sensibilities I'm trying to foster in myself are downright mortified. I grab his elbow and drag him to his father, convinced he must have been beaten or struck by a gruesome disease. But the man just laughs nervously and says he hadn't noticed. I drag them both to the infirmary.

Sidibé receives us, congratulates me on my discerning eye, and says wistfully, "In the early days I used to want to save everyone too." He gives Daouda an anti-inflammation shot, berates his father, and sends the two on their way. Sidibé wants me to learn the ropes myself; he doesn't say that the swollen eye is a reaction to a bee sting. African bees have a vicious bite—too many at once can kill a person. The boys, however, tempt the bees on a regular basis, climbing straight into hives to collect honey.

All of a sudden, I'm hyperaware of the state of the kids who frequent my courtyard. Tiny girls show up at my screen to ask if they can have my bucket. "*Wel nawa luo gun,*" they say. We want to pump water. They come back with a few gallons wobbling about on their little heads. They blink with satisfaction, droplets on their eyelashes. Sita is maybe seven. She insists on carrying my biggest bucket when we go to the pump together. Her skeleton looks too fragile—like it might buckle under the weight—but she scurries on, matchstick arms stretched to the lip of the bucket, matchstick legs walking awkward and fast. I find myself naively swearing I'll never refuse her something to eat.

One evening, as the boys crouch over their papers by my flickering, blackened lamp, raspy cries waft in through the back window. Mandou and Daouda glance at each other over the Scrabble pieces. The cries are coming from their courtyard. When I ask what's going on, Mandou grunts that his youngest brother, Drissa, is sick. The child's wrenching cry pierces the black silence of the village night.

Early the next morning, I'm at Mandou's mother's door. Massieta emerges from her smoke-filled hut with Drissa on her arm. Her face looks tired, and she tells me frankly in broken French that Drissa *chauffe*. I put my hand out to his scalding head and his dulled eyes light up with horror. He is petrified. How to help a child who won't let me near him? I show her how to put wet cloths on him to calm the fever, and she copies me silently. I fill a cup from a basin of water dyed purple with medicinal bark and pour it straight on his head. I am no longer just scary. I'm the enemy.

A few hours later, when I come back with a thermometer, Drissa's father is holding the boy's naked body over burning charcoal. According to myth, fevers break in the face of greater heat. Drissa's temperature reads 104. He is one year old.

You really should go to the infirmary, I tell Massieta. She mutters the catchall phrase: *"Il y a pas l'argent."* There's no money. They are one of the poorest families in the village—but the lack of money is so often used to wiggle out of responsibility that I take the excuse with a grain of salt. I can certainly spare a dollar to cure this child. Or I could tap into my personal aspirin supply. Yet this is risky: everyone knows I'm here to work with Sidibé, but they're not quite sure in what capacity. They've heard stories of white people giving out free medicine, and some assume I have a full pharmacy hidden in my bedroom. But I'm not here to be the village repairwoman—I'm here to teach *them* how to prevent and cure sickness. At what point, though, do you realize that a little boy's life is at stake, and dismiss concerns about precedent?

I bring over a bucket of fresh water and have Massieta plop Drissa in it. He squeals and squawks as if it were a bucket of fire. This, I tell her, is what he needs; bathe him every few hours with fresh water. And then, as I'm sitting by Massieta and her ailing son, a merchant pedals up with enameled tin bowls on his bike rack. She buys two bowls! No money to save her son from malaria, but she really needs those bowls today. I get up and go, thoroughly disgusted. Yet throughout the day, I hear splashes and screeching, and I peek out my back window to see Drissa in the bucket. I bite down little surges of satisfaction that *finally* I have taught *someone* something about health.

The next morning Massieta is at my door, with burning Drissa on her back. The fever hasn't broken, and it won't without medicine if it's malaria. I order her to go to the hospital. Massieta stalls a few minutes, hoping perhaps that my conscience will kick in and I'll offer up medicine or donate money for a clinic visit. Then she nods imperceptibly and walks out of my courtyard, arms swinging. She heads in the direction of the clinic.

"That's the problem with health in the village," says Sidibé later, as he swathes an axe wound on a young girl's shin with cotton soaked in alcohol. The girl is biting her lip white, but she makes no sound. "No one ever shows up for treatment when the illness is just beginning. They always wait for it to get serious. They think if they ignore it, it will go away."

The clinic is painted yellow on the outside, though the bottom two feet of the walls have been washed gray by rain and riddled by insects burrowing homes in the cement. There are two small consultation rooms lit by windows and covered with old tile. Serious cases are allowed to spend the day in a dim convalescence room across the breezeway from the rest of the rooms. No one is allowed to spend the night. Electrical cords bristle from holes in the plywood ceiling, waiting for the day when Nambonkaha lights up. A shiny faucet and sink end in truncated pipes below. In Sidibé's office, there are a few thin cots, a wide desk, and a tall cabinet whose doors hold the only glass in the village. At the beginning of the month the cabinet is filled with vials and boxes and bottles. Today it is nearly empty.

I've come to make sure Massieta made it here. She did come this morning, Sidibé says, and he treated Drissa. "They don't like to come here because they haven't paid for the last few visits and they know I'll lecture them on credits due."

This is another reason the village loves Sidibé: he doesn't turn people away. He usually charges an overhead of one hundred CFA per visit—less than twenty cents, enough to buy four boxes of matches or several little piles of tomatoes at the market. Then he adds the price of whatever medicine he has to administer. The total rarely exceeds one thousand CFA, about $1.50. Nonetheless, his record book, covered in looping scrawl, has a credit column without many checks in it. Most borrowers will, someday, straighten out their account. But for now Sidibé just makes sure everything is well documented, and pays from his own pocket.

He runs out of state-supplied medicine about three-quarters of the way through every month. The rural health-care base in Ferké has strict rations, and their shipments from Abidjan are often late or incomplete. Instead of relying on them, Sidibé buys his own stock of basics at the pharmacy in town and sells it at a small profit. Considering that state nurses haven't had a raise in eighteen years, any money on the side is welcome. For antibiotics and more serious medication, the best he can do is write pre-scriptions, and hope that someone can get to Ferké to fill them and back in time to actually help the patient.

The next patient is a naked one-year-old, clutching his mother in panic. She and her husband sit in the chairs opposite Sidibé. He pelts them with questions, and they answer meekly. He is not condescending, but they expect him to be. They anticipate being treated like inferiors and criticized for neglect or stupidity. They seem to exude guilt, as if they're to blame for the son's illness. (Of course, sometimes they are.) The little boy's nostrils flare rapid-fire; a tear winks out of his eye, rolls over his cheek, catches momentum on his neck, and slips across his belly, leaving a shiny dark path on his dry skin. "Pneumonia," declares Sidibé and gives the father a packet of malaria medication and a prescription.

"If it's pneumonia, why do you treat him for malaria?" I ask later as we cross the courtyard to Sidibé's house for lunch. He tells me, "Seven out of ten patients who come in probably have malaria. Since Africans have built up a resistance to it, the disease often shows up in different forms. It's always better to treat it just in case, especially for children, who don't have immunity to it yet."

Abi always prepares as if the whole village might show up unexpectedly for lunch. There is inevitably a plate for me. "Have the vaccines come in yet?" I ask as we hunker down over our bowls. Sidibé pulls a chicken leg from the sauce and shakes his head. "Not yet." There are annual national vaccination campaigns against polio and meningitis and measles. They flood the country with billboards, T-shirts, and visors with motivational slogans.

For the polio-eradication efforts, men and women armed with oral drops hijack bush taxis and buses as they stop in at major gendarme checkpoints, and dose every child under four. But routine vaccinations—for diphtheria, tetanus, and whooping cough—are left to the discretion of the local health authorities. Sidibé has chosen to make them available every market day, and while some women come in months off schedule and others don't come at all, a fair number start as soon as they've delivered and keep to the program.

But yesterday was market day and there were no vaccinations to be had. Nor the market day before that. The health base in Ferké insists that the vaccine shipment is coming, but we've been waiting over a month.

We ball up bites of yam foutou and talk about sick babies and vaccinations and negligent mothers. Sparks sputter in my head—there's room here for improvement. I've spent several months trying to figure out how to approach health in Nambonkaha. I have dabbled with teaching mothers home remedies, but so far my work has been one-on-one. The only evidence I have of these mothers following my advice was the sound of Drissa's cold baths yesterday.

I know what tack I want to take—I want to teach preventative care; I want mothers to feel that they have some control over their children's health. I just need some structure. I ask Sidibé how easy it would be to get a baby scale, so that we could start weighing. He scoffs a bit. "I could ask at the health base in Ferké, but I really don't think they'll give one up."

He tries to be optimistic about the doctors at the rural health base in Ferké, but it's hard to skirt the glaring facts. Apparently Dr. Kouamé, the head doctor, and his deputy are involved in an ongoing feud that recently erupted into a fistfight on the hospital lawn. "Kouamé broke his deputy's wrist! *Vraiment!*" says Sidibé with a bitter smile. "What can you do?" He scoops the last of his sauce into the hollow of the foutou and chews pensively. Suddenly he pops out of his seat, his eyes lit up. "We *have* a scale! I forgot! My predecessor left it in the storage room! I think it needs some repairs, but at least it's here."

Minutes later, he emerges from the infirmary, arms full of white metal coated in dust and scampering spiders. It jiggles and squeaks at every step. He brings out one of his ailing stereos and puts on an old Rolling Stones tape as I start cleaning the scale. Then he disappears inside. Abi sits by the fire, frying up plantains. She's heard all of our conversation and remained silent. "It's a really good idea," she says now, watching me struggle with the awkward contraption. "Women here really have no chance to take care of themselves or their babies, since there's no maternity clinic."

Support from Abi is like a medal. She is not easily impressed, and she has the power to motivate and set examples for the village women.

Sidibé leaps out of the doorway in a pale blue boubou and prayer cap. "I was thinking," he says as he heads to the plastic water kettle for his ablutions, "if you weighed babies, I could start doing prenatal consultations for women. You know, nothing embarrassing, just checking their pulse and measuring and making sure they're not anemic."

One hour in three months of questioning, and it all begins to fall in place. Mick Jagger battles feedback on the stereo. The refrain of "Wild Horses" whines out over the courtyard, and then

Sidibé's voice rises up in undulating Arabic, fading in and out with the melody.

Fourteen-year-old Mandou says tonight, "How is it that you're a woman and you have money and I'm a man and I don't?" I ask him first why a woman shouldn't have money. Then I revert to my stock response that I'm a volunteer and don't have much money. His face twists into a look of disbelief, and as I hear my own words, I realize how ridiculous they sound. "Look at your radio and that funny flashlight that sticks to your head. Look at your house with that table and a stove and all those books." True, a lot of it is gift or on loan, but it's presumptuous to try to come off as poor. I have parents who will bail me out in an emergency, I have job prospects when I go back home. He points to his clothes. "This is what I have." I have no answer.

Seydou, who goes to school, comes by to stand silently and watch me, as he usually does. He's always dressed nicely and does well in his classes, but he never has anything to say. He stands next to Mandou in my courtyard. They are about the same age. Mandou looks him up and down, pride and resentment dueling on his face. "I work in the fields and still I know French," he says, with a cluck of his tongue. "You go to school. You sit in a chair and turn pages in your books all day long. You get to go to Ferké and eat attiéké. I go to the fields and tire out my arms and work in the sun. I have no books and I don't go to Ferké, but still. I know French. What does that mean?"

It means something. Mandou is an opportunist, and smart. He proposes this afternoon that we go to a funeral together tomorrow night. He stands on my stoop in faded pants cut off at the knees and a shirt with a stringy, gaping hole in one shoulder. He plunges into an inspired speech about what he's going to wear for the occasion. "I'm going to get *sapé*," he says, "I'll wear my jeans and this shirt I have that's really white. And my tennis shoes!"

·   ·   ·

Past midnight the following day, I am tramping circles around Nambonkaha with Mandou ahead of me and my other miniature guardians tugging on my hands. Without them, I might be lost in the bush somewhere by now. Generator-powered fluorescent bulbs glare on walls that are used to ambient sunlight—the new perspective transforms the village into an unfamiliar collection of huts and cluttered spaces. City vendors circle through the crowd, selling batteries and little cakes and cigarettes. Several women have set up fire rocks and iron woks, in which they fry yams and millet fritters. There are no boundaries: the ceremony threads through private courtyards and public areas alike. Spots usually bare and open are lined with rented chairs. I'm thoroughly discombobulated.

A dozen moving bands perform at once, looping into one another, the music blending and clashing. The married women stand in a circle off to the side, dancing slowly to the snare-drum shake of calabash gourds covered in nets made of shells. They take turns in the middle, singing to relatives they have lost, to the ancestors. Across the way, old women sit on short stools, thudding a beat on calabashes sunk in basins of water. The deceased is an old woman, and this is the vieilles' traditional celebration of their departed sister. At intervals, an old woman puts down her stick and dances in a slow circle. Trilling flutes, jingling thwack of drums, balafons thrumming—the musicians eddy breathlessly, carrying swirls of dancers.

Abi appears suddenly beside me. "They say there are going to be masks tonight!" I look at her skeptically, but her helper, Tenen, stands beside her and nods excitedly. "*Des vrais, vrais masques! Beaucoup même!*" Abi says most funerals just have a few bands and dancing all night, but this woman must have been *really* important. "Or else her relatives are rich," she suggests, raising an eyebrow.

And then there are screams, and a stampede of children melts into the crowd. A figure covered in burlap slinks by, and space widens around him. Rings of straw sprout from the figure's cuffs and collar. Eerie eyeholes are pinched unevenly out of the burlap face. I'm mystified. The villagers are petrified. "Where's the mask?" I ask Abi, expecting something carved and sinister. She just points at the costumed figure. The whole outfit, the whole creature, is called a *masque*. A few yards behind him, another burlap figure follows. This one dashes madly into the crowd and scatters shrieking women and children. When he turns, dried bones and horns and tin cans rattle around his waist. The third mask has a dead hedgehog tied to his back. But everyone's already been scared off. He prowls through the empty channel in the crowd, stops abruptly, and looks back.

Behind him, the final mask steps forward slowly. The musicians play on, but the rest fall silent. The last mask wears a tremendous hat of flared straw and sewn cowrie shells. It covers his head in a steep tent and throws a shadow on the rest of his figure. He is much larger than the rest and moves slowly—one leg forward, bending low at the knee, then the next leg forward. Silence surrounds him, menacing almost, and his movements are deliberate and deep. He seems like some sort of animist Grim Reaper.

It's too dark. The moon is slimming. The mask is covered in shadows. He looks spooky, like a ghost that might lash out suddenly. No one has told me anything. All I can see is his hat and the shadow below it. He's stepping, bending, plodding toward me. I *have* to get a better look. I flick on my flashlight and edge the beam up his side. I think I'm being sly.

Abi nearly tackles me to the ground. Her niece Kharidja and Tenen grab my wrists. "This is the most sacred one!" they rasp. "The one that represents death and the other world! You can't shine your light on him! Eh! *Wallai!*" In the name of God! Kharidja, the eleven-year-old, shakes her head as if to say, We can't take you *anywhere!* Tenen stifles nervous giggles with her palm. The mask slides past me without pausing.

Tonight there is a crazy sense of agelessness in the air. I try to count every modern influence on this night and can only come up with the glaring fluorescent bulbs. Drums beat, women and children dance in wild circles, the night, the dust, the song—it feels old, so primordial, so lasting, as if watching it, I can see centuries back.

6

Edifice

In the middle of July, word of another major event passes through the village. The *préfet* is coming. The préfet is the regional representative of a government whose power base is in the southern, mostly Christian part of the country. His outpost on the outskirts of Ferké is a walled villa surrounded by bougainvillea. The préfet is the government chief for miles; his halls fill daily with people seeking justice. But at the same time, he is stranded in a sea of political opposition: his posting in the mostly Muslim, less-developed north means he is on the outer edges of the political loop.

Nambonkaha is the hub of over fifty smaller villages and campements. Its residents have not been bashful about what they need from the government: they want light. Ever since electricity came to the north, they've been petitioning to have the village hooked up. Last year the prefecture of Ferké sent power lines up the main road to Burkina. The villagers chopped down a lane of mango trees and demolished several mud huts to prepare for electricity. Power lines followed the train tracks to the west of the village. Electricity poles poked up promisingly along the road all the way from Ferké. They went up on either side of Nambonkaha and just kept going—till they reached a smaller village five kilometers north. That's the native village of the préfet's deputy. It has no school, no clinic, no mosque. But it has electricity. Nambonkaha is sandwiched between two sets of power lines, yet it lingers in the Dark Ages.

Early in the morning the main road is lined with village elders in brilliant boubous. The balafon musicians play to herald the préfet's arrival. Women in their fanciest outfits dance at the entrance to the village. The youths have set up an awning in the center of the village and arranged the plush armchairs for the *grands types,* the important guests.

Sidibé and the school director stride rapidly through the crowd, looking official in dark slacks and pressed pagne shirts. Kinafou is right on their heels, wearing a regal lime-green boubou. She sees me in the throngs of women and waves. All of a sudden I feel important.

The préfet is one hour late. That's to be expected. The schoolkids leave their little clusters to form a corridor of checks and khaki along the main dirt road that crosses the village. Sidibé's daughter Adjaratou stands in the middle, clasping a bouquet of orange flowers clipped from the mayor's tree. And there they wait. The préfet is two hours late. But that's okay! It's a rule of hierarchy—he's important, and we're just villagers. The music stops. The women drift to the sidelines to chat.

And then, finally, a black car noses over the hill, and then another, and soon a whole motorcade slithers up to the crowd. Considering the fanfare, I'm fully expecting *Son Excellence le Président.* Instead, when the car doors ease open, a dozen men of dubious distinction hop out. Certainly the préfet doesn't need *that* many bodyguards—they must be the token itinerant males, the bodies needed to convey a powerful image. A few stocky figures in uniform emerge from the cars, and then a large pouting woman unfolds. That's the deputy from the village up the road, Abi whispers. Finally, a thin man wearing big glasses and a captain's hat steps from a Mercedes. Our students stand straighter. The entourage walks briskly through the dancers, looking straight ahead despite the singing children on either side of them. I slink back behind the women, hoping to somehow blend in among the crazy collection of fabrics. But the préfet shines a toothy smile on me and sticks out his hand. Hundreds of villagers dance and grin for him—*please love us, we really want electricity*—and I'm the only one he chooses to notice.

He takes his place flanked by his deputies on the couch set up under the awning. The school director plays translator, since he speaks Niarafolo fluently. He relays all the formal introductions, speaking through a battery-operated microphone. What follows is a ceremony that unveils the gulf separating the authorities in Abidjan from the humble cotton planters of the north.

The préfet refuses to use the microphone, fearing that it is unclean. He speaks instead as if the entire village were sitting across a coffee table from him. In a barely audible voice, he mutters rhetoric and formalities. He looks at the ground, looks at his feet, then drones on in a monotone. And says absolutely nothing.

But the chief refuses to play the game. He shoots direct questions at the préfet, and his tone is not fawning. *He* is president in this little village. He details the history of Nambonkaha's nonelectrification and demands an explanation, or at least a promise to pursue the matter. The préfet's response starts with indifferent, wandering words, and ends noncommittally. Then, with a curt nod, he indicates that business is done. The chief brings out his offerings to the cause of electricity and government favor: a sheep for the préfet, a goat for the deputy, some chickens for the rest. They issue token words of thanks, obviously not impressed, and sit looking bored while the balafons clang into action again. The village women spin and shake and smile in front of them, as if all their prayers have been answered.

Sidibé brings out the tea set after the ceremony. He wants to know what I thought of the performance. He is trying hard to mask his own disgust. I tell him of American politicians kissing babies, shaking hands, bellowing feel-good words. He shakes his head, and his voice sounds incredulous. *"Tu as vu ça?"* he says again and again. "They call this a democracy too, but somehow everything is turned on its head. In your country the people can make the politicians dance. Here we have to dance for them. We grovel and scrape to get noticed. It's like they only exist for their own good. We have nothing to do with it. Nothing ever gets accomplished."

Sidibé spoons sugar into the teapot and pours in the tea. "You saw what they did at the end? After no help, no agreements, no compromises, they gave him *gifts!*"

African French Lesson No. 1: *Bouffer:* Slang term for "to eat." Example: *J'ai bouffé tous les gâteaux.* I ate all the cakes. More prevalent use: "to line one's pockets." Example: *Il a bouffé l'argent de la caisse.* He has emptied the till. Often substitutes for "to steal." *Bouffer* is the gentler fleecing of funds conducted by an insider.

Côte d'Ivoire supposedly has the third largest economy in sub-Saharan Africa. Money *is* here, but in fine Third World form, it saturates the upper level of society and never seems to seep through to the rest. Corruption has become something of an accepted cultural norm. People *bouffe* in proportion to the funds they deal with. The big guys in President Bédié's circle *bouffe* international donations: funds for the betterment of the country are skimmed off. They have the safety net of other government officials with secrets to hide, and their rackets are rarely exposed.

Local heads of government are known to doctor their budgets or neglect to report a few major transactions. On the next level down, customs officers and gendarmes run their own nationwide laundering scheme: at checkpoints along all roads, they solicit bribes from immigrants and merchants in the name of customs and immigration regulations. And since the president and his wife, the ministry heads, the local authorities, and the gendarmes all *bouffe* with vigor, lower-rung fonctionnaires and villagers figure they might as well *bouffe* too.

The préfet's visit is a perfect example of another important force in professional and political society: the power play. Every echelon of life is ruled by the *patron*—or boss—mind-set, a checks-and-balances system based on age. The elders, mellowed and wiser, have the last say. In the professional realm, the *patron* can be just or unjust, he can be enlightened or myopic, but the employee is always the peon, the sycophant. Cooperation and communication are often achieved with a pathetic interplay of brownnosing and condescension.

Add bureaucracy to corruption, and you've got the formula for stagnation. Bureaucracy ensures that nit-picking, insignificant things get done so that the important, life-changing things won't have to. The préfet's arrival is a perfect illustration. Ivorians have an undying love of decorum. Every meeting, project, festival, or official visit is occasion for an elaborate opening ceremony. If it runs smoothly, nothing else really has to. If there's a meal afterward, the project is already a success. A good ceremony fills the void left by unfulfilled goals and promises.

Sidibé arcs the tea back and forth between teapots. He says, "The only reason they ever leave Ferké to do rounds of the district is to stock up their courtyards with cows and sheep."

David comes by late in July and stands at my door with his hands in the pockets of his clean blue jeans. He wants to talk about America, he says, so I invite him in. He is twelve for certain— he was born in a modern hospital, and all his statistics and dates have been documented. His head looks like sculpture: patrician brow, full lips, straight nose. David is an unusual strain of village kid: his father is a *grand type*, a cadre. In the village, the phrase carries connotations of untouchability, success, and condonable arrogance. For most cadres, returning home is an ego trip— they're the village's success stories. They tend to revel in their celebrity. But David's father blasts the stereotype. A tall man with a mustache that wiggles and jumps when he speaks, Siaka is eager and honest—and deferential to the villagers. Siaka lives in the city but prefers that his kids be brought up in the village where his father is the patriarch and his ties remain strong. Siaka has done well working on the business side of a large rice cooperative in Yamoussoukro, the administrative capital. He has a car, and a driver as well, and he appears in the village at least once a month for ceremonies or to check on his kids. David is fiercely proud of him. But his father's importance makes David quite precocious. He sees himself as better than the village kids, claims with a smirk that he doesn't understand Niarafolo, and instead speaks slightly pretentious French. Scrapes and cuts repulse him;

physical labor exhausts him. He is not like the others. He is never dusty, never too loud, never at work in the fields.

David is reserved with me. It seems that he expects me to consider myself superior, and he's already got his defenses up. As he perches in my chair, he asks me about the Kennedy assassination. Where he's learned about American presidents, I'm just not sure—his sixth-grade textbook draws an overview of the founding of the United States and then briefly discusses crops and computers and exports. Other than Sidibé, few have asked me about the history of my own country. It is too far away and too alien to concern most villagers. When I explain the events of 1963 to David, he listens with arched eyebrows, nodding solemnly.

"I used to hate white people," he says out of the blue when I've stopped my short lesson. "They did so many bad things to my people." He is not referring to the slave trade; his concerns are closer to home, involving stories passed down about French colonists who directed forced-labor rings in the early part of this century. He knows that the pocked road that curves by our village on the way to Mali and Burkina Faso was built with the sweat of Nambonkaha's own villagers. "Now," says David, "I know that I have to leave what was in the past behind. Now my parents have white friends, and President Houphouët-Boigny, after all, went to France all the time. He must have seen something good in white people. And I'm sitting talking to you. Maybe the world is good now."

When David speaks of school, his words come with halting confidence. Everyone assumes he has aced CM2, the equivalent of sixth grade. But we are still awaiting results of the national exam. Regardless of all his good work throughout the year, the only way to graduate is by passing a long and difficult cumulative exam. David won't say how it went. He just shrugs his shoulders and looks out the window, murmuring, "We'll see . . ." But occasionally I catch him speaking of next year, when he's at school in Ferké . . .

Abi's daughter Adjaratou and niece Kharidja meet me at the pump in the afternoon. These two are eleven, fluent in French, and my little sisters. We lift big buckets onto our heads and wind back to my house on the overgrown path. Adjaratou is a smiley face, all dimples and happy eyes. She flutters through my calendar, reading the words in awkward English. "Apreel" shudders in her throat. "Toooosdaiiii."

The girls are in CM1, fifth grade. They won't take the national exam till next year, but they're nervous already. They've heard bits and pieces about it from their CM2 friends, and next year just seems scary. When I ask how they think school went this year, their faces straighten out and they give short answers. Final grades for all the classes will be announced when the CM2 test results come in. They've probably done fine, but they don't want to jinx anything.

Kharidja, Adjaratou, and David are the lucky students. Their fathers know the benefits of schooling; they know what's beyond the boundaries of Nambonkaha; and they'll cover the expenses of education without thinking twice. For other village kids, getting through school is an independent struggle.

Children are born into designated roles according to their place in the family. The eldest son usually helps in the fields; the eldest daughter stays home to care for grandparents and younger siblings. The second son might mind the cows (often six-year-olds spend all day *en brousse,* in charge of giant beasts with finely sharpened horns). Among the succeeding children, girls are conscripted into fetching water and pounding corn as soon as their arms are strong enough. Girls and boys alike are expected in the fields during the planting season. School is a distinction: a few or maybe just one in each family attends. In the first- and second-grade classrooms, boys and girls are equally represented. But the female population ebbs in the older classes; village fathers have only recently decided that daughters are teachable too. Even Sidibé says that schooling a girl is risky. So many return home pregnant that one never knows if spending all that money is a good bet.

At least half of Nambonkaha's students come from elsewhere. They live in the campements or in the villages down the road. One father dutifully putters in on his moped from a neighboring village every morning with two tiny twin daughters in frocks clutching on behind him. Most kids don't get an escort. They walk several kilometers to get to school before the seven-thirty gong. At five o'clock, there's an exodus of students returning to the campements. Often when I go running past the ancestors' bridge at dusk, I come across a straggling group of kids in uniform heading home. They'll hurtle behind me, leaping and laughing, but when I ask them, "How was school?" their uniforms seem to stilt their tongues. They have trouble lapsing back from the rigid protocol that's enforced at school. They get home when the sun is teetering on the horizon and are immediately enlisted into doing chores.

The school director stands behind his desk, waiting for the room to fill. A long slab of cement planted in the wall and painted black serves as a chalkboard. Usually it is filled with paragraphs of tight script—illegible, I'm sure, from the desks at the back of the room. Today it is clean, with a line of chairs backed up against it, in preparation for the graduation ceremony.

Ibrahim, the first- and second-grade teacher, sits on the end chair. Originally from the southern coast, he is tall and easygoing and can't help smiling at the wide-eyed antics of his students. Alidou, in the next chair over, comes up to Ibrahim's shoulder. He is the master of the third and fourth grades. His round belly is a rarity in the village, and he holds it aloft pompously. He is obsequious around me, but—I hear—heavy-handed with his classes. He regularly puts on shiny shorts, pulls up his socks, and ties on cleats to play soccer with the village youth, who make do with plastic shoes and torn shorts. He and Ibrahim are a lopsided pair, like an old comedy team.

I am seated, curiously, with the president and chief at the front of the classroom. My only role at school so far has been that of occasional observer, but the director himself has ushered me to my seat. We face forty fathers and Abi, all crammed into beat-up bench-desk ensembles meant for their children. Some fathers wear pants and printed pagne shirts; others wear faded boubous. The room echoes with greetings, nervous laughter.

Each of the three school classrooms is painted dingy apricot and lit by shuttered windows. The wooden furniture, which occasionally requires a kick to keep its shape, suffices for most classrooms, though some of the first-graders are packed in three to a desk. Ibrahim has strung the ceiling in his room with colored paper chains. Alidou's walls are bare. Posters about hygiene and bees deck the walls of the fifth- and sixth-grade classrooms, and a smug picture of President Bédié watches from behind the director's desk. Each room has a bulletin board posting the school rules and the education ministry's slogan: "Union Travail Discipline." The school schedule is regimented, without room for creativity. Along with the expected dictation and mathematics, there are daily segments on morals and manners.

On most days, as soon as the gong at the foot of the giant baobab is clanged, the children pour out of the doors and resume their usual running and playing. But the students swarming just outside the door today are reduced to sharp whispers. Their futures will be announced in the next few minutes.

The director's walleye serves him well in his profession. His class is split in two: CM1 on the left, CM2 on the right. He can literally keep an eye on both sides of the classroom at the same time. Today he stands anxiously, one eye out the door on the throngs of children, the other on the collecting fathers. For all those kids, only forty fathers have showed. School is still struggling to be a priority in village life. Some 120 kids have attended school this year—about a quarter of the eligible children in the area. Not all of them are here today. Oumar, for instance, is weeding the rice fields, since his father has migraines.

The men quiet down, and a second woman slips into a seat near the door. She is Siaka's older sister, daughter of the patriarch. She has come to support her nephew David. She has been to Abidjan and speaks French better than any other vieille—she is almost a *grand type* herself.

The school director braces his shoulders and clears his throat. The kids hush and cluster in two groups outside, creating a corridor that passes in one door, between the special guests sitting against the blackboard and the desks stuffed with fathers, and out the opposite door. It will be the walk of shame for some, leading straight to a beating at home.

Ibrahim rises to deliver the verdict for the youngest classes. Rank is everything. Being "premier" is the biggest honor around—even illiterate, Frenchless vieilles know who's premier in each class. As he names them one by one, the kids bite down smiles, walk down the corridor, and stand facing the fathers. The rest of the students hover outside, clapping politely for their classmates. The fathers of the named children breathe out a little sigh, but not a single one applauds. Any congratulations might indicate to the child that he's already succeeded and doesn't have to keep working hard. I clap loudly for each one. David's aunt takes it a step further, hooting at every name and yelling words of encouragement raucously as the students walk forward.

The line of tiny graduates stands in front of the classroom while Ibrahim issues brief congratulations. Then they file out the opposite door, their order collapsing before they're outside. I can see them jumping gleefully on the stoop. Ibrahim's voice drops, and he quickly lists the children who didn't pass. They walk fast right through the room, in one door and out the other, chests tense and faces knit in shame. The fathers cluck and shake their heads. The last to be announced is a tiny paunchy girl in a fluttery dress. She scrambles right through, tears streaming.

Alidou stands rigidly and begins to announce his names in a high voice. When Oumar's name is called, I clap even though he's not here. He's passed in spite of long absences and complaining joints. Then the director stands to announce the results in his classes, beginning with CM1. He clears his throat and declares, "These are the kids who worked hard," and lists off the names of about fifteen students. Adjaratou ranks number three, and Kharidja is seventh. They walk through with their hair newly braided, chins held level. They glance at me with quick grins and then return their eyes modestly to the floor. The row of students is a model of ideal African child behavior: they look down so as not to be too proud or presumptuous. They are quiet and humble and respectful. Kharidja and Adjaratou grab hands just as they pass out of the doorway.

Finally we get to the cliffhanger—the CM2 class. The others' grades have been determined by a few tests throughout the year and their general conduct in class. But the fates of the CM2 students rest solely on the national exam.

The director lists the winners: a tall dark boy from the village down the road is premier. Siaka's sister sits up straighter and glances worriedly at her nephew. David is number two. It's a shock—we all expected him to be first. But his aunt doesn't care. She yelps in unabashed joy and pretends to grovel behind him as he passes.

After the director names the third student, he stops. Only *three* out of twenty-eight have passed sixth grade. The room buzzes with clicking tongues and sucked teeth. The director continues with the failures, still in ranked order, naming first, with a sigh of regret, those who just missed it. Fatoumata, a sixth-grader for years, missed by a half a point; the director's own son needed two more points. Then he grimaces, and his voice comes out a growl: "These are the ones who don't even know how to read. Kids such as these waste space in my classroom. Next year send them to the fields." But these last students must have predicted their failure: only two are around to sprint through the room and bear the brunt of the village's disappointment.

In reality, most village kids never do pass sixth grade. I've just assumed that most of the young men who spend their days in the fields have always spent their days in the fields. But a surprising number of them are somewhat literate. They have had the luxury of learning to read, and they choose not to put it to regular use. Most villagers tend to look at school as a six-year commitment. For those who *want* to continue their education, the odds are piled high. I've sat in on a few classes in the past few months to see how they work. There are children in the third and fourth grades whose French is so skeletal that they can't understand the most basic instructions. But though they can't express themselves, they *can* recite the various sentences and facts that they've been taught to memorize. And that is what merits their promotion from grade to grade.

Learning disabilities do not exist at the village level; either you do well or you don't. There's no encouragement, unless one considers a thwack across the hand positive reinforcement. One-on-one help is available only to those who pay for it, like Siaka, who pays the teachers to tutor his children several days a week after school. Sidibé's kids study around a lamplit table every night. Kharidja and Adjaratou teach their brother, and Sidibé teaches the girls. Other students are in a lonely league of literacy in their communities. Their parents can't read or write, and chores eat up the hours when they could be studying. The overall philosophy is perhaps that of health and life in general: the ones who can tough it out will succeed; the ones who are weak will not.

When Kharidja and Adjaratou and their brother Tidiane get home from school after their graduation, Abi awaits them with a pitcher of bisap. She is not full of praise, not fawning. Sidibé doesn't yell out congratulations or hug his kids. But there's something about their tone of voice that is softer, and everyone can feel it. It's as if a victory parade were winding silently, invisibly through the courtyard. After dinner there is popcorn dusted with sweetened powdered milk. Sidibé, Abi, and I sit in the circle of light from a lantern. The girls crouch just outside the edges in the dark, but they are still for once. Not washing dishes, not washing siblings. Just still and allowed, this night, to revel softly in their good work.

Oumar's family doesn't seem to be aware of his graduation to fourth grade. They must know—the village grapevine is as good as a newsletter. But his father suffers, his mother is pregnant, and the fields are a lot of work for one little boy. School doesn't really matter right now.

Village gossip breezes over the successes and delves straight into the glaring disappointment of the CM2 test results. Within a few days of the graduation ceremony, sundry explanations arise for the failure of our sixth-grade class. None of them have to do with hardball teaching methods or an impossible exam. Apparently the number of children passed into *collège*, junior high, is in part determined by the number of places available in the secondary schools. The methods for securing a place in these schools and the testing system itself are often plagued with corruption.

A child I know in Ferké studied hard for weeks before the national exam. When he finally showed up to take it, the proctor wrote down all the answers on the board and the whole lot of students passed. If you don't pass, there are seats for sale. Some parents aren't concerned that their child isn't academically ready and buy off spaces in *collège*. The villagers shake their heads, wary of the system, wary of preferential treatment given to city children. Gradually the onus shifts partly off the students and fatalism surfaces. How could Nambonkaha's kids compete with so many conniving forces in the city? The director, perhaps worried about complaints that the failure stemmed from his teaching style, is quick to place the blame squarely on his predecessor, who left years ago but who obviously gave these kids a shaky foundation upon which to build the rest of their studies.

And finally, as a safety net in case all the other complaints and assumptions don't hold up, the villagers point to sorcery as the culprit. Dramane tells me that chicken feathers and blood had been found around the school on the day of the exam. No one talked about it then because they didn't want spoken words to confirm any malicious deeds, but now they all remember and nod. The witches step in conveniently to relieve negligent parents and a flawed system of responsibility.

7

Récolte

Several weeks after the end of the school year, the ancestors' bridge succumbs to the rains. Most elders and women with babies stay in the campements because they can't get across the water. I take a detour on my way to Abi's fields one day to see the situation. But I don't even get close. The road is a sea between walls of reeds, and water swallows the start of the bridge. A man rides up slowly on a dented old bike. His home lies across the river, so he strips off his shirt and his shoes, rolls his pants way up past his knees, balances his shoes on his head, tosses the bike over his shoulders, and glides in up to his chest.

Abi's fields are, happily, on this side of the water. The growing season is in full swing now, and the grasses are six feet high in some places. During the day, the village is vacant. Men and boys leave for the fields around dawn. Women and daughters pound corn all morning, stir sauces in big pots, and disappear into the bush around ten, balancing basins full of axes, empty rice sacks, and stacked bowls of lunch for the rest of the family.

Everyone has fields to tend—even the *boutiquier*, even the imam, even the fonctionnaires. Some have over a dozen hectares of many different crops. The mayor, for example, has fourteen hectares of cotton—the local cash crop—as well as hectares of peanuts, three kinds of corn, and millet. Two tired-looking cows latched onto a rusted metal contraption plow his fields. It's a sign of his success: most villagers hack up the dirt on their own.

Each season is perfectly orchestrated. Cooperatives of all shapes and sizes spring up as the crops ripen. Young men come together and draw up a schedule for working in certain fields, sometimes their own, sometimes those of potential fathers-in-law. Neighbors pitch in to help neighbors, friends to help friends. Harvest means twelve-hour days spent in the sun, bent parallel to the ground. It means getting scratched by cotton thorns and bitten by various mites and ants. Vast acres of rice are clipped stalk by stalk with a paring knife. Peanuts are yanked from deep earth and plucked one by one from their stems. But no one bellyaches about the work. Somehow every inch of farmed savanna gets planted and weeded and reaped in time.

Abi has a hectare of peanuts with hibiscus plants on the periphery for bisap. She's trundling through the rows when I arrive, looking over her plants. I offer to help, but apparently there's nothing to be done. Her neighbor's son is taking care of pesticide, pacing the length of the field with a can full of poison and a spray nozzle. The mayor stands with his hands on his hips, shouting tips to the boy.

Discarded pesticide cans lie at the edge of the field. When I lean over to inspect them, Abi and the mayor both yell out sharply, "Don't touch those cans!" Abi explains that this poison is extremely lethal, and the mayor chimes in with a story of a new cotton pesticide sprayed on the fields of a nearby village. "One family had a garden of greens planted right near the cotton," he says. "Their son went to a friend's house for lunch, and the rest ate at home. When he came back, his entire family was dead.

"Some villagers put pesticide in the stream," he continues. After all the alarm about the pesticide cans, he announces this so casually! "Why?" I demand. "They think it's the most efficient way to fish. No broken lines, you don't need bait. Just dump in some pesticide and dinner floats right up." He chuckles. "I've never done it, but there are people who do."

My guts twist all up; my temper comes tremblingly close to snapping. "*How*, how, how can they?" This is the "sacred" stream, the one the ancestors inhabit, the one where women douse their children for good luck! How can you be so careful with an empty pesticide can and then baptize your baby in poison, feed your children toxic fish? This is too much. This I can't just brush off. "When I got here, people complained of their lives." I'm speaking rapid-fire to the mayor, trying to curb my anger. "They said, 'Guissongui, why does everyone die here?' But meanwhile, people eat *poisson à la pesticide* and bathe in poison and then wonder why they're sick? They have no regard for the day after tomorrow!" Abi raises her eyebrows and cocks her head. The mayor snorts. But there's no retort or assurance or clarification. My anger just hangs in the air.

It's all just helpless. I want to yell, Well, *that's* why you're stuck in the last century, that's why you die early, that's why progress slips through your fingertips: pesticide in the water, empty memorized phrases at school, four uneducated wives at home with no rights. But I curtail my harangue—it's useless. The problems are so much bigger than this village. The mayor chuckles at my horror.

The next morning, Sidibé runs into my courtyard at seven, yelling. "The mayor's wife had a baby last night but something's wrong. Come fast!"

The mayor is nowhere in sight, so we enter his second wife's hut alone. It's like walking back into night—the hut is black and smoky, and only after several minutes do my eyes adjust to reveal the dim figures inside, lit only by a slit in the wall. Mendjeta, the mayor's second wife, sits on a pagne with her legs out straight, leaning back on her hands. Her infant daughter is swathed in pagnes a few inches from her side, still plugged in to her mother's insides with a pale cord.

There is a feisty gleam in Mendjeta's eye as she spills out a long discourse in Dioula to Sidibé. He tells me the child was born a few hours before dawn, but not everything came out. Mendjeta looks fed up and derisively amused. I find a stool and cram my nose in the book, squinting hard to make out words and pictures in the smoky shadows. Sidibé stands shiftily in the doorway for a few minutes before muttering, "So you can handle it, right?" and disappearing into the sunlight.

I look up *Placenta, stuck*. All I find are dramatic drawings of naked women splayed and dying, their wombs turned inside out by an inopportune tug at the umbilical cord. "DO NOT," it says in highlighted boxes under the pictures, "pull out the placenta! You may KILL the mother!" But Mendjeta can't remain restricted to a foot radius of her baby forever. I read the chapter over and over, hoping that some saving sentence will suddenly appear out of the darkness. Nothing.

Vieilles pass in and out of the hut. They've delivered the child, but they won't get near Mendjeta's umbilical cord. I ask her to nurse the baby to stimulate contractions. She looks at me as if I'm crazy, and says, "I don't have milk, just water, there's nothing to feed her." I repeat my mantra: "The water is good! Give it to her." She concedes, shaking her head, but to no avail. Her contractions have completely abated. Minutes swell into an hour. My throat is dry with smoke, my eyes strain in the dark. Meaningful communication is paltry now that Sidibé has gone. The stakes are too high for any rash action. I jump up from my stool and tell her I'll be back.

Back in my own house, I read the placenta chapter thoroughly. The book illustrates placentas that have come apart and membranes that remain in the womb. These are two distinct possibilities. It's not my place to be tinkering with someone else's organs. But there's really no choice—getting her to the hospital in Ferké on public transportation with a baby hanging from her would be absurd.

Bright skies filter a little more light through the chink in the wall when I return. I've got a flashlight now, and rubber gloves. The beam of light reveals a bloody, lumpy cloth shielded behind her body. This could be the key to the mystery. Can I see that? I ask. She shrugs her shoulders disinterestedly but shoves it over. The cloth opens on a coiled gray mass. The placenta. Strange thing—this great feeder of life. It looks like a brain, feels heavy, important. I turn it around in my hands reverently, a little concerned to be touching this object considered so sacred and personal. It looks whole, no pieces missing. The problem must be the membranes knotting her baby to her insides.

I motion that I'm going to grab the cord sticking out of her body, conscious of personal space and body awareness like a good American, though I know she's accustomed to doctors with gruff, impersonal hands. Three vieilles crowd in the door and crane over my shoulders. How did I become the expert all of a sudden? I'm just deducing what's wrong. With my fingers at the top of the pale tube, I pull steadily, holding my breath. It seems quite possible that I'm about to yank out some major piece of Mendjeta. A lump of gray tissue eases out with a little pop. A chorus of astonished *Yeh*s greets it. Mendjeta's eyes flicker in surprise, but then she laughs. "Eh, Guissongui!" The vieilles stand up straight, clap their hands together As soon as I step back into the blaring sunlight, people materialize from all corners of the courtyard. They shake my hand and say, "*An y bara!*" Good work! It's as if half the village has been waiting for the conclusion to Mendjeta's birthing trauma.

The news sweeps across the village. I stop by Tchessilahana's outdoor boutique to pick up some beignets, and she grabs my shoulder and looks me in the eye, "*An y bara,* Guissongui." When I pass through the imam's courtyard on the way home, his wives stop what they're doing and say, "*An y che.*" Thank you. They are all solemn and grateful. My desperate tug might have just branded me midwife. The mayor comes over that afternoon with a rooster for me. He is all smiles and gratitude, hands clasped behind his back, bowing slightly at the waist. Abi tells me later that he brought the chicken at Sidibé's urging. Apparently, he is trying as much as he can to distance himself from the whole situation. Mendjeta may be free from her baby, but she is still all tangled up in a courtyard drama. Several of the vieilles have consulted charlatans about the Real Reason for her delivery troubles. Charlatans—regular villagers themselves—get paid five francs to chat with the spirits about events in the village and come up with causes. Their findings are taken quite seriously. As two charlatans have been consulted, two answers come back: Mendjeta has a) insulted her husband and was creating *palabres,* or fights, with her cowives and/or b) cheated on her husband. Word spreads quickly. A simple glitch in delivery has tarnished this woman's reputation for good.

According to Sidibé, the mayor's nightly complaints about his wives have gone from abstract to concrete in the past few weeks. His first two wives—Mendjeta is his second—are uneducated village women with no French and fertile wombs. Between the two of them, he has sired about ten kids, though he has to stop and count when asked exactly how many. His third wife spent some time in Ferké. She's more sophisticated, comes from a distant village, and speaks French. She is the most modern, the most demure, the least contentious, and the one he likes to show off the best. But she is barren.

The fact that the mayor likes her best despite her inability to give him children offends the first two. They are bitter about his lopsided love, and criticize him regularly when they're in the fields out of his earshot. The third wife hears it all and, still insecure about her sterility, tattles to the mayor.

Their courtyard life heaves and splits. The first two wives *won't* speak to the third, the mayor will *only* speak to the third, and all the agreements inherent in polygamous arrangements fly out the window. Generally, each wife is entitled to a hut of her own, an allowance of her own, and a certain number of designated nights of the week with her husband in her bed. This is her right. But the mayor is furious. He refuses to go near his first two wives, let alone sleep with them, and days after Mendjeta's delivery, he still has not seen the baby.

The Niarafolo name their children eight days after birth, in accordance with Muslim tradition. After five days, Abi comes to my courtyard on her way back from Mendjeta's hut. "The mayor won't go see her," she tells me. "He is our friend," she says, idly inspecting a mango on my table, "but I can't stand to see him treat his wife like that." Maybe since he's your friend, you can approach him about it, I tell her. She bites her lip and nods. "*C'est compliqué, hein?* Maybe I'll tell Sidibé to talk to him." She plunks down the mango and looks up. "Maybe I should just talk to him myself," she says.

On the seventh day, the mayor begrudgingly meets his daughter. Conversations with Sidibé and Abi have paid off. He announces the baby's three names in an unceremonious grouping of whoever is around. Everyone in the village has a family name, a Niarafolo name, and a Dioula name. The family name is no big deal—there are only about ten options, and lots of young women and children aren't even quite sure of their own. Dioula names are derived from Islamic tradition. Niarafolo names are statements relevant to circumstances surrounding birth, generally long and hard to pronounce. The Dioula and Niarafolo names are interchangeable; people go by either or both.

For instance, Moussa, Mandou, and Oumar are Dioula names, but their mothers call them Kpayirgué, Kagnédjoulokon, and Gnignéri. Some Niarafolo names are tried and true: I know at least a dozen other Guissonguis in the village and the campements. Others are more whimsical. The chief's name means "I don't have a name."

The mayor's brand-new daughter has been known as "*Piéchaplé*," Baby Girl, till today. Since her parents are feuding, she wins an extra name. The mayor calls her a name that means "You should rest now," which is a shorthand message to her mother with various interpretations. Three possible meanings, translated by Dramane, are "Don't come into my fields anymore," "Stop sleeping around," and "I'm not coming to your hut at night again."

Mendjeta isn't about to put up with that. The name she gives her daughter means "I don't do what other people tell me to do." But we just call her by her Dioula name, Sawa.

The bridge built by ancestors is whole again in a matter of days. Mere mortals have taken care of the repairs, though I really can't imagine how. Water surges under it now, flooding the trees up to their midriffs. I push my bike over the tied branches and ride up the hill past the adoration ground. I'm off on a promotional tour of the campements beyond the stream. The vaccines have arrived; the baby weighing station is ready. Sidibé has met with the village men to explain the importance of bringing pregnant wives to the infirmary for a monthly checkup. Saturday is market day and the kickoff for our tandem preventive-care programs. We have activated the bush telegraph system by announcing our project to the chief, the elders, and the clinic budget committee—a collection of representatives from the village and different campements. It's a telephone tree without cords: elders tell their communities, a team of messengers visits each campement and tells each subchief, and the message trickles through the bush till every last villager has heard it. I'm visiting the campements personally to rally the mothers who hide from modern medicine. If I can lure them in the beginning, by whatever means, maybe they'll understand why they should come of their own accord in the end.

The road slopes upward, through groves of cashew trees and long blowing reeds. It rains brilliantly just in patches; the sun threads through dark clouds, and the savanna glistens. The air is humid and cool at the same time—it's like biking in a glass of ice water. And then the first path veers off to the right and I ride into a little Oz. The names of campements are usually burbling mouthfuls, as they often include the chief's name. This first campement, one of many along the dirt road that stretches twenty kilometers into the bush, is called Koufoungobavogo. It means "Koufoungo is here Village." Its mud huts *dazzle* in the crystal sunlight.

Probably eight families live in Koufoungobavogo; their huts crouch together as if to ward off the bush. Women pound corn in the sun, flat breasts flapping with each thrust of the pestle. Most know me from the market, but my appearing unannounced in their little settlement has surprised them. They can't stop giggling. Children who have never been to Nambonkaha flee from me in terror. A middle-aged man who works with the vaccination campaign invites me into his hut. Ancient pages of a French magazine cover the walls; on one, a white woman, fuzzy and orange with age, steps out of a sedan. It doesn't matter who she is—it's having pictures that counts. The three traditional steps of welcome follow my arrival: he invites me to sit, offers me water, and asks me for *"les nouvelles,"* my news.

"C'est un bonjour," I say, as is custom. "There's nothing serious. Everything is well." *"Bon, bon."* He nods, leaning back in his chair. Now I can state my mission: "Since we are doing vaccinations and weighing on market day, I've come to remind the women that they must come." Dramane has supplied the "must." According to him, my inclination to beat around the bush *(I would really like it if . . .)* will get me nowhere working with villagers. "You have to give orders," he says, "and then everyone will listen to you." The vaccination worker nods some more, accepts the message, confirms the dates and times. Some pleasantries pass. And when I'm ready to leave, I must "ask for the road."

The next campement nestles under a mango grove set off from the road. It is deserted and dark under the branches, and the whole place smells vaguely of animal urine. The owner of my house is the chief here, and on other days I will find it full of children and scampering chicks. Today I pass through it, finding only a man with cloudy eyes who teeters on the edge of insanity. He has no one to weigh. I bike on down the road to the next campement.

The path winds back from the ancestors' bridge, bumps across the railroad tracks, and cuts into the village, past the long wall around the clinic and Sidibé's house. When I roll by, Abi is standing on the porch. "Come eat alloco!" she calls. Alloco is a personal favorite. I wobble through her gate and hop off. Sidibé emerges from the house with a grin and a stack of children's health-record books. "I just picked them up at the health base," he explains as Abi hands us a plate of fried plantains with hot pepper sauce.

Sidibé and I visited the base together a few days ago to explain our child health-care project in detail to the deputy doctor. "We are going to weigh babies," we told him, "and teach illiterate women to understand growth charts and nutrition. The clinic is going to start doing prenatal exams, so that troublesome pregnancies can be sent to Ferké before it's too late." We perched on the edges of our seats, hoping for the doctor's blessing. The deputy sat back in his rolling chair, flicking a pencil and nodding with his chin on his chest. The cast from his scuffle with the head doctor still covered his left wrist. A blasting air conditioner turned the office frigid. The deputy paused after our explanation, ran his eyes from my head to my knees, and said, "You've gotten fatter."

It's a compliment, actually, but it doesn't go over so well with Western women. Whenever I arrive back in the village after a trip, like clockwork the villagers first say, "You stayed away too long!" no matter how long I've been gone. And second, "You got fat!" regardless of whether I look any different. It generally means You look healthy! or You must have eaten well! But the words were lascivious in the deputy's mouth. I wanted to kick him. Just in case I had forgotten: I am first woman, and *then* health worker.

Nonetheless, he rationed us twenty-five health-record books, or *carnets,* for our village-worth of tots, and a high school notebook to use as a register. As we got up to leave, he said, leering, "Come back soon!" I couldn't help just a little dig about his cast. "*How* did that happen?" I asked. Sidibé stifled a smile.

With little more backing than some lukewarm words from our superiors, we plunge into the project. I fashion some wooden planks into a measuring board and paint it brightly with acrylics brought from home. I cut a strip of cloth to measure arm diameter, an indicator of malnutrition. Finally, I scrub our scale and graph pages for the register.

Saturday morning, Tchessilahana, the rice and sauce maker, is first in line. The infant in her arms is her daughter's son. He wears a scrap of pagne for a diaper. He is a small, serious baby. He lies still on the jittery scale while I shoot across the weights. Without a sound, he allows us to measure the diameter of his forearm and head. Then I stretch him out on the new measuring board, a little brown body against the newly painted wood, and he lets out a long, nonchalant stream of pee. Acrylic will never work. Colors meld and run all over the board. Tchessilahana picks him up, laughing. His bottom is smudged lavender.

The women come fast and furious. With the help of the president and Sidibé's assistant, dozens of infants are measured, weighed, and documented. Along with the babies shrieking at my paleness, there are a few unforeseen complications. Some mothers aren't sure of their baby's last name. Others can't even begin to imagine how old their child is. We ask, "Was he born before or after you planted cotton? Were you still pregnant during Ramadan?" Many just smile embarrassed smiles and say they can't remember. Otherwise, Nambonkaha's first baby weighing moves along swimmingly. In a few hours, we introduce fifty women to the importance of regular weighing, outfit twenty-five of them with record books, and vaccinate all the children in sight.

The next market day, I move the whole operation to a spot wedged in between an old woman with a trembling jaw who sells eggplants and tobacco and a crew of women frying up fish and fritters. Sidibé has donated a rickety table that he used as a door to his chicken coop. I've painted it blue and drawn some propaganda: pictures of smiling mothers weighing pudgy babies. I transport all the equipment from a corner in my house across the village with the help of small friends' heads. Little Sita balances the scale on her head; Moussa upturns the table on his; a few others are conscripted for the measuring board, my stool, and a basket of supplies. I bring up the rear, watching my baby-weighing station, disassembled, bob through the village in a speeding, wobbly line.

Mothers come to weigh in droves at first, perhaps still impressed by the novelty of it all. I man the station myself and attempt to explain the process at the same time. When I come across underweight babies, I try to give tips on weaning in broken Niarafolo: "He's going to drink porridge with peanut paste or egg or greens." They nod and laugh. "*Ao, le?*" they say, Oh really? They understand my words, but they must be baffled by my intentions. I want them to add protein and vitamins to their weaning babies' diets, to acknowledge that there are important steps in the transition from sucking breast milk to eating kabato. But in my attempts to enlighten them, I'm recommending that they combine sweet gruel with ingredients used in salty sauces. It's culinary blasphemy at best. Peanut paste goes with vegetables and fish, not porridge, Guiss! And everyone knows that babies who eat eggs will grow up thieves!

The sun is teasing the trees to the west when the market finally dwindles. My basket holds sugar and soap. My hands have been full with babies. I have been peed on and screamed at. I haven't had a chance to buy my supplies, but all the vegetable sellers have returned to the campements beyond the stream. I am hungry and tired. Far across the school field, Angélique bends over a giant bowl on the fire. I send my weighing tools back on the heads of my small team and wind my way to her courtyard for a calabash of chapalo. I take a low stool next to her fire rocks so that we can chat. But she doesn't sit still. She moves from her pot to the dim pantry where the chapalo is kept, serving up gourdfuls to a line of slurring men sitting behind the hay wall.

One of the men wears a sweatshirt with Santa peeking from behind a Christmas tree. The man raises his eyebrows when he sees me sip the beer, but hell, *he's* the Muslim. Dragging up a stool and ignoring all but the most basic greetings, he launches into a long tirade, of which I understand nearly nothing, then waves at Angélique to translate. Running her fingers through a bowl of uncooked rice to check for pebbles and bugs, she flashes me a smile and restates his lecture in her singsong voice. "He says how come you weigh babies? He says what can that do for them? It doesn't make them grow. It doesn't keep them from getting sick. He says all you get from it is a number of kilos."

I'm only too glad to explain. "Mothers can keep track of their child's growth. They'll know if something's wrong when he loses weight or doesn't grow, and plus it's a good way to give mothers a sense of responsibility for their kid's health." Angélique translates. He makes a sputtering noise with his mouth, and continues.

Angélique says. "He says that *they* don't know all that! And even if they did, how can you tell them what to do when their kid isn't growing? They just look at this chart and see lines and dots." Here are all my anxieties, spelled out by a stranger. I know I need to meet with the women to explain just why they should weigh, but I haven't set a date yet. I know I need an assistant who can communicate fluently. "Give me time," I say. "This is just the beginning." He grunts and sloshes the last of the chapalo in his gourd. With a flick of his wrist, it shoots out into the dirt, an offering for the ancestors. Then the man with the Santa shirt shakes my hand and walks away.

Every day merchants haul out their wares and fill up the wooden market stalls lining the main street of Ferké. It is the second largest town in the north and a hub for all transport headed to or from Burkina Faso and Mali. But on Thursdays, the official market day, commerce spills out from behind the cement buildings and lean-tos and swamps the street. Malian fabric merchants come down from the north and stack pyramids of tight rolls of cloth on the side of the road. Yam and charcoal sellers bus in from the villages and set up shop inches from traffic. Men bike by with trays of eggs piled high on their handlebars; women haggle boisterously and switch down the road with their purchases in wide basins on their heads. The thoroughfare bustles and chokes. Rattling trucks on their way to Mali or Burkina hurtle through the crowd, barely missing toes and bodies.

Abi always goes to Ferké on Thursday. I always go any other day. I often ride my bike into town, and it's so much easier to maneuver when you're not sharing the road with milling masses, taxis, trucks, and stacks of fish. But the week that Sidibé goes south to his family's courtyard, I leave my bike at home and take the badjan into the Ferké market with Abi. I wear a pair of drawstring pants and a T-shirt. After giving me a once-over, Abi shakes her head. She can't believe I don't dress better. Market day is a chance to show off. She wears a blue pagne complet with a large orange flower print and a scarf tied above her forehead. Pinned to the sides of her already monstrous shoulder pads are two stiff six-inch roses made out of crepe. She has to enter the badjan sideways.

We stop first at Sidibé's uncle's boutique to greet him. This involves drinking a Fanta and idly watching a butcher across the way slice apart a goat as if it were made to be dismantled, then deciding that maybe we should buy some grilled goat meat, waiting for it to cook for a half hour, and eating slowly. Finally we hop into a taxi to go a half mile to the heart of the market. Abi heads first to her hairdresser, a woman with a chair set up among the stalls. She has a comb and a mirror, and bags of artificial hair of all shades hung up on a string. But Abi doesn't want extensions; she wants a wig. Usually she tames her hair with pomade and partitions it into braids or tufts. Sidibé's return from the south, however, is occasion enough for a whole new look. The woman slicks back Abi's hair and fits on a wig. Lustrous, plastic black hair falls down her back. Then she brandishes shears and gives the wig a haircut. A bob, to be precise. Abi pays her five hundred CFA—under a dollar—and leaves with her chin a little higher, her expressions a little more controlled, bearing the strangest resemblance to Jackie O.

Abi always buys in bulk. She gets a giant sack of locally made soap and a dozen bottles of talc for her own market stall in the village. She buys twenty onions, a whole pile of hot peppers, and several large, hairy yams. We'd need a grocery cart to haul it all, but she doesn't attempt to carry anything very far. Instead, she leaves each bag by the side of the road with strategically placed merchant-friends. Later, when we pick up a taxi to head back to the village (a two-thousand CFA splurge that she makes a habit of), she asks him to stop at seven different spots along the street to load up.

There are nine hills to Nambonkaha. They are faint, rolling, deceiving, long. I know each rise, each rut from pedaling into town several times a month. I have biked them with eggs and watermelons wobbling on my bike rack, colossal planks of wood listing over my head, chickens dangling from my handlebars. For each torturous climb, there is always a short breath of ecstasy. Nine moments that are worth it for the wind buffeting my face, ringing in my ears, filling my shirt, for the brilliant streak of rice fields beside me.

Our taxi swerves around large red scabs in the asphalt, dodging strands of men on bikes heading home from the market. I can close my eyes and know just how much longer till the village. Second hill, the hardest climb: swoop through the rice bog where green was born. Fourth hill: nose up near the rusted cattle-merchant sign. Seventh hill, and the tufts of thatched roofs peek out from a village tucked back from the road. Eighth hill: the cargo box of a truck tipped months ago is still pitched in the grass; the fields open out in front of us on either side. The land sweeps up to two stalwart baobabs on the distant ninth hill where the village begins. Old women walk single file along the road, hips rocking under the weight of stacked firewood. Boys in smudged rags dangle their latest catch by its tail, hoping to lure a buyer from the cars that hurtle by. They are my neighbors. I know them by name.

When Sidibé comes back on a Sunday in September, he's gained two little boys and a dog. Abi doesn't even flinch. His brother and his uncle consider Sidibé's education and his civil-servant salary reason enough to make him guardian of their own young sons. The arrangement eases their financial burden and guarantees a good upbringing for the boys. So Sidibé and Abi's little band expands to eight, out of which only four are their own.

Sidibé never skips a beat; it seems perfectly natural that his list of dependents should expand on such short notice. He's charmed by the addition of these two small boys to his mostly female courtyard. But just for a fleeting second, there's trouble in his eyes. His extended family assumes his generosity is bottomless and his salary steady. But life hinges on his next paycheck, and it often comes late.

The dog is for me. "I named it Dick," says Sidibé, as he thrusts it into my arms. It's a ball of brown and black fluff, cowed into corners by pecking chickens and small grabbing hands. But I've already decided, after much debate, that I don't want a dog, that it would be too much responsibility for an animal I'd just have to give up after two years. Plus, there's not a bag of dog food between here and Abidjan, and who really wants to cook meals for a pet? "No problem," says Sidibé, scooping him up, "we'll keep it. I always wanted a dog anyway."

Abi cooks attiéké and grilled chicken for Sidibé's first night back in the village. The mayor comes by just after we smear our plates clean. I have recently been traveling too—east to a small village and then south to Abidjan and the beach. "You were in Abidjan?" the mayor asks.

"I've been to Abidjan before," he says, stretching his long legs out in front of him. "But just once." What did he think of it? He shrugs his shoulders. Abidjan is overwhelming—all those crazy skyscrapers and looping overpasses and fancy cars. "You just end up spending all your money and feeling alone," the mayor sighs. "*C'est trop chaud-chaud.*" It's too hectic. "Despite everything, I was happy to get back to Nambonkaha. *Nambonkaha n'est pas compliqué.*"

The mayor hands a coin to Sidibé's son Tidiane and sends him off to buy a cigarette at Tchessilahana's boutique. Paying twenty-five francs for every craving somehow seems less costly than paying five hundred for the pack. He says, "Guiss, you've been north and south—which do you like better?" I suppose he expects me to choose the south: it's the land of television and *toubabous*, where there are beaches and big towns and restaurants with more than just rice and sauce. But I find the south too humid, not only the air, but the people too. My lingering impression is of sweat beading up even on my shins, and little hands all over me. Children would thrust out fingers as I passed, to catch my legs or my hands. All was sultry—the oppressive laziness in the air, the lascivious game of sex (more blatant in the less conservative south), the tension between tribes and men. Southerners seem more prone to *palabres*—fights—and crime. The north is known for being "*tranquille.*" Maybe it's a Muslim thing. "I like that tradition is still strong up here," I tell the mayor. "I like the huts, the obscurity, the dryness of the savanna. I like the music. And I like that people here are easy to get along with."

He thinks a while. "Me too," he says. "Down south," he continues, "there are lots of Ghanaians and Senegalese. They don't

really work. It's always *petit commerce*. It's never real work."
Sidibé nods in agreement. *"Vraiment,* only the Ivorians and the
Burkinabes know how to work. They go to the fields from sunup
to sundown without a break." A round of grunts serves as hom-
age to their work ethic. Tidiane sprints back with a cigarette and
some change. The mayor lights up and blows blue smoke at the
stars. "And Malians, they are just plain lazy."

"But!" says Abi, looking up from her stool by the fire with
animated eyes. "A Malian woman, since she hardly works, knows
how to get a man. She spends hours braiding her hair, fixing up
her face, and putting on jewelry. She takes forever deciding which
expensive pagne will make her the most sapé. Then she's all sweet
and pretty with the men. *Elle dit, Mon cheri! Cheri coco!"* Abi
bats her eyelashes. "Here we just grunt and beckon to our husbands." Her laugh starts out low, then burbles up, loud and deep.
Sidibé and the mayor grin.

It's idle stereotyping, but when the laughter dies down, it
leaves an awkward ring in the night. In the south, a wave of anti-
immigrant sentiment is sweeping areas where Burkinabes and
Malians provide manual labor on large plantations. There are
reports of murdered laborers, of Burkinabe families running back
to their home country. It is a fervor fueled by the president himself, who, concerned about the popularity of the northern, Muslim opposition leader, is stoking the fires of ethnic tension. This
despite the fact that over a third of the population—and much of
the labor force required to produce cocoa and coffee, the country's main source of income—comes from neighboring countries.

In the north, however, ethnic friction remains mostly muted.
Nambonkaha's butcher is from Mali. Our main mechanic is a
Burkinabe. The non-Ivorian families in the village are well-
assimilated and important parts of the community. Villagers are
proud to be Ivorian, because everyone knows that Côte d'Ivoire
is the most stable and prosperous country in West Africa. But in
the end, they treat nationality like a last name—it's a distinction
that doesn't mean much. They are first and foremost villagers of
Nambonkaha.

Despite his innocent demeanor, Dick the dog creates strife in Sidibé's courtyard. The kids think he's a great toy, Sidibé is rediscovering the meaning of man's best friend, but Abi is livid. She throws evil glances at the little pup and sucks her teeth long and loud. "That ugly beast keeps sticking his dirty mouth in my pots," she booms. *"Je vais le frrrrapper jusqu'àààà!"* Her palm wags threateningly. And so I accept him, partly just to keep him out of range of Abi's hard hand. My house is a bit small for the two of us, but he's fuzzy and clean. (Most puppies here seem to be born with worms and sores.) "I'll train him," I suggest, "and then you keep him when I'm gone." Sidibé clenches his jaw—he's annoyed that his wife is dictating the dynamics of the courtyard. But he agrees.

The first thing to go is the name. The practice of naming animals at all is considered borderline lunacy in West Africa. Cats, cows, chickens, and all other domestics go unlabelled. Most dogs are just referred to as *"chien-là,"* that dog, but those with names don't fare much better. Every dog I've met so far answers to Dick or Bobi. As a compromise, and so as not to confuse the dog who thinks he's Dick, I name him Nick.

Dramane and Bakary show up together for lunch. Bakary claims to be just past twenty, though it's possible that he's guessing. Like Dramane, he is a village "might-have-been." He did well in school, but not well enough—repeating eighth grade three times before quitting—and has come back to an elevated status among their peers. Sidibé selected him to tutor his four school-age kids several nights a week. As a rule, Bakary comes to tutor a little early, hoping to accidentally arrive in time for dinner. He has cheerful eyes and a quick, bright grin. He wants to do something important in the village, and he hangs around me just in case I should stumble across such an opportunity.

Today I have invited Bakary and Dramane to lunch, my first stab at entertaining. I make vegetable curry, breaking all laws of African cuisine. First, none of the vegetables are mashed. Second, I don't use Maggi cubes for flavoring. And finally, they can trawl through the sauce all they want, but there's not an ounce of meat to be found. Preparing meat or fish requires gutting, cleaning, and in some instances killing, which would likely perfume my house for days. It doesn't occur to me that I've committed a horrible faux pas in cooking a vegetarian meal for my guests until they're at the door. I douse their servings with palm oil before presenting them in a vain attempt to compensate for the oversight.

The two of them spear chunks of carrot and green pepper, eyeing them curiously. They nibble gingerly at first, Dramane squinting his eyes like a seasoned food critic. Bakary looks up from his plate. *"C'est intéressant."* In English, "interesting" is a polite evasion. In African French, happily, it means tasty.

Lunch is a pretext for discussing the future of the baby-weighing station. I finish up my curry first and explain my intentions. I need at least two helpers—I would really like one of them to be a literate girl. And I want to hold a meeting to explain to the village mothers why weighing and buying carnets is important.

The meeting is no trouble. We set a date in September, and the two remind me that we have to ask the chief's permission. They offer to be my assistants—which I've been hoping for. "But a girl," they say, "that could be difficult." They're hard-pressed to think of a literate girl who's still in the village. "The ones who pass CM2 go to secondary school," says Dramane, "and often the ones who don't pass go to sewing or typing school in Ferké. There are two or three who went to school and quit early, but most are in distant campements." Altogether, they can only count a handful. There's Fatoumata, who failed the exam by a half point, but she's trying to finagle a spot in *collège* by other means. There's Bintou, but her village is several kilometers away, and anyway, they think she's married.

Compounding the paucity of schooled girls is a more basic problem, which is revealed when I visit Fatoumata. "Since I don't have a husband, it would be shameful for me to work alongside unmarried men," she tells me. "The whole village would think I was sleeping with them." I stick with Dramane and Bakary as my health assistants, and begin planning my first course for the village women.

In order to establish the current health condition of village children, I've charted on a large growth curve all the weights and ages recorded so far during the weekly weighing sessions at the market. The resulting collection of dots shows that children are well nourished until they hit six months, but then many level off instead of growing. Clearly the problem lies in popular conceptions of weaning. We'll have to discuss that at our first meeting with the mothers. I spend the afternoon on the stoop drawing visual aids—pictures of different foods good to feed a six-month-old, a ten-month-old, and a one-year-old. Eggs and peanuts, tomatoes and greens are all easy enough to depict. Meat is more complicated. I draw a fat, red T-bone steak, which baffles the kids I test it on. "It's meat!" I explain, but they just look puzzled. So I redraft it, sketching irregular brownish chunks. They still don't recognize it by themselves, but when I explain, they nod excitedly: "Ahhaaaan!"

Daouda appears in my courtyard one afternoon, strides right up to the puppy, and wallops him across the nose. I kick him out. Hitting the dog has been explicitly forbidden. He's outraged, but he knows he's done wrong; he shows up at night anyway. But I am exhausted and my head throbs. I say to the boys outside the screen, I'm sorry, but could you please leave? And I have never really asked them to leave this early in the evening, so should they heed me? Maybe not. Anyway, I'm not even asking them the right way. I find out later that there's a simple key to kid management: Follow procedure as if you were a chief. Explain the message to the eldest present and it becomes his mission, his responsibility, to make your wishes happen. It works like magic. But this one night, I just ask the whole crew once, twice, three times, and then I yell in English, "Can't you just go home!" Everyone hushes. They think that maybe I've insulted them in my language. Or cursed them. Then I fumble; I plead. "I give you pencils and paper to draw with and cards to play with. Yesterday I gave you candy, remember? Please just do me this one favor." And *that* is a serious slight to their pride. As if they can be bought off with treats! Hah! They're irate, and Daouda is ringmaster to their rebellion. They take turns standing akimbo, their backs to my door—it's the ultimate insult to turn your back. They click their tongues and suck their teeth, most just following the leader and not sure of the source of their own fury.

I am one of the few adults who do not shout at them, who don't raise a hand to them. I've thought the reason we've gotten along so smashingly is because I respect them. This is the catch, however. *Because* I respect them, perhaps they don't respect me. In fact, their actions make it obvious: to fight back with an adult is unheard of, and yet here they are, all lined up with their backs facing me. If I set these kids in their place with the back of my hand, would they respect me then? Clearly my pacifist approach has turned all custom on its head.

Daouda drags everything I have given him back into my court-yard—the giant box that my bike came in, flattened in the middle now from children sleeping on it; sheets of alphabet practice; an old *Newsweek*. Moussa follows suit, cluttering my stoop with dirty pages full of loops and shoving his prized ballpoint pen under my door. He's a little laughable, huffing around as if I'm *just* outrageous, though he doesn't really know why.

I have to shut the door on them—the metal door that means Guiss is asleep or something's vastly wrong. It's like I'm spelling the end to my happiness in the village, closing out these scowling faces. I have never shut my door on anyone. What would I do if the kids abandoned me? They are under my skin, in my blood. It would be so lonely without them. But how do I wield some grain of control and win back their respect?

I talk to Dramane the next morning. His eyes twinkle when he hears my angst-filled story. "But Guiss," he laughs, "they're just *kids*. Give them a week and they'll be clamoring at your door again!"

Daouda comes by the next evening to perfunctorily explain that he will no longer respond if I greet him in the street. He is proud and stubborn. He does not clamor at my door for another year.

In this poisoned atmosphere I hold my first meeting with the village women. Saturday morning I'm up at the crack of dawn, arranging my posters and visual aids, setting up benches and chairs under the twisted roof of the market terrace. At ten o'clock one woman appears. By eleven there are about ten mothers assembled. I'm feeling antsy about making them wait but fretting that no one else will come. "They'll come," Bakary says sleepily. He has the makings of a bureaucrat—he likes to reaffirm his own importance by dozing or disappearing at inopportune times. At eleven-thirty, I stride fiercely through the village to call on people individually. Evidently, this is what it takes. Kinafou, the president of the women, expects that I'll extend a personal invitation to her—it's a sign of respect for her position. The rest just need a little urging. There's a slow exodus to the marketplace, and at noon, just three hours behind schedule, we begin our meeting.

The young women in the group are mostly too timid to answer my questions or voice their own. This is the first course they've ever attended; they have never had to read pictures or understand graphs like the ones that show the progression of their babies' weights. But Dramane has a splendid knack for translating. In fact, his translations go on much longer than my words. He is illustrating, explaining, and reexplaining, giving analogies and making jokes. It becomes clear that I just need to supply a skeletal version of the topics and he'll flesh them out.

Despite their sluggish arrival, the fifty women at the meeting are an alert audience. They may not say much, but they listen attentively. We tell them about making enriched porridge—clarifying the gibberish I had offered during my early weighing days at the market. They recognize my drawings, and a few of them reiterate what we have said. I'm under no illusion that I've changed their weaning habits in an hour, but at least I've gotten the information in front of them. At least now they'll understand when I tell them to put peanuts in their porridge.

As we wind down, Kinafou stands, her eyes lively and the whisker scars, carved into her face decades ago, moving with her mouth. As she is the head of the women, her words make the difference between their hearing my advice and heeding it. I have offered the facts; she has the authority to order the women to profit from them. She uses all sorts of aphorisms and colorful illustrations, but Dramane doesn't bother to translate them all for me. "I want you all to buy carnets," she says. "It is a very important way of recording the identity of your child." This is a slightly different spin, but I suppose that for now, motives are secondary to action.

The women get up saying, *An y che! An y bara, Guissongui!* Thank you for your work! They are eager to buy carnets. I have bypassed our health base in Ferké and stocked up hundreds of health-record books on the black market in Abidjan. On their way out, the women pick up the benches and tables and run them back to the school canteen, from which I had lugged them myself early in the morning. In seconds the market terrace is empty, and the stress of hours of waiting evaporates. I think, just maybe, this was a success.

I head home and curl up in my chair, exhausted. My courtyard is unnaturally empty for hours. At last, as the light blinks through the leaves of the mango tree, there's a little rustle outside the door. I hear a gravelly *"Bon schwa!"* Little Moussa peeks his head around the doorframe. One eye first, then the grin. I want to grab that dusty child and not let him go.

The next morning, Oumar shows up on his way to the fields with a sack slung over his shoulder, sewn by his father in the days before his sewing machine got cursed. He pulls out three cobs of braised corn and hands them to me with a shy smile. There are times when so much love fills up your gut that you don't know what to do with it all. Maybe you just cry. I stuff a sturdy envelope with roasted peanuts for him, send him on his way, and burst out crying.

The *moulin* comes to Nambonkaha at the height of peanut season. There's been talk of it for weeks: they say the cadres secured the corn-grinding machine with the help of a foreign embassy. A square cement hut was built in anticipation months ago, and the machine finally arrives in September. Abi's son Tidiane and I encounter it one day on the way back from harvesting peanuts.

The mill stands in a patch of wet cement, its engine unwieldy and full of teeth, its power hinging on a revolving rubber belt. It looks like an artifact from the industrial revolution. The giant generator that will feed it energy sits next to the door. Bakary has been designated keeper of the mill. He says, "See, the big one is for corn and millet. But the attachment can grind peanuts too." I'm not so excited about this. Tidiane is thrilled. The eastern sky billows with gray clouds; a tall sheet of rain slants just outside of the village. The clouds above us glow red. "*C'est joli,*" says Tidiane as we walk back to his house. I smile, assuming he's referring to the sunset. "The sky?" I ask. "*Non,*" he says simply, "*le moulin.*"

The next morning I am not awoken by the usual crescendo of knocking pestles. There is no beating rhythm in the village, no sound of life save for the self-righteous crowing of roosters and the vomiting bleat of sheep. Instead, around eight, a loud motor kicks up across the village. It hums for hours, sometimes shrieking like a chain saw, drowning out the babble of yellow weaver birds in my neighbor's tree. Women are missing from each courtyard, gone to join the line outside the moulin. Granted, they have shaved hours off their daily chores. They can now rest their strong arms and enjoy some respite from labor. But there's a saying here that if ever you're lost in the bush, listen for the beat of the pestle and follow the sound. Now the sound belongs to a motor. Something precious is lost—the rhythm of the village is thrown all out of kilter. I can't help thinking that this is the first step toward fast food.

Within a week, the rubber belt has unstrung itself and the engine needs repairs. The tools, the replacement parts, and the repairman are six hundred kilometers south in Abidjan. The moulin is cemented to the ground in Nambonkaha. Needless to say, it remains defunct. The *tok tok* returns to the village, a summons for the day, a salvo for the noon sun, a lone thumping late at night. I, for one, am silently elated.

8

_____

Verdict

"Women," says Dramane, "can't go a month without sex."
"*Quoi?*" I yelp. "You've got to be kidding me! What about the
men?" I ask. "They're the ones who *cherche femme* all the time!"
He laughs. "If they didn't chase women, they'd never have any
luck. You have to make an effort to get noticed."

An interesting quirk in our friendship is that our cultural differences, which might make other communication somewhat
awkward, actually seem to facilitate frank discussions about sex.
Dramane tells me that village men are often out of luck when it
comes to picking up women. "Unless you have money, a woman
won't sleep with you. Women want to know they can get nice
pagnes out of you, or jewelry. They hold all the cards." I have
heard this complaint before. Sidibé and the mayor say that mistresses are a luxury that comes with affluence. Having a mistress
means that you can *afford* to have a mistress—with all the inherent financial burdens of wooing. Ferké supplies the mistresses for
a few of the successful villagers of Nambonkaha. In general, village women are not mistress material. They seek husbands and
the security of a courtyard, not the scandal and disrepute of casual
affairs.

"People should have built-in meters to show how many people
they've slept with. Someone should invent something like that,"
continues Dramane. "Shame, at least, might keep promiscuity
down." But the village already has a well-entrenched system of

sexual vigilance. It is called female genital mutilation in the Western press. In other circles, it is called female circumcision or excision. In Uganda, there are horror stories of chopping and sewing till all that's left of a woman's sex organs is hardened scar tissue that must be torn open once the woman is married. Other cultures clip away all flaps and folds. The Niarafolo practice a milder form of circumcision: they snip out the clitoris with a bare blade. The same vieilles who deliver babies administer this awful ritual. Dramane tells me the procedure generally happens just days before the woman's marriage. Supposedly it will keep her faithful; it also signifies her transition from maid to matron. The heart of the ritual, villagers insist, has little to do with the actual circumcision. Just before the cut, the girl has to name each man she's slept with. "The anticipation of pain scares the girls into telling the truth," Dramane says. It's an age-old inoculation against sleeping around, but I wonder if there are actually consequences when the list of lovers is long.

Female circumcision is not on the wane in Nambonkaha. It's not an old-fashioned tradition but a full-blown modern-day practice. The girls accept it as indisputable, a part of being a woman as inevitable as cramps and childbirth. Or maybe they just realize how puny their voices are against the dictates of the elders. When I ask Dramane how village women feel about it, he looks at me funny. "I've never asked a woman how she feels about it," he says. "Nobody would ask that." Then he adds, with confidence, "Women who are not circumcised are likely to never have a child that survives infancy. Either she never gets pregnant, or she miscarries all the time, or her babies die. No one can explain it, but that's the way it is. The village is cursed."

There's a timid clap just outside the screen. I'm crouched on my floor, drawing visual aids for a health project. The woman I find on the stoop is a very pregnant stranger. She speaks soft French and tells me at the tail end of our greeting, "Water came out." I take this to mean that her water has broken, and I wonder why she isn't being attended by the village vieilles. My house is no delivery room, and despite my handful of delivery experiences, there is no possible way I could go it alone. Why did she come to me? She answers my questions about contractions but tells me no more of her situation.

I recently diagnosed a miscarriage with the aid of my trusty manual. That woman's stomach was tight and hot and hard, but this woman's feels normal. I tell her the baby should come out by tomorrow and say that if she starts bleeding, she should go straight to Sidibé. She nods, hesitates, a flicker of uncertainty in her eyes, then thanks me and walks off. I return to the drawing board with an inkling of guilt. I'm not a midwife, so I did the right thing in not leading her on. But could I have done more? Was I too quick to dismiss her?

The next day I start laundry after lunch. Abi would be horrified if she saw me—everyone knows laundry is a morning affair. It takes hours to scrub through my large piles. As I finally set everything out to dry, I look up and realize that not only is the sun plunging west, but it is plunging behind thick clouds. Once more defeated in my attempts to impersonate an African woman, I hang up my clothes in the rain. Tidiane comes running into the courtyard, his face alert with an important message. He halts first, though, to survey my strung-up clothes streaked with rain. "Guiss, it's raining," he says. *Merci, Tidiane.* "Papa says come help a woman at the clinic. She's trying to make a baby."

My guest from yesterday is prostrate on a cot in the dim, vacant convalescence room of the infirmary. The window above her affords no slats of light. Incessant drizzle spatters on the roof, shushes on the ground outside. Cold gray legs stick out of her body. She's too weak to push out the rest of the child, so she just sits with a lifeless head trapped inside her. She has no pink scar. I open my birthing book. The section breech babies tells me how to manage so that the legs stay together and no arms break. But it says nothing about how to deliver a dead baby. I rotate the body and pull just a bit. The head inches out.

My book says, "Take precaution!" There are a hundred different ways to kill a baby fresh from the womb! But this boy, legs dangling, arms limp, is dead already. Helping out the placenta, my gloved hand—just for a second—smothers his squeezed-shut face. It makes me feel terrible, as if I just suffocated him myself. How must it feel to give birth to death? In my own culture, we grow so attached to the creature in the womb, painting bedrooms in pastels, toying with names, stocking the house with all the infant must-haves. A miscarriage or stillbirth will seep into dreams and haunt us for years. But here, they place no expectations on anything, afraid to jinx work or life or health with the confidence of prediction or planning. Self-pity is an indulgence. The mother looks crestfallen, but is it the horror of losing a child or merely the result of the blood loss? They are groomed to expect death and move on. They seem so psychologically resilient and physically strong—but what if all the hurt is just tucked away in a pile of Things That Aren't Expressed? When that pile gets tall enough, does it become *folie*?

Dramane's mother takes the boy from me, wraps him in a pagne, and carefully places the bundle headfirst in a bucket. His feet protrude grimly from the cloth. She sops up the puddles of blood on the bed with a rag, and helps the hobbling woman out the door. There will be no bed rest, no time to heal. She'll just get up again. She balances the bucket on her head, turns out the infirmary gate, and walks a ways behind the brick wall that rings the property. Atop her head, where there has been firewood and water and corn—signs of everything alive—there are tiny gray feet, death in a bucket bobbing along above the wall as she walks.

There is no visible sympathy for the woman. Like Mendjeta's rabble-rousing in the mayor's courtyard, a miscarriage undoubtedly means that some more serious sin has been committed. Potential explanations for this mishap fall in line quickly. Her betrothed brushes it all off—he doesn't care that the little corpse was a much prized son. They say it wasn't even his child. There's a rumor that she's seeing a boy from the city. Abi's voice is hard: "That's what she gets for fooling around in town." But the strongest reasoning lies in the absence of that pink scar. Abi is not circumcised herself, and she despises the custom. Since she's not from the village, Nambonkaha superstitions and rumors don't generally faze her. Yet she won't dispute the power of a curse. Abi looks me in the eye. "You know why her baby really died?" she asks. "Because she wasn't circumcised." Why did she come to me instead of going to the usual vieilles? Why didn't anyone except Dramane's mother step in to help her delivery? Because no one wants to fiddle with a strong curse.

First comes the president's mother, hands knotted behind her back, scarf swooped around her face, calling out the day greeting: "*Fochanganan! Piera mon djigi lé?*" Are you washing dishes? Content she guessed right, she moves on. My neighbor, an old, usually shirtless woman I call Ya, or mother, sings out my name as she strolls by. Then come the mayor's mother and aunt, and Kinafou following on their heels. They nod and call out hello, but keep moving. Men pass in twos and threes, dressed in old boubous, faces serious. The signs are clear: there has been a death in the village. I cross my courtyard, scrubbing burned rice off the bottom of a pot, and peek around the hay wall to see where everyone is going. They've stopped in a courtyard just around the corner from my latrine.

Whoever died did not die in my neighbor's courtyard, however, but in the campements. The cemetery that serves Nambonkaha and all its campements is just south of the village, through a lane of teak trees on the other side of the market. In line with Muslim belief, the deceased must be buried within twenty-four hours of death.

Today, Dramane appears out of the stream of elders and calls out, "Ko ko!" to announce himself. He is wearing a navy blue cotton blazer, and there's a pint of beer on his T-shirt. "Guinness is good for you" is emblazoned across his Muslim chest. "There is a ceremony for my great-uncle who died a few days ago," he says. "I think you'll find it interesting." So I finish up my dishes and follow.

The old men sit in a cluster, mostly in chairs, under a mango tree. Women sit on logs, rocks, bowls, stools in scraps of shade.

It can't be a burial, because Dramane said his uncle died a few days ago. No one is shaking hands or whispering blessings. Plus, in place of grieving family members at the center of the congregation, there are two unfamiliar men. They hoist a branch wrapped in cloth onto their shoulder. The one supporting the front of the branch wears a pink sweatshirt in the burning sun. He shuts his eyes and speaks in staccato bursts, pausing at length every few sentences. The onlookers watch silently. Just behind him, a woman holds a large calabash full of dried corn and tosses handfuls to the ground rhythmically. There is a bushel of leaves tucked under her pagne like a bustle. Other women have leaves tied around their ankles and their wrists.

Clearly something beyond conventional Islam is at work: the imam is nowhere in sight. Occasional clucks rise from the sitting women; a few men shake their heads. I throw Dramane a glance that says, "What is going on?" but he just smiles and closes his eyes slowly. It goes on and on, monotonous words, tossed corn, silence. Finally, the branch is hefted to the ground. As the assembly disperses, Dramane is called off to a group of elders. I'm jumping with curiosity, but there's no one around to explain, so I simply return home.

Dramane stops by before long and flops into my wooden armchair with a sigh. "Eh, Allah!" Then he lurches forward, elbows on his knees, eyes lively. "I just found out my uncle was a sorcerer!"

It turns out I've just witnessed history's most humane witch trial. The villagers of Nambonkaha wait until the accused is *dead* before investigating the crimes. "I should have known!" says Dramane, threading his fingers together and tapping his chin. He explains, "The swaddled stick represents the body of the person who has died—in this case, my uncle. The man you saw holding the shroud was communicating with my uncle's spirit." Dramane says the man is a professional mystic, hired from Ferké because of suspicions about his uncle. "So it's a séance of sorts?" I ask. He doesn't know that word, but he describes the ritual. "The elders ask him questions, and he communicates with the dead man's spirit, and speaks for him. The corn that my aunt was tossing is supposed to entice the spirit to talk." "Why do some women wear leaves?" I ask. Dramane tells me, "They are the female relatives of the dead man. The leaves help the spirit recognize his family. Each relation has a designated spot for them. For instance, all his daughters wear leaves around their waists, and all his granddaughters wear them around their ankles."

Dramane says that the verdict was established early on in the ceremony. The spirit admitted without shame to being a witch: he killed or hurt many members of his own family. In order to be victimized by sorcery, you have to have a witch in the family—they can't harm those with whom they don't share blood. Most offer up their own family members only on occasion, as a duty to the other sorcerers. "There are a few, however," says Dramane, "who offer their own kin for sacrifice even when they don't have to." He is nervously relieved. It's as if he had just missed being run over by a truck. "Thank Allah he didn't remember me!" he breathes.

Of course, Dramane's uncle is not guilty of outright homicide, since he only figuratively "ate the souls" of his relatives and thus triggered their demise. The man in the pink sweatshirt, speaking as the spirit, listed a handful of deaths that occurred over the past decade (*Remember Souleymane, who went south and got sick . . . and Sita's daughter who died before she could walk . . .*) and proclaimed himself responsible.

Doesn't anyone ever just die of bad health? I ask. "Sure," says Dramane. "My uncle did. No one questions death of old age. It's the ones who die young whose deaths must be explained." I'm in no place to doubt that there is a legitimate basis for the magic that underlies this society: too much is unexplained and unbelievable to dismiss it. But how much is chicanery? Is this mystic just full of well-worded nonsense? Should the witch-trial tradition be shelved with a chuckle along with the psychic hotline? Or is there a nugget of truth in it all? The more I learn, the less I know, it seems.

Dramane is fiddling with my shortwave—all buttons and digital display, compared to his dinky little dial contraption. Suddenly he puts it down. "You know, my uncle's sorcery *has* affected me, actually. I was premier in my class for most of elementary school, but I couldn't pass the CM2 exam for two years. Everyone thought I would do the best of all the students, but I failed it. When I finally got into *lycée*, I went through until *troisième* [the equivalent of tenth grade] and again I couldn't do well on the exam. I repeated the year twice, but could never pass the test."

Dramane's eyebrows shoot up as he continues: "A few months ago, my uncle was really sick and thought he was dying. I went to visit him one day and he took me aside and told me that he and my aunt had been responsible for destroying my chances at school. It seemed so strange that he would admit it. At the time, I thought maybe he was just going a little crazy with sickness and age and everything. Now I see. He told me because he expected to die right afterward. After all the evil deeds that he confessed to through the mystic today, I believe he might have been telling me the truth."

So what do you do when you find out your uncle's a witch? Is there some sort of cleansing ritual? Do you seek a féticheur to hex his spirit? Apparently you just dance. I accompany Dramane out the door and walk with him a ways. Married women have returned to the courtyard around the corner. They've changed out of their faded pagnes and T-shirts into clean, matching complets. Their heads are tied in scarves, and some have gold-painted earrings on. They stand in a line against the wind, tossing up waves of rice with winnowing baskets. Clouds of husks blow off with each flip. "Are they still going to have the funeral?" I ask. "Considering it's someone who harmed the village, do they really want to honor him?"

Dramane smiles and responds: "*Mais, oui!* The corn's already pounded and the rice is getting cleaned!" It doesn't matter that the dead man was a scoundrel. No one really wants to give up the chance for free food and a party.

Drissa squawks in my arms. Months back, I helped plunk his burning body into a bucket of chilly water. Now I'm suspending him over a slick, cold, rocking scale. I am scary and pale *and* completely insufferable. Drissa is a big baby, full of wriggle and indignation. He's hard to keep still on the scale, hard to straighten out on the measuring board. Massieta, his mother—mother of Moussa, Daouda, Mandou, Dramane's designated wife, Senata, and several more—chuckles a bit at her littlest child's revolt. Dramane takes over for this one. "You write," he says as Drissa squirms in my arms, "I'll do the weighing." Even after six months, I still strike fear in the hearts of most babies. The color of my skin is, of course, horribly upsetting. Plus, I'm associated with all evil measuring contraptions that they're flattened onto at the market. But it's my eyes that seem to inspire the most terror. The children see green like the grasses where they are accustomed to seeing brown. They shriek and kick, grabbing for mothers or anyone else comfortably dark. But their eyes remain transfixed on mine. It's just the color, I know, yet the way they look at me is unsettling. It's as if they've seen bad things in my soul, as if they've seen a sorcerer.

Massieta and Dramane take turns cooing at Drissa to still him long enough for the cranky old scale to make up its mind. I fill out the date and his age and wait for his Dramane to read the weight. We started out as three at the weighing station this morning, but Bakary keeps disappearing. This time he's gone on a brief jog to the other side of the market in pursuit of a girl from Ferké selling bags of yogurt and bisap on her head. He doesn't want yogurt; he wants the girl.

The novelty of weighing has tapered off, and just under twenty mothers have come on recent market days. Most are so anxious about doing the right thing that they weigh their one-year-olds weekly, though monthly would suffice. Among the campement mothers, however, weighing seems to be a dying fad already. We taught them why they should weigh their babies in our course last month. We never promised that it was a cure, but maybe that's what they heard. I imagine they believed weighing would somehow shield their children from mysterious illnesses. Maybe some thought that sitting on the scale would help make their babies pudgy. Maybe they hoped their good intentions would be enough to warrant good health. Yet week after week we just draw another dot on the chart. We tell the mothers that it's good news or bad news and suggest things to feed their child. But what if they don't want guidance and coaching? What if they just want a cut-and-dried answer to this one fundamental question: What can you do so that my baby won't die? It's hard to fathom how a line of dots on a chart might be a reassurance.

Clearly, we need to stoke our campaign to lure the mothers. When we've finished with the last baby in line, I wind through the market to greet people. The vieilles selling hot peppers and tomatoes ask after my husband again and hoot and clap their hands when I say I don't really need one. I pick up a loaf of sweet bread at Angélique's table and offer it to my assistants. As we sit chewing warm rolls, a hush ripples through the marketplace.

Three figures have appeared shrouded in black. They are women with fleshless faces—bony features with the skin pulled tight around them. Their skirts, dingy and gray, appear duller still against the flaming, fighting colors of the villagers' clothes. Several wide brass hoops are stuffed through holes in their ears. Their hair is rolled into a thick matted pillow that hangs over their foreheads, and then braided irregularly everywhere else. The older villagers of Nambonkaha bear marks of the old scarification rituals: whiskers like Kinafou, small dashes on the cheekbones, or an outline around the whole face. These women have blue designs tattooed on their hollow cheeks. I just stare.

It seems as if they've blown straight out of the Sahara on an eerie wind. The Peuls are nomads from the southern Sahel. They are beautiful and exotic, but approachable. I greet them with my five words of Peul when I see them; I buy milk from them; I weigh their babies once in a while. But these women are more foreign than anything I have encountered in my life. One of them has wild eyes; the whites glare and the pupils roll. Her teeth splay out of her mouth, and her cheekbones are so round and high that the rest of her face falls into a weak triangle underneath. The one with a basket on her head has refined features and bright eyes. But the first one is too peculiar—she gives the threesome an air of disheveled creepiness. "Dramane, where do you think they're from?" I whisper, my eyes still plastered on them. My months of being stared at have disintegrated any idea that it's impolite.

"I think they're from Niger," says Dramane. "They came this time last year too." But I want details. I drag him up to the women to translate my questions. They are Wodaabé nomads from Niger, they say. These women loop south each year to sell traditional medicine.

One lifts a basket from her head and crouches down in front of a village woman. I peek into the basket, expecting to see leaves and bark and mysterious powder concoctions—the stuff of local indigenous medicine. Instead there are beads and strings. The two women—a stranger in drab black and a neighbor in a toaster-print pagne and an orange velveteen T-shirt—communicate in thinned Dioula, reconciling their different dialects. Dramane leans over my shoulder to translate as the Wodaabé woman draws each item from the basket. The first medicine is a few inches of twisted string with a bead at the end. "This one you take if you want your baby to learn to walk faster." A slightly thicker cord makes a woman produce more milk. The Wodaabé woman pulls out a braided string and weaves it fluidly through her fingers while she lists its qualities. The mother nods quickly; that's the one she wants. The medicine seller draws the string back and forth between her lips, sputtering faintly. She could be whispering prayers over the medicine, but it seems like she is just spitting on it. A hundred francs changes hands. The string, Dramane tells me, will prevent a teething child from having diarrhea. Teething occurs around the age when babies learn to crawl. They are curious and newly mobile, and dirt and dirty things become a significant part of their diet. Villagers blame the resulting sickness on teeth. Evidently, teeth are the scapegoats in Niger, too. The Wodaabé woman hands the little string to the mother and says, "Rub the string on the child's gums and he won't get diarrhea."

I can't take my eyes off the odd women. They eat nothing. They buy nothing. They meander through the market hawking their wares and then disappear for a year. Where do they sleep?

Are their husbands and children tucked away in the bush somewhere? Have they walked the whole way down from the desert, or do they pay their way on transport? Do they follow the roads or filter through the browning grasses, wary of gendarmes? They are like phantoms, like strange icons from a wild and ancient past. I am spooked, elated, but also refocused on reality. This is what we're up against—magical string.

"Guiss," Dramane says when we're back at the table, sitting on stools and scanning the market for more babies to weigh. "You know, we can't just keep working here like this." Bakary agrees.

Bakary tosses his bisap bag on the ground. "When we had that meeting with the women, remember we asked the chief's permission to hold it? Well, we didn't do the follow-up right. We should have notified him when it was starting that morning, and we probably should have invited him. The chief was angry. Some people got in trouble for it." Oh, the rules—there are so many! Protocol in the village is an unending obstacle course, and I trip over it on a daily basis. Dramane says that the chief reprimanded the president, but really he's upset that we started working as a team without his sanction.

I've emerged without a scrape. I can still get away with a lot under the heading of Ignorant Toubabou. "If you want us to work with you as assistants, we *have* to ask the chief for his permission," Bakary explains. I understand that the village runs on a generally benevolent authoritarian system. I go to the chief to "ask permission" to hold meetings, to "ask permission" to weigh babies, to "ask permission" to go on trips. Basically any major decision or plan must have the chief's blessing at the onset. Yet when I was choosing competent people to work with me, it didn't even occur to me that the chief had the last word. He oversees the village staff—those who work for the community—so he gets to appoint them all. "No problem." I say. "I'll just go see the chief, then." Bakary's eyes slide sideways to Dramane.

As it happens, I must notify a sizable crowd in order to petition the chief. First I ask Sidibé to explain my plan to him. He asks the president to accompany us and explain it to the chief; the president says he has to consult the mayor before he can propose it to the chief. In the end, somehow, the health contingent gets squeezed out of the process entirely, and the president and the mayor go by themselves to see the chief about my health team. "By the way, Guiss," they say when we're sitting at Sidibé's one afternoon before they approach the chief, "you never *tell* the chief anything—you *ask* and *he* decides." In a situation like this, for instance, you can suggest your preferences, but the final decision has to look like his own.

The verdict comes back quickly: Bakary in, Dramane out.

The chief, the president tells me, understands that this is important work, and he has offered to recruit a different villager to take Dramane's place. His choice is a married man from the campements who has a few children and two wives, who speaks halting French and hasn't written a word in a decade. He discards the one who translates best, who takes initiative, the one with the capacity and the desire to help the village, and chooses a man saddled with a large family who's never expressed an interest in health. There must be a story behind such an inane decision.

There is. Dramane is young, but he's already admired and respected in the village. The last chief was actually his grandfather, but Dramane has earned a good reputation on his own merit. Several nights a week, he conducts literacy classes by lamplight for villagers who missed the chance to go to school. He's part of the vaccination team. He acts as my translator. He weighs babies. None of these jobs bring him any remuneration. The cadres recognize his potential. Siaka is his mentor of sorts and pushed to hire him to manage the tractor. When the rains came this year, the chief, working with Siaka and the other cadres, selected Dramane for the job. Dramane worked hard, spent nights away from the village. He was able to pay off the tractor's debt and even brought in a profit. And profit is what got him in trouble. He passed the revenue figures directly to the cadres who had nominated him as manager, bypassing the chief, and therefore forfeiting any cut the chief might have demanded. The chief was outraged—but had no recourse. What Dramane had done was completely legitimate.

When the president and the mayor meet with me to explain his choice, they look hopeless. "He declared that Dramane has seen the end of his village responsibilities," says the president, raising his palms to the air.

I'm not sure if there's an avenue for appeal in this one-man village court. I don't know if the chief has the last, uncontestable word. But I'm willing to take advantage of my good relations with the chief and my singular status to buck the system. Sidibé, who realizes how crucial Dramane is to the health team, speaks to the president, who speaks to the mayor, who speaks to other elders, and slowly, subversively, we start a quiet uprising.

The harmattan wind blows in from the Sahara, sucking up all the green from the earth and turning the ground from mud and moss to dust within days. The air turns so dry my throat and nose wrinkle as soon as I step outside. Along the road to Ferké, the grasses turn soft gold, then fade. Leaves on the trees skip the color show, crumple up, and drop. Haze hovers above the trees and washes blue from the sky. The sun sets flat and pallid, slipping into the nebulous gray far above the horizon.

9

Harmattan

For a small minority of Nambonkaha residents, Ramadan is a time of fasting and atonement. For the rest it means a month of talking about fasting that ends in a big party. Islam, apparently, has a caveat for those who need sustenance to continue their work—an emergency exit from fasting—and as field laborers, most villagers excuse themselves that way. The others might fast a day or two out of respect for tradition, but holding out for the month is really too impractical.

There are two days a year when every self-respecting villager dresses up and strolls the lanes of Nambonkaha. One is the end of Ramadan. The other is the spring sheep sacrifice called Tabaski. People save for months to buy a new outfit and a choice piece of meat for the sauce. Villagers define their year by Ramadan; it's sort of a season of its own. I expect, on the January morning that marks the end of Ramadan, to wake up uncommonly early with that kid feeling on Christmas morning that the day ahead will be full of magic. Instead, I sleep late, jump into my boubou in a panic, and sprint out to the mosque by eight-thirty, afraid I've missed morning prayer.

But there's not a soul in sight at the mosque. So I walk to the imam's courtyard and ask my favorite of his wives what's going on. She looks up from the gourd where she's washing rice. Her eyebrows bend up and her eyes dance. She looks at my boubou, which I seem to have put on inside out, watches anxiety flit across my face, and then her whole body bursts out laughing. *"Wel na sro suoh!"* We have to prepare the food first! I have forgotten the morning routine: festivities wait till the water is pulled, the wood chopped, the courtyards swept.

When I come back to the mosque an hour later, the drab space is crowded with spots of brilliance. Men flash by in glossy bou-bous and prayer caps. Knots of women—elders and married ones only—show off chaotic new pagne prints decked with lace and eyelets. There are smiles, handshakes, and all the inevitable ques-tions and answers. I thread through the crowd, shaking hands, reiterating the nonexistence of my husband and children. Dra-mane finds me in the crowd and grabs my hand. I have been gone for a few weeks and haven't seen him since my return. But I can read good news in his face before he says it: "Did you hear, Guiss? I can be a health worker!" Then he puts up a palm to halt my questions. "Don't ask now. I'll explain it all later."

Then some tacit signal causes a simultaneous unfurling of a hundred plastic prayer rugs, and the whole scattering of villagers is suddenly tamed into ordered lines facing east. The mosque is just a plain concrete rectangle, off axis with the rest of the nearby houses so it can correctly salute Mecca. On Fridays it is filled to capacity, and fields of flip-flops spread out from each doorway. But holidays outdo it—villagers stretch into long lines in the courtyard.

The imam, with his one puckered eye, sits at the center of the first row with the village leaders—the patriarch, the chief, Sidibé, the president, the mayor—on either side. There are several more rows of men before the women's rows begin. The imam sings out an Arabic prayer, the ranks standing and kneeling and touch-ing their foreheads to the ground in time with his words. Curved backs glare blue and pink and gold under the hard sun. It is perfectly orchestrated, this solemn Muslim performance of vil-lagers who believe in witches and make sacrifices to the ancestors. The men stand up and circle the imam. They hold a woven blan-ket over their heads, and the imam crouches beneath, still inton-ing. The blanket is a symbol of Allah's protection. I wonder if

He knows the ancestors have blankets, too. Where does Allah's jurisdiction end, and where does that of the spirits take over? The villagers must need to seek as much spiritual armor as possible; they cover their bets by honoring both entities.

The lines break. Many younger women scurry back to the courtyards to change out of their finery and finish preparing the meal. The men cross their arms and discuss weather and crops and other hot topics on the village agenda, then split off in a slow game of musical courtyards. The women at home are cooking not only for their husbands but also for anyone their husbands happen to bring by. It's like a giant village bazaar, and the men mosey from one friend's courtyard to the next, helping themselves to a full plate at each stop.

It's taken for granted that I'll eat at Sidibé's house. Otherwise his invitations are coveted; since he is a salaried fonctionnaire, it's expected that meals at his house will be rich in oil and meat. The president comes; so do the mayor and Femme Claire's husband and a few members of the clinic budget committee. Generally, because of my strange Third Sex status, I eat with the men. Today I miss the boat: I've stood around the mosque too long, chatting with vieilles. When I finally arrive at Sidibé's, the men are already leaning back in their chairs, legs stretched out to accommodate full bellies, talking idly about last year's cotton crop. I take a seat by myself on the porch and dig into a big plate of *riz gras,* rice and vegetables cooked in oil.

Abi was too busy cooking to come pray. She spent the morning in an old 4-H T-shirt and a faded pagne. But now she emerges from the house in a frothy pale blue dress covered in ribbons. She puts on a tape of modern Abidjan music, and the kids practice a new bum-wagging dance that's the current craze. Angélique comes by in a crimson boubou with a bowl on her head. Her family celebrates Christmas all alone, so they might as well crash the party on Muslim holidays. Femme Claire shows up in emerald, balancing a gourd. All over the village, women dart around with bowls on their heads, bringing foutou and sauce or a piece of meat as gifts to their friends.

When the meals finally wind down, kids are scrubbed, patted

with talc, and stuffed into new outfits. It's like someone waved a wand over the village. Even the poorest, the most ragged, the ones who appear in my courtyard wearing nothing but grayish underwear dress up. Girls' hair is braided in lanes down their scalps or twisted into little tufts. Boys' heads are shaved. Girls don neon-colored polyester dresses covered in bows and plastic flowers. Boys wear matching shorts and shirts, button-downs with lots of pockets and crisscrossing patterns. Moussa strolls around in a cheap denim ensemble with striped shoulders. Mandou is wearing his prized jeans. Even a dusty little girl named Maimouna has agreed to bathe today and wears a yellow slip of a dress, obviously a nightshirt in a former life.

The children can't keep the lid on their excitement, in spite of the fancy clothes. They form bright little packs and race from courtyard to courtyard as if they're trick-or-treating. Every time they wish an adult "Happy Holidays," they get a coin or a piece of candy. They arrive breathless in my courtyard. No one warned me of the need for a supply of coins on this day. Embarrassed, I hand out pieces of old candy I sometimes give out for chores. But word comes that a few elders are giving out fifty-CFA pieces. They sprint out of my courtyard, jingling.

In evening, the balafons play in the chief's courtyard. At funerals, the musicians must play brief tributes to all the elders before the real dancing starts. Tonight, however, the elders retire early, and the band plays on for a younger troupe. The dancing chain turns around the mango tree at the center of the chief's courtyard. A lantern in the dust at the middle of the circle throws spastic shadows of leaping children on the walls of mud huts all around. Hundreds of feet, shuffling, stamping, jumping, pound up a haze of dust. Men toss buckets of water in among the crowd to tamp it down.

Dramane and Bakary find me in the crowd and beckon, "*Viens danser!*" Dramane's breezy laugh has come back. The two do an easy dance, moving outside the women. I step in behind them. The musicians, lugging their giant balafons, chime on unstopping for hours. From tiny children to teenagers and mothers, no one misses a beat—they dance relentlessly, as if quitting for a while might halt life.

I, meanwhile, am folding to drowsiness despite the beat and the crazy energy. After a round of excuses to my friends still dancing, Dramane walks me home. We step in the trail of my flashlight beam and Dramane tells the story of his redemption. "The elders got together and petitioned the patriarch. You understand how long that takes, right? It's not like they could just ask. They had to pass on the message to all the other important elders. About ten approached the patriarch, and debated for a long time. And finally the patriarch agreed to meet with the chief to ask pardon." We skirt a few cows tied up in the middle of the road for the night. "So what about your relationship with the chief?" I ask. "Does that mean it's all better, just like that?"

"No, it's not that easy. I have to be really careful with him. And you'll have to make sure to tell him about everything. Don't ever let him feel left out of the loop, or he'll spoil your work."

My house is quiet, but the night vibrates with the earth noise of balafons. Children sing on in the distance, unwilling to give in to sleep, squeezing out every last drop of scrumptious holiday. At the first stroke of sunlight, they'll find themselves in rags again.

By the end of January, Nambonkaha is baking again. Dust hangs in the air, hazes the horizon, fades the trees in the distance. And then there's the smoke. Villagers ride by on bikes and mopeds with surgical masks or bandannas over their mouths and noses. We are smack in the middle of an annual epidemic of drought and fire. I cross the paved road with Nick at my heels, jog down the embankment to a spot that was inundated during the rains. The stream that once buckled the nearby dam and spilled all over the rice fields is nowhere in sight. The streambed is split like thick reptile skin. It seems impossible that this hard and lifeless slab of gray is the same earth that harbored a luxuriant pelt of grass just two months back. All that fertility, gone.

I run to the east toward the dam, dust scraping my throat, stinging my eyes. The path used to be a narrow cleft between walls of green. Now it is a gutted, drab, tire-trod mess. And instead of bluing sky and moon sliced thin on the eastern horizon, there is smoke—black and roiling. Chains of fire ring outward in the dead grass. It's not a wildfire: there are boys in charge of the flames, doing a job that everyone in the village deems necessary. The slash-and-burn method has been used for centuries. Not only is it a quick way to get rid of old growth and fertilize the earth, but obliterating the grass will keep the Peuls' cows from tamping down the furrows to graze. And the villagers despise grass anyway. They've waited all rainy season for the chance to get rid of it.

I stand in the low trees watching too much annihilation. The boys are quick, agile, leaping with torches of fiery weeds to urge on the flames. They are armed with slingshots to ambush any animal trying to escape incineration. Energy trickles out my toes. Last year, the burning season was past when I arrived. There were blackened spots in the savanna, but the grass grew again. This year it seems like the end of the world.

The fire boys are not courtyard regulars. I know their faces but not their names. They do not go to school; they do not speak any French. They see me behind the trees, not waving, not smiling, and decide maybe it's better just to greet my dog. This is a source of some confusion. Some yell out, "Lick! Lick!" because it means nothing, just like Nick. Others cry, "No! No!" since that's all they ever hear me call him. But Nick is wary of village boys—their fists are so unpredictable—and he's nervous about the sizzling ground. He sticks by me.

Bracelets of fire flicker and dwindle and spout. The noise is like a tank coming through the bush, or the sky falling on the trees, brittle snapping against a roar. The sun sets as I stand there—white, flat, the unblooded, unliving harmattan sun, behind a curtain of dirty smoke. It trembles as it falls.

Harmattan is a lean season. The granaries are full of corncobs and rice bushels. It's yam time, and the market is also full of green onions. But money is needed to make anything edible out of starch and onions: money for oil, Maggi cubes, and meat. A farmer's pay period is a whole year long. Traders show up in February or March to purchase Nambonkaha's cotton harvest. The mayor, as head of the cotton cooperative, deducts the price of fertilizer and pesticide from each planter's earnings, and the end result is one year's salary. If there has been a death or a marriage during the year, part of the windfall is put straight toward hosting the ceremony. If there is a house to be built, then some of the cotton returns go directly toward construction. And by harmattan, last year's earnings have dwindled to a few thousand francs for most. Cotton prices aren't predictable, and neither are the traders. January is an anxious month.

It is also the month for vaccinations. Mothers and children have no fields to tend; the roads are less treacherous without the rain. The Ministry of Health launches an annual national campaign, replete with cheap silk-screened T-shirts and stickers. During the last weekend in January, we are combating meningitis and measles. Most vaccines are free. This one—good for kids of all ages—costs under a dollar. Nambonkaha's villagers, however, are waiting for their cotton cash.

When I arrive at the infirmary the morning of vaccination day, the line already stretches the length of the breezeway. An unsmiling man from the Health Ministry is stuffing bills into a covered can and trying to fill out vaccination cards for each villager. Sidibé and the president are armed with disposable needles and tiny vials. They direct me to the seat beside the stranger so I can help him register children. It seems funny that *I* should be a liaison between this Ivorian and his countrymen, but I can ask names and ages in Niarafolo, and he cannot. The first in line is Little Sita, the imam's daughter, who carries my baby scale and water. The second is her little brother, and the third her older sister. Look down the line: the first twenty children belong to the imam. And there are more coming.

The imam spent much of his childhood learning to write Arabic and beg for alms in Koranic school in Ferké. French eludes him, but he can sing prayers in Arabic. His courtyard stretches over two lots, and on any given day they're both packed with a gaggle of children under three feet tall, teenagers, and several wives. They are my neighbors—women I pound corn with, children who show up regularly on my stoop. Early on, I pulled a literate daughter from the fray to figure out the family tree. She is one of three who attend school. Her father, she said, counting on her fingers, has five wives. Five! But I thought the Koran only allowed four! Um, well, he has five. She listed all the children that belong to each wife. "One, two, three . . . nine for Sita, except two died. Drienchen has . . . six, but she'll probably have some more . . ." Between five wives there are well over twenty kids.

Among the older ones there is a man in his early twenties called Américain. Américain has thinking eyes—they want to believe good about everything. His teeth look like a panicked crowd trying to flee his mouth in all directions. He is the leading comedian of Nambonkaha. I didn't understand this until after I saw him at a funeral wearing sunglasses at midnight, puffing a cigarette so fast a permanent cloud of smoke billowed around his head, and jerking his knee in time to no music. He looked like an extra from *Saturday Night Fever,* and I just laughed at him, thinking that the village concept of "American" was certainly absurd.

His status as the village American was severely shaken when I arrived. "Why don't you speak English together," his friends would joke. "*Bien sûr!*" he'd cough with an affected swagger, but he couldn't hold up the ruse. I'd take off in casual English, hoping he could play along, but under his act he's too earnest. He just got flustered.

He is one of Dramane's literacy students. Slowly, slowly he is learning to write in Dioula. "Why did the imam send so few of his kids to school?" I asked him once. He waved a hand in dismissal. "Oh, the imam's not my father." And thus the explanation unfolded: the imam has three wives of his own and two adopted from his dead older brother. Apparently, half his brood are nieces and nephews.

Nephew and son are interchangeable when a man has gained his dead brother's family. When it comes to something important, like vaccinations, there is no preferential treatment in the court-yard. The imam shepherds children of all ages to us with each wing of his white boubou. He makes little bows as if to apologize for hogging the vaccines, and then dashes back for more. His absent eye is shriveled into many crow's-feet—it makes him look as if he's always about to laugh. He pushes forward a tiny girl, scratching his head to bring her name to his tongue. "So many, you know, you begin to forget..."

The mayor's children stand in line, mingling with the presi-dent's family. Most other families bring at least the little ones to the needle. Moussa's father, however, says, *"Il y a pas l'argent."* Only the baby—out of nine children—gets a shot. And Oumar's dad looks guilty and shakes his head when I show up to summon them. My two friends come from the poorest families in the vil-lage. I've convinced myself that Moussa's family won't spare the dollar because it buys only an intangible health benefit, and not something to eat or something to wear. But Oumar's family is plagued with illness, strange migraines and flaming joints, and yet usually determined to do the right thing. Oumar has a clean school uniform and treats schoolbooks like treasures. Moussa has quit chasing lizards to go to school this year, but he wears a hand-me-down uniform from a sixteen-year-old on some days, and a faded Star Wars T-shirt on others. He doesn't have any school-books. These two families, and a few others, don't even grow cotton. Their barely lucrative cash crop is rice, and they're just waiting, waiting for the proceeds to come in. What if there really *isn't* even a dollar to spare? Not for food, not for meat, not for medicine or kerosene for lamps?

The villagers are so good at keeping up appearances, at work-ing hard all day in the fields, at pounding and stirring like the rest. They'll dress up with the others for Ramadan, but what if they have nothing to offer the friends who come over? Poverty no longer means rags to me. It doesn't mean mud huts and no beds, because that's how most here live. It doesn't mean starving kids, because most of those round bellies are just swollen with worms; serious malnutrition seems more of an accident than an obstacle. Poverty is something I nearly forget in the village, because it's so well disguised in the good sense of community and the homogeneity of life. The villagers are too proud to let it show. It takes shape in the things you can't notice just passing by. Maybe you can see it if you look closely at the dinner bowls: Is the starch slowly edging out the sauce? Is there macaroni in the sauce instead of fish? The villagers seem so smiling and care-free, seem so happy, make me sure I could be glad to have noth-ing too. But how much do they suffer quietly? How much hunger do they swallow with a smile?

Headlights slink up on my wall at dusk. They sound like screech-ing metal and feel like so much dread. No one in Nambonkaha owns a car, and visitors rarely pull into the village past sunset, especially to my house. Bad news from home would come in the shape of a car arriving unexpectedly in my courtyard. The car door slams, and I'm tense and cringing and just hoping the visitor is heading elsewhere. Cologne wafts through the screen door. Then a throaty "Ko-ko." At first, it's a relief. On my stoop in the gray light stands a plump gendarme in a shining gold boubou. He looks quite pleased with himself. I want to hide.

Gendarmes are experts at the streetside ambush. They hail you down urgently, calling, *"Madame! Madame!"* as if you've dropped your wallet or they have an important message for you. And once they have your attention, they glint at you and say suavely, *"C'est madame? Ou bien ... mademoiselle?"* I have a standard lineup of evasions that generally fend them off, but sev-eral have pried my address out of me. On occasion I get letters replete with drawings of teardrops and roses and grateful phrases about the divine hand that brought us together. My mailbox is neutral ground: far off in Ferké, metal, and surely censored. My village, on the other hand, is my haven, my hideaway, my terri-tory. To have it trespassed by this reeking, leering man makes my gut rise.

This particular gendarme first sped by me as I was riding my bike on the road to Burkina a few days ago. Jolting to a stop, he reversed at high speed back to me, then stopped his car in the middle of the road. He stepped out, smoothing his uniform over his paunch, and launched into the Generic Flirt routine: *"Mais! A white woman in this heat! Ça te gêne pas?* It doesn't bother you? *Mais tu es forte!* And you live out here *en brousse?* In the darkness? *C'est formidable!"* He really wants to learn English, he said, and he likes to have white friends and maybe he could stop by the village sometime . . .

In most circumstances I can fend off these requests with a few smiling fibs: "The village is so far from Ferké! And really, I'm hardly ever there." But this one caught me defenseless, alone on a road not a kilometer from my home. He knows just where to find me, and as a gendarme, he and his colleagues control my passage through Ferké. I couldn't say no and pedal off—he could make every transport experience hell. "I don't have regular hours." I told him. "I go into the campements a lot. And I work all day long, not much time for visitors really." But he wouldn't give up. "Maybe I'll come once a week," he said. "That way we can really get to know each other." It was no use. "How about every couple of months?" I suggested. "That would suit me better." He just grinned then shook my hand for so long I had to yank it away.

So he pulls up in a different car as the sun sets tonight, and swaggers in as if he owns my courtyard. No electricity, darkness descending. A man showing up at a woman's house at night means only one thing: he expects a red carpet unrolled to my bedroom door. Gendarmes aren't used to naysayers. They're paid well—bribed for loyalty by the state and then bribed again by unfortunate travelers without *cartes d'identité.* Women flock to them because they're famous for treating their girlfriends to lavish gifts. The road out of Ferké is lined with villas built for mistresses whom they've since abandoned. They are hedonists to the hilt— they drink beer in the morning, send petits for food all day long, entertain their girls at work. And in a region where so many are lean and humble, gendarmes are greasy with fat and power. I am not afraid of this man—this is my territory, after all—just disgusted to be considered prey.

I bring my most uncomfortable chair *outside* and shut the door firmly. Nick greets him with his typical crazed hyperactivity, which I usually try to quell with sharp words. Tonight, I smile apologetically and say, "He really likes strangers" as the dog mounts the gendarme's leg relentlessly.

It begins innocently enough: "So what exactly do you do here?" But he doesn't listen to my answer, just nods absently and looks around. "How can you stand this? No light? No television?" When I tell him I like it this way, he feigns disbelief and replays his lines about my incredible strength. The decency can't last long; his tame questions take a prurient turn. *"Je suis fonde de toi,"* he breathes. "Are you a virgin?" Eh, *pardon!* "Do you have a boyfriend?" Of course! Stateside boyfriends materialize reliably in situations like this. (They also commit to marriage readily.) There are hushed voices in the black outside my courtyard; silhouettes pass in front of the entrance and then dash off.

The gendarme leans toward me. "Is your boyfriend the only man you've slept with?" My guts twist up; *damn,* I want to hit him. Against all impulse, I remain unruffled. To let him know how much he's pissing me off would only encourage him. I stonewall every question, but I have to tread lightly—he has the power to stop my bike, stop my badjan, ransack my bags every time I pass the Ferké boundary.

The village grows dark. Hunger aches in my bones, but jockeying on the defensive has given me energy. Oumar appears scrubbed clean and cozy in his black-and-white sweatsuit. He looks at us with wide eyes and sits silently on the stoop. I'm so glad to see him. *"Ça va, Oumar?"* I smile at him and ask about his family. I need to somehow show this gendarme that tight-lippedness is not usually my nature, that my coldness is reserved for him. "This is your *petit frère?*" the man asks, chuckling patronizingly. I glare at him.

I mention that it's about time to start my nightly lessons with the kids. He nods and leans back. Mandou walks in, stops short, and turns on his heel. "It's okay!" I holler, maybe a bit desperately. "Come over! He's leaving soon!" My two boys sit on my stoop, glancing at the man sideways. But the gendarme won't take any of my hints. He slumps quite comfortably in my rigid chair. So I pull a village move: I turn my back to him and start talking to the kids. "Did you do all your homework? Did you bring your workbook?" Question after question, though I know all the answers. The man shifts and clears his throat, shifts again. Finally, he sits up. "I need to ask for the road," he says. "Take it," I tell him, and stand up abruptly. I am starving, I am livid, and I just want to be with my boys. The gendarme leans in close and whispers, "Next time I come, I'll bring you a rose!" I smile and lie: "I'm allergic." The dark figures hovering around his car disappear as he walks to it. The engine starts smoothly. His headlights retreat, like two groping hands shoved back into their pockets.

I spring into a rampage, pacing and jumping all over my stoop. Villagers emerge, lingering just outside the courtyard. Gendarmes make them nervous. Even those villagers with their identity papers in order live in perpetual mistrust of gendarmes. This unsolicited visit seems to have turned my courtyard into hostile ground.

Oumar and Mandou sit on the stoop still, watching me rant. It turns out they weren't all sure if I had made a new friend or if maybe the man was my boss or something. They were neutral, ready to accept my choice to entertain a gendarme, even if they didn't like it. Now my diatribe about disgusting old men and their stupid power trips calls them to arms. They jump right in on the anger; their faces are indignant, and they suck their teeth loudly.

Bravado is part of Mandou's act. Tonight, he brandishes a fist and growls, "*Celui-là,* I almost hit him myself." His squinted eyes dart around the night. "If that ugly man comes again, ohh! *Il verra . . . !*" Oumar feels pretty righteous too. "Next time he comes," he says breathlessly, "we'll get the whole village to come chase him out. Some people have guns here, you know!" I can't imagine the gendarme would be much daunted by an army of musket-wielding elders. Dramane comes in to investigate. He shakes his head when I tell my story, and offers a few solutions. "Tell him your boss doesn't allow you to have men over. Think of arguments you can have every time he comes, so that you're not worth the bother." Later on, the chief sends word that he'd be happy to complain to the captain of the gendarmes on my behalf. My friends back home have asked me anxiously if I feel safe in Africa. I have rarely felt safer. I never see the man again.

Oumar follows me close through the door and sits right up next to me. This crippled boy wants to protect me. As the kerosene in my lamp is gone, I've lit a candle for the lesson. Spry shadows of pots and pans dance on the wall to its flicker. Mandou sits across from me, etching his name in crooked capitals. I pull out a *Newsweek* to identify letters with him, but he gets impatient, just wants to look at pictures. *Newsweek* provides my only illustrations of world events. They tend to arrive several weeks late, so that I finally glimpse Monica Lewinsky long after Clinton denied misconduct, and I get footage of war in Kosovo weeks after the treaties have been signed. To me, the pictures and articles are belated peepholes into so much I am glad to be missing. But to the villagers, they are glossy colorful photographs, perfect for decorating the inside of your house, no matter if it's Milosevic who reigns over the salon.

The boys are becoming quite familiar with the Clinton family, and they search for the president in every issue. Mandou looks for the white head of hair, indiscriminately jabbing at Newt Gingrich or Ted Kennedy. Oumar is more precise, always glancing at me sideways for affirmation, dangling a finger over the right Bill before he announces, "*Ça c'est Cleenton!*" He has a favorite little speech in which he lists all the people he thinks are nice: "*Mon mama est très gentille. Guissongui est très, très gentille.*" Invariably, Clinton is included. "*Et Cleenton, il est très, très, TRÈS gentil.*" Hillary, they're convinced, is actually me, since we have the same color hair, and Moussa has decided he'll marry Chelsea.

Tonight I've got a pot of oatmeal on the stove before the lessons end. Mandou leaves quickly, but Oumar stands near. I light his rusty old lamp for him. He tucks his textbook under his arm but lingers. "Guiss, you know," he says, looking at me with wide warm eyes, "that man that came tonight. At first I thought he was Cleenton, coming in here with that big car and everything."

The world shrinks and expands in seconds—Nambonkaha is all, and everything else lies just outside its borders.

An aside on our country's illustrious scandal: Marilyn Monroe is a foreign garble in my mouth, Madonna and Princess Di ring no bells. But among the young village men—the ones who tote around their buzzing radios, listening for soccer scores—the name Monica Lewinsky is well known. Not many of them care about politics in America, but a fair number over the past year have stopped to ask me what all the fuss is about. Infidelity on a man's part is run of the mill; it's an art to be perfected, a luxury that comes with stability. "Why," wonders Bakary, "are Americans making such a big deal out of a little diversion? President Bédié must have dozens of girlfriends." Dramane and Sidibé agree that America must be problem-free, that everyone is just looking for something to talk about. I've tried to explain the significance of a president lying to the people, but they just raise their eyebrows at my naïveté. "Eh, Guiss! Who's ever heard of a president who *doesn't* lie?" No matter what I say, they just chuckle wistfully at our idealistic nit-picking and go away convinced that America is made of bliss.

IO

Source

I have tried to dash back from a film festival in Ouagadougou to meet Abi for a trip south to her hometown. But the train from Burkina Faso *never* dashes. It shrugs through the gray Sahel, past arid bastions of civilization isolated among the acacias. Six hundred kilometers take eighteen hours. It is deep night by the time we're allowed across the Côte d'Ivoire border. Somewhere near the end of the line, the train passes within throwing distance of Femme Claire's house. How lovely it would be to fling myself off like a vagabond and sleep in my own bed! But all is blackness outside, and as hard as I try to distinguish the tall tree by the road to the ancestors' bridge, the shadows are confounding.

In the morning, when I finally pull up to the village from Ferké in an orange taxi, Abi's son Tidiane is waiting by the side of the road. "Eh! Maman has gone! Just now! She didn't know if you were coming." The three hours to Abi's home village seem like nothing compared to last night's journey. I can catch up. So I run by Sidibé's to tell him I'm off. I pull a few things from my bag and put a few other things in, and within twenty minutes I'm back on the road, waiting for transport to Bouaké.

The great thing about Africa is that, armed with only the name of a village and the name of a person, you can travel confidently without the faintest clue where you're going. All you need is patience. In Bouaké, when I tell a taxi driver to take me to the Tiébro bus, he drops me off at a lot packed with ancient station wagons. Token itinerants are draped over benches and plastic chairs. Some are drivers, some ticket sellers, some drivers' mates, but all the roles appear to be interchangeable. A car has just left, they tell me, so I'll have to wait till this next one fills up.

By the time the car finally fills an hour later—a *"sept-place"* they call it deceptively: seven people fit snugly, but they rarely leave with less than nine—the itinerants have become friends. I've been entrusted with greetings for Sidibé's brother, who is apparently a great friend to all of them, and messages for a gas merchant in Tiébro, and the woman who sells eggs just past the teak tree. Doors slam shut, there's a bang on the roof, and every man in the vicinity pushes us out of the lot till the engine wakes up. My new friends run alongside, heads bent in my window, gasping wishes for a safe journey.

The driver zips along a smooth paved road—this is Baoulé territory, the land of the ruling ethnicity. There are some days when Abi considers herself Baoulé. Her dead mother came from that tribe, but Sidibé and his family are pure Dioula, and her father is half Dioula, half Peul. Out of habit and practicality, she's taken on Dioula tradition.

Tiébro sits at the conjunction of savanna and forest, not far from the large, shallow lake that sprawls across the center of the country. It is a village still, but large and electrified. There's running water even, though for most this just means an outside faucet. An hour's ride takes me to the village center. I step up to a stray man loitering around the depot, ask where Abdoulai the mechanic lives, and immediately have four men detailing directions to Sidibé's brother's house.

The infamous progenitor, bulky and tall, is leaning over an ailing moped when I walk into the courtyard. He looks up in surprise when I greet him in Dioula. There are women on stools, a few elders in chairs, and a collection of kids under a mango tree. They simper and stare as I move to shake hands. No one has any idea who I am until Abi jogs out of the house with a yelp of joy and nearly knocks me over, crying "You've chased me all the way down here?" Pride glints in her eyes as she grabs my bag and then my arm, pulling me alongside her into the house. "But I just got here myself!" she exclaims, showing me the room where we'll sleep. Her voice is breathless as she translates the story of our near miss for her in-laws over and over. Still clinging to my arm, she brings her face close to my ear with low words, then pulls back with that resounding belly laugh. A tiny nag in the back of my head says she's showing off her American friend. I want to squelch the thought, but it lingers stubbornly.

I want so much to trust her. I want her to always be the good Abi—the one who looks me in the eye and tells me I've done the right thing, the one whose voice goes soft when she talks about death or injustice. But there is a side of Abi that disturbs me. She is a comedian by nature, but I have to wonder sometimes if it's all in fun or if menace bubbles under her words. At home she is often flippant with her criticism—she mocks my weaknesses, makes fun of me in Dioula so that I can't understand. She is a traditional West African woman, with almost no formal schooling and few ties outside her family. I am Western, educated—and very good friends with her husband.

In front of her in-laws in this crumbling courtyard, Abi is all smiles and inside jokes, without a hint of the condescension she occasionally resorts to in Nambonkaha. I fear sometimes that maybe my friend is just shallow; that maybe, in the end, I'm her doll, to be dressed up and cuddled or thrown under the bed, depending on her mood.

Yet there is *something*—it was in her eyes right when I got here, in her breathlessness—something genuine. And it comes in flashes now and again. When her relatives are not looking, she gazes at me with lively eyes and asks me to tell her all about Burkina Faso. She says one day she would really like to be able to travel, too. There's a sense of realness that's more important than her pretenses. She is surprised, touched, that I've gone out of my way to find her. Despite this strange burst of girlish attention, despite her capriciousness and my wariness, it seems like my following her here has changed something. Possibly it has proven that I'm truly her friend—maybe she wasn't sure of it before.

Maybe she's used to treachery and disloyalty. In spite of everything, I have a sense that my coming has knocked our relationship a notch deeper. At the bottom of whatever charade she's playing, there is some silent understanding, some kindred connection, and *that*—finally!—is something I can hold with both hands.

Abi has come straight to Sidibé's family courtyard, though her own family lives just up the street. Within an hour of her arrival, she's on a low stool cleaning rice. In traditional Islamic cultures, a woman gives up responsibilities to her own family when she marries. Abi is clearly showing what a good wife she is to Sidibé's parents who sit in chairs outside a shabby cement hut. Sidibé's father is dissolving, a frail body swimming in his boubou, a face shriveled into wrinkles and fringed with a scraggly beard. His wife dwarfs him. She fills up her chair with a thick body that looks like it can still work, although the feet stretched out before her are swollen till they shine. She is the matriarch, and her main duty seems to be calling out orders and comments from the chair.

Sidibé's brother and a few of his older sons spend the day under a corrugated iron roof on poles that serves as the repair shop. Mopeds putter in once in a while, and several of the idlers mosey into action. Sidibé's brother is boss, which means he directs the work from his chair and only gets up for complicated cases. When there are no mopeds to fuss over, he and the men at the shop drink rounds of tea and fiddle with spare parts. This is the occupation with which he proposes to support nearly twenty children.

He has a benevolent face dominated by a long, thick nose. For all his hulking shoulders and heavy presence, he utters very few words, and seems almost shy around me. His two wives, on the other hand, cluck and chatter nonstop. The courtyard teems with children of every size; both wives have large babies at their breasts. There is a disheveled sort of bustle about the whole place—comfortable, but unexpected, considering Sidibé's own orderly courtyard.

Abi heaves a gigantic pot of rice off the fire rocks, ladles steaming white mounds onto a tray, and spreads them out to cool.

Then she scoops the rice into a bowl the size of the one in which I wash my dishes and my clothes. "For the men," she announces, handing it off to a boy, who scurries across the darkening courtyard and plunks it down in a circle of males.

"Look at this," she says gesturing to the rice still in the pot. "All this rice for one meal. Rice that Sidibé sends so that his nieces and nephews don't get hungry. How can we ever have money like you?" she whispers. There's a vague tone of triumph in her voice—as if she's hoped for ages that I'd understand these dire straits.

My first impulse is a hackneyed denial of being rich. I stop short—to trivialize their need would be tawdry. Besides, I am rich, because money in America versus money in Africa is like gold versus cowrie shells. And I am rich with opportunity, and I am rich with education, and I am rich with the knowledge that there will always be hands to catch me if I fall. *"Aidez-nous,"* Abi whispers as she fills the bowl for the women. Help us.

The bowl for the men is set upon immediately by a dozen right hands. Every male, from Sidibé's brother down to a two-year-old son, crouches around the bowl and eats quickly—any pause means a handful less. The women and girls of the courtyard circle around the second bowl. Such mealtime segregation is routine in traditional households, but it surprises me. I suppose watching Sidibé and Abi eat from the same bowl, I expected that he learned the practice here. Despite my protests, Abi serves me on a separate plate. Conversation halts; all are occupied with devouring their fair share. Within five minutes, the bowls are empty. There's still plenty on my plate. The prized fish head stares at me from my rice accusingly.

At seven-thirty sharp, young and old bring chairs and plastic mats to a corner of the courtyard that I somehow hadn't noticed before. All eyes are glued to a large television screen. This is the supreme irony: Sidibé, the financial provider, relies on a tiny black-and-white box of snow powered by a battery. His brother, who can't support his flock and yet breeds on, spends what he has on a sleek black television, a status symbol even though everything else visible here undermines status. Apparently, the television set takes priority over self-sufficiency.

Despite broken clocks and absent watches, in Côte d'Ivoire, everyone who can turns on the television at seven-thirty. Marimar is on. The Mexican soap opera is a phenomenon I have missed entirely, thanks to the lack of electricity in Nambonkaha. It is dubbed in French, and though many, including the cluster in the corner tonight, don't understand French, Marimar seems to transcend linguistics. The ones who really don't get it can easily get a full recap of trysts and scandals—many viewers will give a rundown on the whole season's plot at the merest mention of the show.

The Marimar craze has hopped off the TV screen and infiltrated pop culture. Marimar, the star of the show, is the new icon, ranking somewhere just below the president in terms of iconography. In the market there are Marimar tissues, Marimar perfumes, Marimar print underwear, and T-shirts with shivery images of her with her hair slicked back in a ponytail and her expression haughty. Women wear outfits made out of pagne material called "Marimar's Mirror," a mustard-yellow background staggered with compact mirrors and hair picks. A rash of babies have been named Marimar all over the country. And sometimes as I walk down the street in Ferké, not in slinky western outfits, without a dramatic expression nor a slick ponytail, I occasionally hear cries of "Marimar!" White skin and light hair are evidently enough to fit the bill.

But I'm fated to miss out on the magic: just as the opening credits blink on and the cheesy music strikes up, Sidibé's friend Joachim shows up for a visit. Joachim is Christian, a fact he reminds me of with a nudge and grin as he invites me for a drink at a maquis up the street. I turn to invite Abi but swallow the words—she's married and Muslim and wouldn't be caught dead in a bar, let alone strolling with a man not her husband. So we amble up the hill, our voices loud on the deserted road. The dingy boutiques are empty; the battered Foosball table at the side of the dirt path is still. There is only silence in this big village and, at the very back of it, the faint din of canned melodrama. Life has stopped for Marimar.

"Rien n'est important à sept heures et demi," laughs Joachim as he pulls out a chair for me on the patio of the vacant maquis. Nothing is important at seven-thirty. "People watch Ivorian comedy shows sometimes, and the men like to watch soccer games." He calls out to a woman glued to a television inside and orders a liter of beer. "This show outdoes them all." His voice is lighthearted, but the subject is serious. Rural Africa has had no chance to grow into modernity. They've missed out on the early stages of technology, and now the flashy fruits of it are flung in their faces. Western contraptions are seductive: their pros far outshine the cons. Addiction to technology doesn't seem like something to look out for but something to emulate.

"Marimar is just a symbol, not so important in itself," Joachim says. "There are grave changes in other places, though. The old medicine men are anxious. They can cure broken bones with the touch of a leaf. They can stop migraines forever with mysterious concoctions. But they say the younger generation isn't *sérieux*. They'll pass on the simple remedies, but the big secrets they refuse to give up. They don't want them wasted on youth who don't really revere the tradition." He peers into his glass. "And in Abidjan, you've noticed, *n'est-ce pas?* Businessmen wear Western suits and ties. They eat croissants and cheese instead of the food we've all grown up on. It's like they think how we are isn't good enough."

A scream splits the night, but it's followed by dramatic music. Just Marimar again. Joachim and I finish our beers in silence, pop culture renegades in a paralyzed village.

The next afternoon, after breakfast *and* lunch of tamarind juice and grilled fish doused in oil, Abi and I finally go to her own courtyard to greet her father. Sidibé's courtyard is packed dirt sprouting with people and animals, but Abi's is a smooth expanse of cement, bordered on each side with painted concrete houses. There is a spacious annex, covered with a giant straw dome. It looks like a posh maquis or a deserted dance floor. There are no children, no chickens, no vieilles. It's empty, lifeless, save for a man with Abi's face and thick plastic glasses, sitting in a corner. He doesn't stand when we come in but watches us with a placid smile. He shakes my hand calmly, and then Abi's, before barking out a phrase to the empty courtyard. As if on cue, women in lacy dresses leap from the doors of each house and pounce on Abi. "These are my aunts," she says, and pointing to the one in the ruffled peach dress, adds, "She is my stepmother."

I'm a little bit shocked. Abi's father is so unlively! So unlaughing, unbawdy, unironic. And he's a foot shorter than his daughter. There's nothing Abi-like about him, except his features and the way they're all pulled toward the center of his face. Abi must be made of her mother on the inside. But her mother died when Abi was fourteen, just as her daughter was learning who she was.

Her father's wife and sisters flutter and flounce around him, all the while gossiping with Abi in fine French. A few of these women live in apartments in Abidjan. All wear rings and gold-colored necklaces. Their voices purr and ripple over news of their own families all grown up and doing quite well for themselves. Next come bubbly questions about Sidibé and the children. Abi answers them with smiles and lots of laughter, but her news hasn't changed. Her response to inquiries is the traditional village reply, "He's there. They're there," but dressed up to match her aunts' bragging.

Sidibé's brother's courtyard is relaxed, unpretentious. Here there is money and no life. I miss the children and the chickens and the unglittery conversation. Maybe Abi does too. We don't stay long. We leave in a high-pitched babble of good wishes and don't speak till we're further down the road. Then, in a voice real low, Abi says, "They have never really pardoned me for marrying beneath our class. They say, 'Eh! Abi! Oh, Abi!' *Quoi quoi quoi!*" she continues. "But as they're greeting me, they're looking at my clothes. That's why I stay with Sidibé's family. They are *sans façon*, and kind." We walk slowly down the hill, toward the worn comfort of Sidibé's courtyard.

"My mother was not like that," she says. I've seen a picture of Abi's mother a few times; she keeps it deep in a corner of her room. The picture shows a young woman leaning against a shelf of photographs with an old television at the center. She looks much younger than Abi is now, and she's smiling mischievously at the camera.

"What was she like?" I ask.

Abi speaks of her mother reverentially, softly. "She was beautiful. She was laughing all the time. Everybody wanted to be around her." She folds her arms in front of her as we walk, and it looks like she's trying to keep herself warm. She smiles faintly. "She made great palm-nut sauce. And she loved to dance." *Here* is Abi: small despite her figure, cold despite the heat, hurt despite the laughter, a little girl who still wants a mother.

As soon as we're back, Abi rinses her hands and starts scaling fish. Dusk falls on the squabble of kids and clucking wives; the wizened vieux and his stoic wife grow dark in their chairs by the house. A fluorescent tube blinks on just above them and exposes the cracks and the scuffs in the cement. It glints off the giant pot of rice boiling again on the fire. Abi's one-year-old and her toddler cousin play at pounding with pestles twice their size. Sidibé's brother tinkers with moped parts under the shed, and Abi's rumbling laugh erupts out of the babble. I sit on a stool in the dark, drinking in good energy. The courtyard is overstuffed and maybe underfed, and it's all worn at the edges. But it hums.

11

Apprentis

It's hard to sleep for the heat. My bed is a loft I built whimsically last November to free up space in my tiny bedroom. Sidibé had laughed then, saying, "Wait till the hot season—it'll be like sleeping on fire rocks." He was right: my mattress is a boiler plate, two meters from the cool cement floor and close enough to the blazing metal roof that it seems to generate heat on its own. The air is suffocating, and inside the skirt of my gossamer mosquito net, I feel Saran-wrapped and vacuum-packed. Nights are salty and airless. I wake early each morning to the dry chafing of Massieta sweeping the dust outside.

The first market day of March falls on a Tuesday. When I get there, the weighing station is bustling already. Storage of the equipment has moved from a niche in my bedroom to a spot in Dramane's house, so that the operation won't depend on me. We've also spiffed up our outfits with the proceeds from carnet sales. My assistants are dressed in natty blue uniform jackets. The splintering, wobbling table that threatened to collapse even under the most malnourished child has been replaced with a sturdy one built in Ferké. I've repainted and varnished the measuring board to foil nervous bladders.

But the transformation is more fundamental than all that: the station's standing in the village has somehow been overhauled. Inexplicably, weighing has, all of a sudden, become less a sideshow and more a main feature. When I get to the station today, there's hardly space for me on the bench. Siriki, the president of the village youth, has taken over the measuring board. Américain, the comedian, is working at the scale for the third week in a row. He's wearing a white shirt, a polyester vest, a bow tie, a little cap, and, of course, the sunglasses—it's always part fashion show with him. Bending over each wiggling baby, he looks like a valet at some tacky restaurant.

Africans have a Tom Sawyer mentality about expertise: the luxury of *knowing* means you can train others to do your work. Bakary and Dramane—the recognized assistants, the ones who know what to do—have passed on the information. Their friends bustle all around us, and my assistants just sit, filling out carnets and dispensing nutrition tips. And I've gone from one-woman-show to adviser.

That our weighing station has become a twenty-something hangout is just one sign of a good change. Health—not death, not even disease so much—is the topic at the market. We're full of orders and advice at the weighing table. Your child is underweight? Go home and make porridge with peanut butter. Try mashing up greens with his rice. Remember to put some fish in her sauce, even if she is just a kid and not worthy. And I promise: eating eggs will not make your child a thief. I've eaten eggs all my life, and aside from a pack of Chiclets once, I've never stolen a thing.

Once in a while, women come up and ask for information on their own. They say, "She's hungry all the time now even though she's always breast-feeding." We tell them how to start weaning. They bring us their babies and show us lumps and bumps, coughs and sores. They want to know what to do. They want to know how to fix. And despite the fact that we won't dole out miracle pills, they are coming to us for help.

The serious problems we send to Sidibé. To the rest we offer home remedies, and tell them to come back in a week to weigh again so we can see how the child is doing. It's like a teaching hospital set up around a table in the dirt. My assistants—the growing numbers of them—listen and nod and translate information I've picked up in all my health books. And the next time around, they explain it themselves.

The line stretches on. A few women just go through the motions, possibly weighing regularly because it's what everyone is doing. There are a good number, however, who will tell us what their children weighed last time, or volunteer that a child has been sick and that's why he's probably lost a little weight. The women *are* coming back. Maybe it's the spiffed-up station; maybe it's the luxury of free time before the rains and fieldwork start again. But preventive health care can't be just something in vogue. It has to be a practice so ingrained that it's taken for granted. And we need some incentive to keep the mothers coming.

So every mother who's stepped up to our table in the past three weeks has gotten a brief rundown on our healthy-baby contest. There are four criteria for winning, and Dramane and Bakary count them on their fingers as they tell each woman. "One: you have to weigh your baby regularly—once a week if he's under three months, and once a month if he's older. Two: you have to have all the vaccinations up to date. Three: we're going to hold courses every month about different health topics, and you have to come to each one. And four: your baby has to be in good health. If you do all that right, you will win and get *cadeaux* at the end of the contest." Dropping promises of gifts seems beside the point, but in the end it's not the lure that's important. This healthy-baby contest will last six months, and that amount of time is hard to fathom in a village where yesterday and tomorrow are indicated by the same word. Even if a few who stick it out *are* just waiting for the carrot at the end of the stick, at least they will have learned from our courses and made weighing a habit in the meantime. The women shrug and giggle and agree to sign up.

My assistants have good fun. They are learning, being useful, and hanging out all at once. But it's not a game. They are concerned—they point things out they don't recognize, and they ask me questions, too. And when this afternoon a woman with pained eyes walks in from a far campement with a tiny, shriveled baby on her back, I can see the devastation in all of their faces. The boy looks straight out of the womb—wrinkled just like that—but his skin is not new. "How old is he?" I ask the mother, assuming a few weeks old at most. "Four moons," says the woman, in a barely audible voice. It almost hurts to look at his face, all slack and bony, and his body wasted. No one wants to touch him—afraid they'll break him, it seems—so they let me do the weighing. The scale barely registers him. "Feel this," I say, lifting the flesh of his upper arm. Dramane, Bakary, and Américain touch tentatively. "See how it feels like it's not even attached to the bone? It's not elastic, just loose? That is the first sign of malnutrition. With this baby it's obvious, but in less evident cases, elasticity is one of the first things to go."

The mother has a beautiful face, with wide cheekbones and a small mouth. She won't look at us. "Don't give him water!" We tell her. "Or cow's milk or kabato or sugar! Just breast milk, nothing more." She says, "I have none. No milk at all." "Milk will come if you yourself eat well," we tell her. "Have meat and greens and just keep trying." She nods quietly, arranges him on her back, and ties him in. He looks lighter than the frayed corn husks that little girls carry as baby dolls. She says, Please, I'd like to join the contest too. It seems useless, because the child is so withered, so near death, but if it gives her something to hope for, maybe that's everything. She leaves, and our chatty bunch doesn't say a word. Stunned, moved, these childless young men look like they've just seen a ghost.

The crowd of workers at the weighing station present a prime opportunity for education themselves. They are busy explaining health to mothers. But what about their own health? As unmarried men who travel often to Ferké, they are, potentially, a group at high risk for contracting AIDS. At a bazaar in Burkina, I picked up some AIDS education materials. At the market today, I nonchalantly strew a comic book and some pamphlets across the table. It doesn't take long for a bite. Printed material remains beyond the reach of most villagers, and those who can decipher words are quick to distinguish themselves. It looks good to be holding a paper in the village and it's impressive to be able to explain it to others. Américain picks up a pamphlet to practice his reading skills; Dramane reads the comic book out loud. There are cartoons of a voluptuous woman with bright red lips hanging on the arm of a dapper, skinny man. The bubbles above their heads are filled with pidgin French. The story line is complete, unbashful: batted eyelashes and slurred compliments move right into night images in dark blue—the man and woman all grins and round lines and a bright red condom zinging like a glow stick. My friends hoot, showing off the pictures, jabbering. The subject is AIDS—not funny. But I'm laughing too.

I tell them I want to hold an AIDS Awareness Day someday and propose that maybe we could do a theater piece. Are there any actors? Actors? *Hah!* Two of the best are sitting right on this bench! Dramane and Américain lapse into banter and send the rest rolling. Dramane's eyes are bright, and his shoulders pop up every time he thinks of something new. "I love theater," he says. "This village needs to be spiced up with something. I was thinking music or a dance contest, but a play would be better." They are talking nonstop, spilling out ideas, story lines, characters.

I am lucky, maybe: I had no predecessor, and all precedents have been mine to set. This village is my clean slate. They've never considered health trouble something they could tackle; most of these young men have not ever thought of themselves as teachers. I have no part in this animated conversation at the weighing table. I am just the one to turn on the taps; I stand back, stifling a sheer sense of glee, waiting to see what pours out.

Before any health contest begins, however, something must be done about our scale. With every child it groans and offers up pathetic numbers. I've charted all the weights each month, and the majority cluster sadly below the optimal curve. We weigh babies who look round and shiny, but they still don't quite make the measure. The thing *must* be lying, but we have nothing by which to calibrate it, and no way to fix it. My only resort is to petition the bosses at the health base.

The deputy doctor in Ferké is on vacation, so the receptionist tells me after I travel seventeen kilometers by bike to see him. The boss, however, should be back real soon. I sit in the room outside his locked door for an hour, listening to the plunking sound of an ancient typewriter, but he does not come. Nor does he appear two days later, when the receptionist has said he'll be there for sure. It occurs to me that maybe being the chief doctor of the second largest health center in the north is a part-time job. Dr. Kouamé, when I finally pin him down, is squeamish about my request for a new scale. He has an unnerving habit of avoiding eye contact. As we talk, he stares at the room as if he's just stepped into *my* office and is checking out the decor. But after smiling shiftily at the filing cabinet behind me, he shuffles into a closet and emerges with a brand-new scale. I am floored. This is my first windfall in a year of working with the health base. I cannot hide my elation—maybe the memory of my joy will wrack him with guilt when he denies me something later.

The new scale is an instant hit because it involves fitting babies into nylon shorts with straps and hanging them from a meat hook. Some ironworkers in Ferké have built us a tripod with a huge dangling hook. Hang the scale on the hook and the shorts' straps on the scale, and the contraption suspends the baby several inches above the ground. It is *far* more entertaining than the old scale. And more accurate: as it turns out, Nambonkaha's newest generation is *not* severely malnourished.

When the first day of the healthy-baby contest arrives, we weigh forty-eight infants with our brand-new scale. It's endless comedy. Our corner of the market is stuffed with onlookers; old men stop to watch; students in uniform run over during every break; the vieilles stand around us, heads cocked and arms akimbo, commenting and cackling. And the mothers just lose it, buckling over laughing as their terrified hanging babies pedal the air.

12

Deluge

The three of us spin down the road to the ancestors' bridge. I am on a twenty-one-speed metallic-orange Trek mountain bike. Dramane and Bakary have one-speed bikes painted blue, with thin, patched tires and numbed brakes. Fringe flutters around their seats; tassels fly from the handlebars. The crossbeams are plastered with stickers: "Les Jaloux vont Maigrir"—The jealous will get skinny, "Rien ne peut contre la volonté de Dieu"—Nothing *can* against the will of God.

We swoop down the graded bank, across the desiccated sandbed that was once a river, past the ancestors' bridge. There is a wedding in a campement tonight, and we are pedaling fast to get there before the bride. We ride by villagers, and greetings dance in the air behind us. The spindly path winds through the trees, around rocks, over gullies, until it melts into a small campement, a cluster of huts pulled close, next to a field of mango trees. We have come so far, it seems like we're in a different world.

The space at the center of the campement is crowded already. I hop off my bike and turn to greet the strangers. But there's Moussa chasing an old bike tire, and Mandou is standing in a clot of teenagers, haranguing about something or other. All the imam's wives and daughters are cleaning rice and stoking fires amid a vast collection of giant pots. My Ya and Kinafou prattle together in a row of sitting vieilles. Oumar's mother is here, as is Abou's whole family, and the president and the mayor, with their respective broods. My entire village has been transplanted ten kilometers into the bush. I could swear half these people were in my courtyard an hour ago.

"So where is the groom?" I ask Dramane. There are young people everywhere, but none stand out as the couple of the day. Dramane points to a man hopping from group to group in an untucked cotton button-down and faded blue pants. "That's the groom." The bride, he says, has not arrived yet. "Usually she arrives before sunset." Dusk is threading up through the trees to the east. "She lives very far away," Dramane continues, "and that's probably why she's still not here.

"The groom has sent a delegation from his family to go get the bride. Traditionally, when such groups arrive in a bride's village, children come rushing out to stop them. They say 'Leave our sister alone! You can't take her away!' It's all part of the ritual. The groom's brothers give the kids a few coins to quiet them, and then they walk into a line of stubborn vieilles." He leans his elbows on his knees and laughs. "The vieilles stage a big fight—all an act, of course. They hide the bride or they form a blockade in front of her. They try to fend off the men as long as they can. Sometimes, if the vieilles are clever, it goes on for hours. Finally, the groom's people either convince the vieilles to let the bride go, or they steal her away when they're not paying attention. She's put on the back of a moped, and her head is covered with a pagne."

"Wait! Is she aware of all this? Has *she* agreed? Or do they steal her against her will?" Dramane cocks his head and chuckles his high-pitched chuckle. "Oh no! She knows exactly what's going to happen, and considers the groom her fiancé. If she seems sad or scared, it might just be because she's leaving the place where she grew up. There have been a few times, though, when the bride has changed her mind before the groom's delegates show up."

The women of the groom's family tend to at least twenty simmering pots. They pour water into giant calabashes filled with dry rice and *swish-swish* rhythmically till the water goes cloudy and the dust settles. They wash dozens of kilos of rice a second time, and a third. A marriage is hardly an invitation-only affair—everyone and anyone who can shows up. And everyone expects to eat. "There's no such thing as a real fête without a meal," the mayor has told me over and over. The groom is expected to provide a plate of food for an entire village of people. What would they think if they knew we throw rice *on the ground* at weddings in America?

A whisper ripples through the scattered crowd: "She's coming!" From across the campement, little girls break out in a disjointed chorus of "Ohhhhhh oo woh!" Women of all ages leave conversations and chores, streaming toward the entrance to the campement, singing. Dramane's mother grabs my wrist and hurries me to the center of the fray. A persistent buzz grows louder. Finally, in the dimming light, a string of mopeds appears. The motorcade pulls up in the middle of us, the drivers flushed and excited as if they've kidnapped a celebrity. There are five mopeds, and the one in front has a bright shroud straddling the luggage rack. That's all. The groom's delegation has brought no sisters, no mothers, no hints of the bride's past life. She is alone and anonymous, her head and arms concealed in a pagne.

The singing women help her off her seat. Her destination is a mud hut not ten feet from the moped, but before she gets there the women have to sing to her to show their welcome. The imam's third wife starts a verse between chants. Another woman picks it up. They are making up lyrics as they go along. I would love to know what they're saying, but this is a female ritual, and none of my translators are anywhere near. The women cloying at the quiet figure speed up the song. They laugh and dance, and their eyes are all shiny. Dramane's mother starts a verse. Her head bobs level with my shoulder, and her voice jingles in my ear. I can hear every word, but I understand only a few phrases. Then the rhythm changes, and my name pops out in the verse, two, three, four times! The poor hidden bride is abandoned for a few seconds as all faces sing to me.

We file into the hut, singing still. The bride sits with her back against the curved wall, flanked by her new in-laws. Everyone is smiling but them. It's like a wedding party crashing a funeral party. They look miserable. Could they be upset at their son's choice of a bride? Or are they just being morose in solidarity with their new daughter?

Dramane's mother is frantic and excited. "Do you want to see the bride?" she asks. "Am I allowed?" I ask, but she's already pushing me through swaying hips. Dramane's mother grins and shouts, "Look who's come!" to the bride, then bends over and parts the cloth. Just barely. The girl's face is all downward curves: mouth and cheeks drawn down, long eyelids nearly shut. This is her wedding! Why is she so wretched? Her eyes slide up to mine, black-and-white crescents that look hurt and dull. "*Changwo-anan!*" I greet her, smiling, but she says nothing. I weave through the dancing women to find Dramane. "What's going on?" I ask him. "Why is everyone so gloomy? Tell me the rest of the story!"

"You'd be sad too! She has to sit in a hot hut without eating or sleeping for the whole night!"

"She can't eat or sleep? What kind of celebration is that?"

"It's just the tradition. Neither she nor the groom is allowed to eat anything from the start of the ceremony to the finish. And they can't sleep at all either. All those women are dancing to honor her, but also to make sure she doesn't close her eyes. Anyway, she has to stay hidden. Men can't see her face, not even her husband, till tomorrow morning. There's no place for her out here—the custom is that she stays seated in the hut till dawn. Then she goes out and fetches water with her new sisters to show dedication to her husband's parents.

"Anyway, Guiss, she probably doesn't want to move around too much, considering she just got circumcised." He says this casually, as if it's only a backup reason for her misery.

"Really? Just?"

"Well, probably the day before yesterday. The vieilles need to get it done early so she can walk before the wedding."

So aside from fatigue, hunger, and nostalgia, it's the blood loss that's dulled her eyes, and the pain, and maybe the start of infection. Certainly riding over a dozen bumpy kilometers on the back of a moped can't have helped.

We watch the *djebi* (flute and drum) band trilling in circles around dancing girls. "So there's no bloody-sheet tradition? No one cares about the girl's virtue?"

Dramane waves the idea away. "*Non.* The circumcision takes care of that. Remember, she has to list all the men she's slept with before she gets cut. Also, marriage is just the celebration of an old agreement. Did you notice that this bride is pregnant already? They've been engaged for months. Tonight is just to make it all official. The sex part is kind of an afterthought."

Amid the pots, the cooks are busy figuring how to divide up the meat and the sauce. Guests of honor get good morsels, and at a good fête, all men should get at least a bite of beef. Bowls are passed around—dozens—and everyone debates how to group up. Six or seven sit around each bowl, rinse their hands, and stick their fingers into the rice. Bakary brings our bowl into a hut. There are only three of us sharing. We have spoons to eat with, because strangers assume I don't eat with my hands. And there are big chunks of meat nestled in the rice.

The air tonight crackles with electricity. A young woman I know passes by, a faithful baby-weighing mother. She's lovely and languid—glittery eyes, deep voice. Tonight she's become Denim Woman in jeans, a jean jacket, and a baseball cap with the bill pointing high. It would be a slightly unusual getup for a girl in Ferké or even Abidjan. But in the village, it's a revolution akin to bra burning. Dramane explains before I can ask him.

"It's just a game, an amusement. I don't know when it started, but I don't imagine it's a very old custom. Some girls dress up like boys, and some boys dress up like girls. I think it is Nambonkaha's own custom."

"Why?"

"Just to make people laugh. It animates the fête." The woman swaggers and struts, hollers to friends, stuffs her hands in her pockets. It's hilarious, brazen. Most Nambonkaha women are boisterous with other women but timid or coy around men. They are always traditional, and that generally means they don't put on such public shows.

The male cross-dressers meanwhile are gawky in three-piece complets. Their broad, muscled chests stick out of tailored bodices, and scarves flop awkwardly on their heads. They speak in falsettos, giggle into their hands, pretend to flirt with their friends, and throw their hips out when they walk.

There is no word for homosexuality in Niarafolo, nor is it acknowledged except maybe in the dark corners of Abidjan. Gender-bending is not allowed. No girl but me wears pants in public; no man, except maybe a fou, pumps water or pounds corn. Tradition is watertight. It's not even a question of conformity; conformity is only an issue in societies that have rebellious elements. In the village, men do men things, women do women things. End of discussion.

This charade is only as deep as the outfits. Their aspects might be altered, but their behavior is not. The tomboys stay among the girls, and the boys in drag never leave their friends. They dance apart, eat apart, talk apart, move as if invisible barriers separate the sexes. Yet somehow, despite the segregation, weddings and even funerals are dating games. I can't see any evidence of courtship, but with only body language, some tacit pact is made. Couples disappear silently from the crowd and merge somewhere in the darkness.

By eleven, the stoops of nearby huts are littered with sleeping children. By midnight some elders have disappeared, and others doze in chairs. But the energy of the dancers blasts on. They've danced hours to the *djebi* band, but when the balafons come out, they're completely reinvigorated. Young girls bend and jump in a frenetic circle, mothers dance fast in a smaller circle inside, sleeping babies rocking on their backs. The long blue figures of the balafon band list around and around; segments of young men shift and slide in loops. Late at night, there's no room for stragglers or anyone with clumsy feet. I go back into the bride's hut and dance to the slow shake of cowrie shells in tin cans. The vieilles are still spinning out new lyrics. But it's sweltering—heat curls out the door, saturates the walls. And the rasp of the cowries is hypnotic. I nearly fall asleep dancing. A sliver of the bride's face shows through her pagne. Her sidekicks are fanning her. We seem like the only two fighting off slumber. The rest dance on.

I want so much to see this night through. But being a foreigner, even now, is always more exhausting than just being anyone. Around three, I look for a good place to nap. I suppose I could nestle down with the kids on the stoop, except they're packed in so tightly. And sleeping in public is an oxymoron anyway: all night I would hear people muttering over me, "Is that Guissongui? Sleeping out here?"

Bakary and Dramane appear to have thought this out. They fetch a mat from who knows where and usher me into a little hut decorated like a junior high gym. Across the ceiling, a string of flattened Marlboro cartons hangs like a streamer. The walls are plastered with faded posters. One displays all the leaders of Africa from some years back (most deposed, assassinated, or otherwise dead). Another wall hanging turns out to be an advertisement for grocery-store specials at some toubabou store in Abidjan. Evidently pâté and canned beans are on sale. Outside feet stamp, balafons chime, and girls sing loudly. I fall asleep in seconds.

The floor of some stranger's hut does not lend itself to long slumber—I wake up at dawn and take a seat under the mango tree. The dance is still going. Daylight seems to mute the music, and the numbers of revelers has certainly dwindled, but the fifty or so who dance on move as if the party's just started.

Bakary and Dramane are ready to go. "What about the bride?" I ask. Bakary tells me she's gone to draw water for her in-laws. I do the rounds, shaking every hand, scattering blessings, thanking everyone. I have come to this wedding out of curiosity and solidarity with my villagers. But it's not enough that I ate their food and danced to their music and slept in their hut. They run back into their houses, scuttle after chickens, and send me off loaded down with gifts. We pedal back toting six huge yams, a bowlful of peanuts, and a hen. The unfortunate bride gets nothing but an empty belly, a cut-up body, and a drowsy, sweating head.

·   ·   ·

One night in late March I go to sleep in a village thick with heat and dust and wake up in spring. It is a *hot* spring day—heat in this season is just a constant—but the air has changed. The sky is blue again all of a sudden, the real, dazzling blue I haven't seen since November. That heavy gray coat of haze has been shrugged off in the space of one night. And there are clouds—not the endless slate of the dry season but brilliant, bulging white ones that sail across the sky as if they've just broken through harmattan's finish line and can't slow their momentum.

I can feel it on my skin, in my nose, stirring in my gut the second I step outside: *rain is coming.* Green is lurking somewhere just under the hard dirt, gearing up for the life push, waiting for the water. In my neighbor's courtyard, when I point up at all that blue and ask, "Is rain coming?" she squints at the sunny sky, wrinkles her nose, and says, *"Chekbul ningbé."* One week. The president shrugs his shoulders and dithers apologetically, as usual. *"Ce qui est sûr, la pluie va venir.* Maybe in a few days."

In the morning, Bakary and Dramane come over to rehearse our first lesson for the healthy-baby contest. The topic is breast-feeding and weaning, and we have a packet of illustrations to be presented gradually so that the progression from breast-feeding to weaning will be clear to illiterate women. Since age in a village without birthdays is mostly irrelevant, there are pictures of different stages of development and, next to each, images of what a child of that age should eat. I tell my assistants, "Make sure you remind them that the colostrum, the yellow water that comes out before milk, is really important. Tell them it's like a free vaccination that their own bodies make."

The breast-feeding segment of this lesson is integral in the scheme of weaning, but it's also somewhat extraneous. The village women know all about that part already. In the cities, some upper-class mothers think of formula as a modern convenience and scoff at the milk they produce themselves. In the village, however, it would be absolutely ridiculous *not* to breast-feed.

It would throw into question your worth as a woman and a mother. (*She can't even produce milk?*) Breast-feeding is easy, and unhindered by schedules or social restraints. Besides, it's free. Weaning might begin at six months, but in the village it doesn't end at twelve, or even eighteen, as our drawings suggest. Most mothers breast-feed until their child is two and a half years old.

Village babies are their mother's appendages. They flop when the firewood is chopped. They shake during vigorous clothes washing. Giant basins atop their mothers' heads splash water on them. From infancy, they are suckling acrobats. They have to be—there's not much time in the day when a woman can sit still to breast-feed. So infants are tied under their mother's arm, and older babies swing under there themselves to grab a nipple. Mothers can breast-feed with no hands, while washing dishes, grinding peanuts, or hanging up the laundry.

In the afternoon, the air blows clear and cool, with flashes of humidity. But the east is still all blue. I gather up a dozen small paint cans and all my brushes and lug them to the school billboard that I've been painting by the side of the road. I am in blistering sun, finishing the last word, when clouds boil up in the east. It's like an oasis coming *to me* in the desert. I can smell those clouds as soon as I see them.

The clouds blacken, march right across the savanna, dragging along gray curtains. I put a sharp corner on the final *L,* gather my things, and walk home—slowly. First comes the wind, warm, crazed, whipping up trees and swirling dust. Chickens dive under granaries. Weaverbirds in the tree behind my house squawk frantically, as if apocalypse were at hand. And behind their frazzled soundtrack, the sky is charcoal and flashing. There is that one climactic moment when the air is electric and the leaves turn eerie and neon against dark sky and women scream out to bring in the last cooking pot and Baba's chair! Children's voices ripple on the wind and birds shriek and Nick's hair stands up straight and goose bumps prickle on my arms and the whole world just teeters on the brink of the storm.

And then down it splashes, staccato on the roof, loud silence hushing outside, water and sky running with dust. This bone-dry village is soaked in seconds. I throw my paints inside and my flip-flops too and run out to be rained on. The kids are out in force, chasing one another with shining, exhilarated faces. This is how to greet the rain!

I shove my buckets under the edge of my roof to catch water, because having the sky as your faucet is so lovely. But the harmattan is a stain that will take several rains to rinse out. This rain is fattened with dust, that old haze is falling with every drop. It rolls off my tin roof into my buckets, collecting grit as it goes.

Night falls fresh and a little chill. The stars wink, and the Milky Way looks like it was just spilled across the sky. Moussa and Abou show up for lessons, and they're clean down to their fingernails. They're my only students these days. Mandou hasn't come since he copied several lines out of a *Newsweek* and signed his name from memory. And Oumar had a run-in with Nick's teeth. The bite bled for days, and despite all my first aid and pleas, Oumar has stayed clear of the house for several weeks.

The boys seem renewed by the rain, too. They sit with their mouths screwed up in concentration as I slide Scrabble pieces around the floor to spell *la, ma, na, lo, mo, no*. At the end, we string together a bunch of easy syllables and come up, to their great joy, with *Nambonkaha*. I ask them to write it, copying from the Scrabble tablets. Abou is earnest and sensitive. He writes painstakingly, shielding his work from our eyes with his arm. When he finally produces his masterpiece each letter is footnoted with its Scrabble point value: $N_1 A_1 M_3 B_3$. Moussa puts on my sneakers and clomps over to a laminated picture of my college friends to choose his wife of the day. Then he says casually, *"Guiss, je m'en vais"* and shuffles out with my shoes still on. I reach a hand out the screen door, grab the hood of his tiny, faded 49ers sweatshirt, and yank him back in. His scratchy giggle gets caught in the clean mango leaves.

13

Rite

A moped buzzes up to the other side of my hay wall just as the sun is burning off morning. I'm drinking boiled coffee, chin deep in Dostoyevsky. There are no words outside. Just the cough of an engine shutting off, the squeak of a kickstand. The door to the next room over winces open. And then, gradually, sobs rise up from the silence. They are soft, genuine. Dostoyevsky drops to my lap. This village is full of wails, but this is crying like I've never heard here.

A girl crouches below the mango tree on the other side of my enclosure. She is young still—eighteen at best. Tears shine on her cheeks. I kneel beside her. "What has happened?" "*Meh pwo, wi kou,*" she chokes. My baby, he's dead. I breathe the death benediction—"*Koro tchélé ka da'uma ma ningué,*" literally "May God chill what's behind us." She burrows her face in her arms.

It should be predictable, that a mother who's lost her child cries. But it's not, quite. Not like this. The prevailing attitude among village mothers seems to be "If I lose a child, I'll make another." They loan their kids to barren sisters or well-off brothers like heirlooms. I actually wrote home a few months ago that children seem dispensable in the village.

It's hard not to think it. Mariam the Burkinabe just waited for her son to die. When I visited last week to check on her newest baby, that grinning heap of bones with his head too big was gone. "Where's Ali?" I asked without thinking. Mariam stopped her sweeping, looked into my eyes, and held my gaze. "*Il a mourri,*" she said in broken French. He died. And all I could see from her expression was "It's sad, but it was coming." How could she just decide that she had created a child unworthy of medical care?

Maybe it's a function of community: the family unit is important, but the individual parts of it are negotiable. And when an individual experiences loss, it becomes everyone's property, so that it's easier to endure. There are scars, of course. Abi is all crisscrossed with scars from her mother's death. Our ace student David lost his mother a few months back. His eyes were full of betrayal, and interestingly, it was Abi who sought to comfort him. But those were mothers. The death of children, in the village at least, seems different. It happens so often. They readily chalk it up to the hand of Allah and the sorcerers and move on. It barely seems to bruise them.

But here's this girl-mother with streaming tears and shaking shoulders. It hurts to see her, hurts bad, so that my throat swells up and it's hard to swallow. I kneel next to her, put my hand on her arm, and whisper, "*Ki ya'a,*" over and over. "*Pardon. Il faut laisser.*" That's what you say, "Leave it." Not "It's good to cry. Let it out." Just "Please, pardon, leave this." She is the one crying the way I cry, and I am the one saying, *Don't, let it go,* because that's what I've heard others here say so many times.

I run back in to get her water, but she goes inside too. Her sobs bounce off the walls of the room next door and resonate in my house. And then there are voices outside. Villagers materialize out of the quiet. Goutoumaya, the owner of my house, has told the chief, and within minutes the entire village knows. They collect in silence under the mango tree, my proprietor in a chair with women on stools all around. When more men appear, they move benches away from the women, to a strip of shade cast by another hut. More people come by, solemn-faced. Each new arrival shakes hands with the family, mutters greetings. The clusters of men and women respond in a single, low grunt, like wind soughing through an open window.

My impatience with these burial ceremonies has rubbed off. For so many months, I stopped by briefly to pay my respects, counting on their faith in my Western busyness to let me off the hook. But I *don't* have anything more important to do than sit for the child of my proprietor's family. It's only natural that I sit. Kinafou, the president of the women, moves over to share the other end of a stool with me. And we sit. Mostly silent. For an hour. Men lean forward, looking nowhere disconsolately, resting their chins on their hands. Women scratch lines in the dust, look at their toes. The sun seems to crackle on the ground. Inside the house, the darkness drips and splashes. And rings with low wails. Solidarity wails. The kind I have come to expect.

I can sit still for ages these days. But I still can't quiet all the questions. I can't shrug off my tendency to immediately search out the facts. How old was the baby? What did he die of? Was he born sick? Was he hungry? Did they take him to the infirmary or treat him with indigenous medicine? No use asking, because to all except Sidibé, who does not attend such funerals, death is just death; it renders all physical cause moot. The three states of being in the village are, roughly, healthy, sick, dead. There are Niarafolo words for all sorts of diseases, but they only come in handy when the person is still suffering them.

The wails subside, and three women carry out a tiny bundle. The old men stand in a line facing east, with the imam in white at the middle. He calls out a prayer in a clear tenor. Goutoumaya takes the baby and turns south, toward the cemetery. The men fall into place in single file behind him. The women follow. It's a long, tight procession, silent and quicker than the regular pace of village wandering. As we near the empty marketplace at the edge of Nambonkaha, the men stride on. As if a cord has snapped, the women curl off the path, the ones in front leading those behind to peel off to the side and find shade. Just as women don't kill the chicken for dinner, they don't go near the cemetery. Women's job is giving life; men take care of putting it to rest.

The months between harmattan and the height of the rains are flush months in Nambonkaha. During harmattan there's not much money; during the rains, dawn to dusk is dedicated to the fields. But in March, April, and May, money from the cotton sale is in, and the rains have just begun, so the earth isn't quite soft enough to start up planting again. Funds and free time overlap, and the village splurges. A year's worth of needs and plans are attended to in the space of weeks. By the end, the villagers have just enough money to cover the rest of the year. The mayor revs in from Ferké on a red motorcycle and redefines "transportation" at the village level. The president buys a tiny television and a car battery to power it, arranging a shrine around it in his salon. Kids show up for a glimpse of Marimar or whatever might be flickering on the screen. The imam decides he'll raise sheep and buys four or five to start the herd.

There's a flurry of construction. Mud walls go up in the imam's courtyard; sandy concrete walls rise in Mandou's family's courtyard and also, surprisingly, in that green field that everyone calls the "maternity clinic." The mud huts are finished in two days, but cement houses are usually built in yearly increments. Next year's paycheck will cover roofing, and maybe the year after that there will be money for metal window slats and a door.

The season is full of rituals too. Couples long together finally throw marriage celebrations; elders long dead finally get all-night funerals. The second most important Muslim holiday, Tabaski, happens when the moon is just a sliver near the end of February or in early March. And all over the north of Côte d'Ivoire, Senoufo boys in their teens undergo their rites of passage.

I have a fairly good handle on marriages, funerals, and Muslim holidays. Sorcery fills volumes in village life, and I've only just finished the introduction. Regarding initiation rites, however, I'm still guessing. Initiation happens in different forms all over Africa. But the Senoufo, more than most groups in Côte d'Ivoire, are distinguished by their rites. Initiation is more important to a Senoufo man than graduating from secondary school, getting married, or having a first child. It defines a man, links him to an ancient order, an ancestral society.

But how exactly? What ritual makes a boy a man, and a man an integral part of his people? I have not a clue. I try to collect clues, but no one talks.

This is what I know.

Each Senoufo village has a *poro,* or sacred forest, usually a thick clump of tall trees just beyond the village bounds. It is conspicuous but not talked about much, and the ones I've seen (from outside only) have a spookiness about them, as if ghosts and genies resided among the branches. Initiates disappear inside for days, weeks, or months, depending on the tradition, and come out changed. Inside, I am told, there are masks and fetishes and tokens from the ancestors. What do they do with them? Dramane, who explains most traditions up, down, and sideways, will say little: "We are shown different sacred objects. We are told stories of the past. We learn certain practices."

I know Nambonkaha's *poro* is a dozen kilometers away, in the ancestral village from which our founder, Nambon, struck out to start a new community. With the whole ritual so far away, it's hard to find out when or how or what they're doing and who exactly is doing it. For two or three months, the boys just bike off every couple of days, as if they're going to the market in Ferké. Then one day they come home real men.

The nearby town of Korhogo is the capital of the animist region of Côte d'Ivoire. During initiation months, it's not uncommon to see young men wearing only loincloths walking the streets. And in Ferké, every seven years, a few hundred teenagers of a certain tribe undergo three grueling months in the *poro.* Some never come out. Those that do must, for months after leaving the forests, wear giant masks, strings of cowrie shells and beads, a loincloth, and nothing else. They shun everything Western: for six months they cannot use bikes or cars or shoes or telephones. As 1999 is the seventh year, I pass them on my bike sometimes, a line of men in long, mirrored masks walking barefoot on scalding roads for days to greet the elders of their brotherhood.

I know that Bakary rolled into the village one afternoon with his head shaved. The teenagers who always hang out by the butcher's stall hooted and yelled, slapped him on the back, knocked him around a bit. Bakary grinned sheepishly, rubbed his shining skull. Américain stepped back from the boys to explain:

Bakary had just been initiated. Apparently his hair, and that of the rest of the initiates, had been kept in the forest as a protective fetish. How was it? I ask Bakary, thinking that maybe such a broad question will elicit a less guarded response. "It just was," he tells me. Come on! Was it hard? Was it tiring? Did you think you wouldn't make it? He shrugs. *"C'était intéressant."* It was interesting.

I know that I'm not alone in my ignorance. None of the women in the village know exactly what goes on in the *poro.* Girls bring food to the edge of the grove so that the initiates may eat, but they cannot go inside, or even look. There are certain local masks, they say, that will kill any woman who sees them. Young boys don't know either. Initiates leave the forest with its secrets sealed inside them. Breaking the silence is a grave sin.

"Do women have initiation rites too?" I ask Dramane. "Yes," he tells me, "but they're not so elaborate as ours, I don't think. And anyway, they don't go through them until they have children." Why? "You know girls," he laughs. "You can't trust them with secrets. They have to wait till they're older and more serious before they do their rite of passage. Otherwise, they'll tell everything to their boyfriends."

Ah, but girls *do* have rites of passage, aside from their initiation. And they don't come back grinning and sheepish.

Weaving back from Angélique's through a thin carpet of new grass, Abi and I discuss a wedding last week. The bride, says Abi, has not recovered from her circumcision. "This morning her husband took her to Ferké to the hospital. *Elle chauffait trop."* She was too hot. Abi shakes her head, yanking leaves from a mango tree overhanging the path.

We walk past the defunct corn mill, its tin doors locked shut. Out of the blue, Abi says, "Kolo cried so much!" Kolo is the daughter of Abi's Burkinabe neighbors. When I arrived last year, she was a little girl, but all of a sudden she's turned into a woman. She walks slowly now, with her new breasts forward and her hips swaying just a little. But her face hasn't grown up with her body. "Kolo was excised with the bride," says Abi, as if it were evident. I gasp. "But that's not the tradition!" I say. "I thought they only got excised right before their wedding." She snorts. "Sometimes when the vieilles have been summoned to do a circumcision, other mothers take advantage of it and send their daughters with the bride. Kolo's sister got excised too." Abi says it so casually! Kolo's sister is five years old.

In Korhogo, it is customary to circumcise girls in early childhood. The vieilles round up all the little girls and take them into the bush for a few days. The operation is performed with a razor blade, and the babies are brought back walking funny, with faces not quite so young anymore. There is certainly no good slant on female circumcision, but in Nambonkaha the women are at least old enough to understand the custom. At least they see it as a marriage rite and abide the pain because their sisters have suffered it too. But for children, there's no justification, no comfort in conformity. There is just a sharp blade and a button of skin they don't even know about yet pulled taut and sliced. And sand to stanch the bleeding. They were just recently babies—they've just gotten their bodies, have years to go before they've figured them out. They are little girls with curling eyelashes, dimples, glittery grins, and bodies old with scar tissue.

Abi and I walk past Tchessilahana bent over a pot of bubbling sauce. When we greet her, she drops the greeting protocol and tells the truth. "I'm here," she says, "but my daughter is sick." She gestures to her daughter, Mam, sitting motionless against the wall of her hut. I assume she must mean diarrhea or something routine, but Abi nudges me, murmuring. "She got cut too." And yes, you can see it on the girl's face; this is more than stomach pain. Her eyebrows are rumpled, and the light in her eyes is out. She looks as if she's been deceived, as if she can't quite fathom what just happened. She is eleven maybe, and so beautiful. Her mother's face looks tired too. "The blood came too much," she says. And Mam just stares blankly forward, wrapped up in so many pagnes, as if to keep all that blood from going too far, as if to protect her from the pain, as if to hold in everything she's lost.

And I can talk all I want, lecture, condemn, expound, but I can't save them. The vieilles will shake their heads in dismay at all the right moments in my diatribe. The mothers will nod eagerly; Dramane and Bakary will agree wholeheartedly that this is a hideous practice. But no one is willing to lift a finger to change it. There is no such thing as rebellion or standing up to the vieilles or curses. My words founder before years of tradition and superstition.

Abi's voice runs gravelly as we pass through her gate. "The only way you can make them stop is by bringing the police in and arresting all the vieilles."

Bakary's hair is just growing back when he slowly meanders into my courtyard one day, his eyes on the dial of a screeching radio. I have just come back from a jaunt south. "How was Abidjan?" he asks, but he doesn't listen to my answer. He turns the dial slowly, slowly, runs over a blip of a man's voice and scurries back to it. In the same distracted voice, he says, "Oh, did you hear that Dramane got married?" The plate I'm washing splashes into the basin. Bakary frowns at the radio, then adjusts the antenna.

"Got married?!" I gasp. "To whom? Senata?" The girl his father has ordered him to marry is rumored to be pregnant with Dramane's child, but Dramane still insists on postponing any ceremony. "No, no, no." Bakary holds the radio up to his ear and squints.

"Bakary!" I punch his arm, laughing, *"C'est qui?"* Weeks ago at a funeral, Bakary pulled me aside and asked me if I wanted to see "Dramane's girlfriend," a girl in her late teens from a far campement. I didn't meet her exactly—instead we watched her from afar as she danced. When I mentioned her to Dramane, he smiled bashfully and waved his hand to dismiss it. Relationships in the village remain undeclared until an engagement can be announced. "How did Dramane get to know her then?" I asked. "Nights like this. They see each other at weddings and funerals. And sometimes at the market."

Dramane has carefully explained the whole involved marriage ritual. The man asks the woman's father, who never agrees straight off but will make a deal. If a certain number of pagnes are delivered yearly, and if the son-in-law-to-be works the father's fields for a certain number of seasons, *then* he will oblige. The waiting period before the ceremony is considered engagement, and just as good as marriage. Weddings happen only when there's money, months or years down the line.

Dramane neglected to tell me of another, less circuitous route, which he has apparently chosen. Just steal the girl. Send a friend to her courtyard or campement in the dead of night and abscond with her. It's not kidnapping exactly, because she's in on the plan. Then a revered vieux from the groom's family will visit the girl's father to ask "pardon." Dramane's father-in-law takes his time returning the verdict. We all wait nervously for a week. His new bride hides in his house. Finally an old man rides into the village with a message. Dramane gets the girl.

Last year was a good one for Dramane. His work with the tractor earned him a fairly steady income while it lasted, and his family's cotton crop had a good yield. He has enough money to hold his wedding a few weeks after getting married. As is custom, on the day of the ceremony Dramane buys dinner for the whole village, while he and his new wife starve themselves and go sleepless. Chapalo is passed around surreptitiously; balafons play till late morning.

I hope, briefly, naively, that his abbreviated courting ritual might mean that the circumcision rite might be overlooked as well. Dramane is completely against it, so why shouldn't he be the first to reject the tradition? He's busy being host, and I can't pin him down alone to ask if by chance his wife has escaped the knife. But when I enter the bride's hut, sweltering with dancing vieilles, the evidence is clear. Dramane's new wife is veiled with a pagne that divides just enough to show her mouth turned down miserably. Her left leg is raised on a small stool, and her straight back is bent slightly over her stomach as if to protect herself. My friend, adviser, assistant, colleague—who loves to chatter about Nambonkaha's traditions, but reviles this one—will not stand up to the power of a curse.

. . .

When Dramane comes over one afternoon at the beginning of planting season, he's toting a friend along behind him. Yakou is an old classmate who made it through all those exams that Dramane failed and is now studying computer technology in Abidjan. He is tall and lanky in this short-statured village, and he's wearing a silky button-down, tucked into jeans. "Are you here for a visit?" I ask, pulling out chairs for them. "*Enfin*, euh . . ." he starts. His French sounds strange, garbling. "I'll be here for a few weeks." He doesn't speak like an African. It's as if different French dialects are fighting for each word. In this humble stretch of savanna, it sounds all wrong.

Dramane and I banter on about our work and our contest, in high pidgin French, all speckled with Dioula and Niarofolo. Yakou sniffs. His mustache bunches primly atop his lip. And then it relaxes. He sits up straighter and sniffs again. It seems that he wants to join in but can't figure out how to speak to us. From my spot between them, it's apparent that a strange dynamic is developing. I suppose I should have more in common with Yakou—he has spent some time in the world outside Nambonkaha; he has gone to university and immersed himself in Western technology. It occurs to me that right here in my tiny salon, sitting on a bucket, speaking about village goings-on, Yakou is nervous and I am comfortable. I am *villageoise* like Dramane.

I've met plenty of Nambonkaha sons and daughters who have gone off to pursue their fortunes in big cities. They are a class apart, and the rest of the villagers treat them like movie stars. They wear trendy rimless eyeglasses instead of the market-bought wire ones with round lenses and the gold stickers still stuck on. They dress in pin-striped shirts instead of boubous or complets. They speak in educated French, drop words like *l'Internet*, carry cell phones that don't work in the village. Returning to the village is usually refreshing and peaceful for them. But Yakou's roots seem to be jabbing at him. He seems awkward in his own skin, not sure of where he belongs.

He starts out with a jumbled non sequitur, and his *r*'s flop in his throat like a dying fish. His long fingers flutter, and he coughs a little and switches to a subject he knows. "Did you attend the elections for the board members of the cotton cooperative, Dramane?"

Last year's board, with the mayor at its helm, went down in the flames of an embezzlement scandal. *Now* everyone understands why the mayor has that manly motorcycle and girlfriends in Ferké. Apparently, his role as head of the cotton cooperative allowed him to skim some fat off the village's earnings. All told, the unschooled custodians of Nambonkaha's main resource were unable to account for eleven million CFA, just under nineteen thousand dollars. Fifty cotton farmers have lost out on a fair chunk of their annual income.

The mayor and his cronies have been summarily relieved of their duties and asked to pay back the missing sum. That's all. They haven't been excommunicated or condemned. Except for the new leadership at the board and the subtle disappearance of the motorcycle, nothing has changed. The mayor still comes to Sidibé's after dinner. He still gets a place of honor near the imam during prayers. It seems ironic that a culture so concerned with giving and sharing would accept such a display of greed. But no one shuns the mayor for tricking his brethren out of their earnings. Sorcery will get you if you don't keep your family fed and clothed, but stealing money outright doesn't seem to bother the witches. Rather, the mayor's misdemeanor is condoned as the inevitable fallibility of a man in charge of large amounts of cash.

It seems logical that Nambonkaha, recovering from such a run-in with corruption, would seriously consider whom to choose for the next cotton board. But village politics do not always proceed logically.

"*Oui,*" says Dramane, "I was at the elections."

"Did you vote?" asks Ibrahim.

"Vote?" he snorts. "It wasn't a *vrai* election, more like a nomination. They picked incompetents again." He shakes his head and jabs at the buttons on my shortwave. "The new vice president made it to CM2 a decade ago. The new president is illiterate. You'd think they would have learned after the last ones."

Yakou pitches forward, elbows on his knees, and says, "Didn't you argue?"

Dramane shrugs. "I don't want to sacrifice my standing in the village."

"What about the forced laborers who built this village and this road? If they hadn't sacrificed themselves, where would you be now?" Yakou's voice is urgent, unsmiling. It's a strange allusion: the laborers didn't *choose* sacrifice. They were forced into it. Dramane is unfazed. "This is Africa—we're always a little *en retard.* That's the way it is," he laughs. "We have to accept it. They'll learn to choose competent people, but maybe only after ten years of idiots. Meanwhile, I'll stay in my place and wait for them to come around."

He'll just wait?! No wonder he condemns female circumcision but does nothing to stop it! He doesn't want to buck the system. He's not apathetic, but is he a coward? Or does he just revere tradition? Nambonkaha was named for a man who bucked the system: unlike the forced laborers, Nambon really did sacrifice himself by standing up to the slave drivers. But that was an alien system—he had no ancestors to answer to when he rebelled against white strangers. How many others would have been as brave? And how much more courage would it take to push it a step further and challenge the infinitely more formidable tangle of elders and spirits that rules the village?

Dramane is all about modernizing the village, but only in superficial ways. He wants electricity, bad. He says, "Wouldn't it be great if we could put up loudspeakers to call people to meetings or play music all day? If we had lights, students could stay up late to study." He measures progress in terms of things, not behavior. He won't meddle with ritual to help the village girls, or suggest better organization to improve business ethics.

From a development standpoint, Yakou is right, hands down. In choosing unqualified board members, the villagers *have* perhaps condemned themselves to another year of inefficiency and *bouffed* cotton returns. How is it at all helpful for creative thinkers like Dramane to remain mute when they could be offering ideas for real progress? The elders are not ogres; they are grandfathers, wizened and wise. And the election of a cotton board is about politics, not ritual. Yet despite Dramane's laissez-faire attitude about change in the village, I find myself identifying with him.

It doesn't really make sense. I'm a so-called development worker, but I understand why he's stepping back. I know why it's not that easy: because in the village, Dramane is still a youngster and the elders hold sway. Messages of change must come hinted at and indirect before anyone will listen to them. And in the village, someone who's too big for his britches, who takes the lead too much, speaks with too much confidence is a prime target for sorcery. This explains Dramane's mantra of "Work hard, lie low."

I get it. And Yakou doesn't. I speak like a villager. And Yakou doesn't. He's forgotten that status quo is solid and safe in the village. I've forgotten that activism has changed other societies for the better. He is a man from the village trying to label himself a man from the city. I am a modern woman trying to recast myself as a villager. Dramane is just Dramane, who'll believe in change but wait for the tide to turn.

And in the end, that's okay with me. I'm realizing that I am a development worker who's not completely sold on development. Maybe I'm just disillusioned with where all the newfangledness of Western life has gotten us. Maybe I see here what we lack: simplicity, community, a noncommercialized, revered culture. I can't dismiss traditions. I can't dismiss respect for elders. I can't dismiss sorcery. I can't accept the shriek of the corn mill replacing the *tok tok* of the pestle, because pounding is social, communal, reciprocal, and the mill just means waiting in line.

Community in Africa still works. The village is arguably the most stable and cohesive unit in West African society. Modern Africans might scoff at their village cousins, who produce a bumper crop of yams one year and give half of them away to relatives and friends instead of reaping the profits. But that's the beauty of Africa, that's its glue in the face of catastrophes like

AIDS and ethnic unrest. In the village, no one falls through the cracks. Knowing how much I esteem their diligence, their adaptability, their strength, I will allow myself to be a bit presumptuous. I *don't* want to watch rituals crumble. I *don't* want to see children's games replaced by insipid images on a TV screen. I want no hand in Westernizing this village.

And then they ask me for change.

Siaka, the *grand type* from Yamoussoukro, drives up one day, bringing another *grand type* named Benoît. They arrive in a cloud of cologne, wearing sunglasses and tailored pagne shirts. Siaka begins. "You've seen those walls that went up across from the infirmary, in that empty space that everyone's called *la maternité?* The vieilles raised eight hundred thousand CFA to build them." How did the vieilles, of all people, come up with that sum? "Well! They sell firewood!" says Siaka, as if it were perfectly evident that this sort of enterprise could gross so much money. Siaka tells me that the cadres pitched in some too, so that the midwife's house could be started, but the vieilles financed most of the work. And now the money has run out. They ask me to contact my liaisons in Abidjan—development agencies, foreign embassies, non-governmental organizations—to see if we can get funds to complete the building.

They've graphed out all the expected costs. They explain who will manage the project and how long it will take. Then they show me the budget. Eight million CFA—$13,000. Do you think you could manage it?

I'm flabbergasted. Not so much by the sum, though it's more than I've seen in my life, but by the fact that the vieilles initiated this project. So many other development workers have had to pull teeth to get a 25 percent village contribution to top off a successful project. But my village *started* without me, and finished a major step before they even came to me. I look the budget up and down. It's a huge undertaking, and I've only got ten months left. The vieilles' hands have delivered nearly every child in the village. They have rocked bellies, cut umbilical cords, pulled babies dead and alive from the womb. Now those old callused fingers are handing off the responsibility, admitting the importance of modern medicine. It seems the end of an era, but they are the ones pulling the curtain. A maternity clinic means a female health authority in the village: one who can save lives in childbirth, no doubt, but also one who can prescribe birth control and talk frankly to women about their bodies, and maybe, hopefully, in the best of all possible worlds, start to dismantle the female-circumcision curse.

I look up at the *grands types* and say, *"Je ferai tout ce que je peux."* I'll do everything I can.

14

Trophy

Our breast-feeding and weaning course in April—the first course of the healthy-baby contest—started three hours late. I paced and swore under my breath, but the women came, around noon, in waves, until there were over fifty clustered on benches, looking bashful. They listened quietly as Dramane pinned up the weaning pictures in sequence, letting the women guess each image. Then he asked for volunteers to repeat the lesson. They tittered and shrugged until finally one of the bold, older ones stood and interpreted the pictures.

Then a younger woman timidly raised her hand. Then another and another. Each volunteer stood up, faced the pictures, and reiterated most points in the right order. Their voices came breathlessly. They knotted their fingers as they spoke. Young Nambonkaha women do not speak in front of crowds, as a rule. Yet when we stopped after four complete reenactments of our lesson, there were many more hands raised. And my women were chattering and pointing and nodding. They could do this! Even though they never went to school, they could look at all those strings of pictures and get it. I knew they could, but I could see in their faces that they didn't.

In May, the course on malaria started three and a half hours late. There were only twenty women in attendance. I had run into a group of my faithful mothers in Ferké the day before the course. They had told me they were going to the women's sacred forest for the initiation. When will you be back? "Ohhh, *chang tanri,*" they said, looking at the sky. Three days. My assistants had failed to notify me of the scheduling conflict. So I checked to make sure I wasn't contending with the ancestors and set a date for a second malaria course.

At that class, we introduced our theme by unrolling a picture I drew of a miserable-looking man. The women snickered and clasped their hands. The first lesson's tension was long forgotten. "Look how he's shaking!" said Dramane. "But he's sweating too. And he's holding his head—*yugo na wir ya!* It hurts so much! What do you think it is?" Several called out, "*Gnuma!*" and the rest nodded. Everyone knows about malaria in the village—it's used to label any prolonged fever or ache. "So how do you think he got *gnuma?*"

Moussa's mother, Massieta, stood up and said, "If you eat too many mangoes, you get *gnuma.*" Some grunted approval, and others clucked the back of their throats. They must not be completely convinced of this one—their kids eat dozens daily. The imam's youngest wife sat up straight. "It's not mangoes. When you're out in the fields, and you have to work all day in the sun, that's when you get *gnuma.* It's from being in the sun too much." More sounds of approval. Such myths are understandable. Malaria abounds during the rainy season, since mosquitoes breed in water. And the rainy season is, of course, mango season and planting season as well.

"But what's the real cause, before mangoes and sun?" Dramane asked them, sidestepping their explanations. We flashed a huge picture of a mosquito. All through the audience, we could hear "Haii!" breathed in surprise. *Mosquitoes are the culprits? Well, then we're doomed!* They come out in invisible droves two weeks after the first rain and ambush the village. They harmonize just outside your ear at night and munch on feet and shins and hands. Tchessilahana sighed, "How can we escape mosquitoes? We cook outside and wash outside and work outside. And mosquitoes are everywhere."

We threw the question back at the women. "You can sweep the trash out of your courtyard, since mosquitoes like trash," offered one woman. Well, not *exactly,* but any reason for cleaning up trash is a good reason. How else? They were stymied. Bakary snapped into action. "Since mosquitoes live in grass, you must cut down all the grass around your house," he offered, making energetic thrashing gestures. "And," added Dramane, "make sure there are no puddles around your house or around the pump, because that's where mosquitoes make babies—in still water."

Such precautions might put a slight dent in the mosquito population, but on their own they won't precipitate any drastic decline in the malaria infection rate. So we plugged Sidibé and the infirmary, reiterating that his malaria pills are better than the rainbow-colored mystery ones sold in the market. We suggested that pregnant women buy chloroquine as a prophylaxis. For our finale, we hauled out a roll of plastic blue screen and offered to sell it by the meter at cost. "At least this can keep them away from you while you're sleeping," said Dramane, unraveling the stuff. The women murmured and nodded, and Mariatou, who walks seventeen kilometers in the morning just to get to these meetings and is always among the first to arrive, said, "Hold five meters for me—I need to ask my husband."

By market day, she had permission and enough money to pay for all five meters, roughly two dollars. Two weeks later, she came back for three more. I am told that somewhere out there in the bush, in Nambonkaha's farthest campement, Mariatou's husband's hut and her own are antimosquito fortresses, every chink in the mud walls sealed with blue screen.

Course No. 3 in the healthy-baby contest will be all about hygiene and vaccinations. But it's getting complicated. There are over eighty contestants, and we weigh around thirty babies weekly. Mothers come faithfully, yet since planting season has begun the courses have lost some appeal. It's hard to justify the benefits of talking about hygiene when there's self-sustaining labor to be done. Plus, the whole idea of a contest that lasts half a year is confusing. So I try to spice up each course so that the mothers will return for amusement's sake if nothing else. For Course No. 3, on a Saturday in early June, I'm making papier-mâché puppets for a hand-washing skit. The kids in my courtyard are horrified that I've turned flour into glue when it could have made a good porridge.

The Friday before the course, a man in tinted shades zooms into the village on a black motorcycle. He dashes around children, sends chickens ruffling, and cuts off the engine in front of Sidibé's gate. Sidibé, Bakary, and I are eating yam foutou and peanut sauce on the terrace. The man introduces himself as Dominique, the president of the local chapter of an international nongovernmental organization (NGO).

Dominique takes a chair and relaxes immediately. City folks always slow down when they get to the village, as if they've arrived at a vacation spot far from their slightly less lackadaisical lives in town. We talk about the weather, discovering, again, that it's rained too much. And then Sidibé gets down to business and asks for the news.

Our guest leans forward, hands clasped. "It's nothing," he says, as formula dictates. "Except that Ferké is host city for the Annual World Breast-feeding Week festivities this year." He is heading up the event-planning team and says he's heard of my healthy-baby contest. "It's a good idea," he says, then sniffs and adds, "So we're having one, too."

My instincts are all crisscrossed. Is this a windfall? With a big NGO at my back, our contest could become a huge success. The awards ceremony would have *grands types,* good food, and *cadeaux*—all the ingredients for a good fête. "Would we work together?" I ask. "*Mais oui!* One big fetê! To celebrate mothers who do their job well."

Yet what does he know about our contest? I explain the premise. He nods excitedly at first, but then his head slows. Eighty women? He was thinking on a smaller scale. And the courses aren't really so important. "So what are your criteria?" I ask him.

He pulls out a sheet—a score sheet—with listings of the measures of good mothering and boxes for points received. "If you could just tally up the scores you have with your contest, and send us the top ten women, we'll include them in the ceremony. There will be many prizes." He lists a few of the items the winning mothers might expect. "T-shirts, maybe some lotion, powdered milk, a trophy." I wonder what exactly a breast-feeding trophy looks like. Bakary pulls his chair a little closer and claps his hands together. He has mentioned that what he'd really like is a job with an NGO, though that was several weeks before he said he'd really like to run his own boutique, which was several weeks before he said he'd really like to go back to school and work in a bank.

The score sheet has a health section including weight and vaccinations. It has a big section for breast-feeding, though there really isn't an alternative in the village, and the final boxes rate looks, dress, and chubbiness.

"We have twenty-five women who are poised to win," I tell him. "We have over forty who have done really well in the contest so far. How will you compensate them? How do you expect them to learn anything or to think they've done anything right when only the top ten are rewarded?"

Dominique laughs primly. "I'm afraid we only have prizes for ten."

Now I sit back and stretch. "Prizes for ten is not enough."

Bakary sidles closer. "Oh, I'm sure it would work just fine. The women will understand. It's so generous of you."

But I'm disgusted. I tell him so. And I'm sure it looks like I'm tossing away a great opportunity, but all I see are empty words of praise and plastic trophies. A few women will have improved standing for a few days, that's all. It trivializes what the women have learned, cheapens their new good habits.

My candor is totally out of line with African business conduct. Bakary throws me a death glance and smiles at Dominique apologetically. Sidibé grins into his shoulder and stays quiet. Dominique won't back down. The picture is clear: they need ten women for a scripted festival. They've written a song all about breast-feeding, the women in Ferké are making uniforms for a parade, the ceremony will be stocked with lots of *grands types* and will probably be televised.

The choice has already been made—by Dominique, with the backing of the Ministry of Health. Ten women from Nambonkaha *will* join the festivities. All that remains to be determined is the role I choose to take.

I don't want to mock the efforts of my women. I don't want to sacrifice the fate of our contest by boiling all the work we've done down to the parceling out of gifts. And I certainly can't match the fancy prizes offered by the NGO with the paltry funds I hope to collect from local businesses.

Course No. 3 starts late, as usual. The women watch bemused as the puppets bobble through the hand-washing skit. *How funny that Guiss wears dolls on her hands!* We hand out Problem and Solution flash cards and have the women with the Problem pictures (rotting teeth, rice covered in flies) find those holding the Solutions (chewing stick, lids for food). We hold up a drawing of a courtyard in shambles with a disheveled woman in the middle. "This is Drianchen. What's wrong with her courtyard?" There are some curious suggestions: "That kid is sleeping!" "The straw roof wasn't made right, rain will get in." But the right answers come too. When we're finished, the women balance the benches on their heads. They call out, *"An y che! Guissongui-yo!"* and fade back into the village. Begrudgingly, I note those with healthy babies and up-to-date vaccination and weighing charts, those who have come to every course, those who have participated unasked. I'm ignoring the NGO's score sheet and using my own standards instead. But I feel like a traitor for selecting so few when there are so many putting forth a good effort.

Later in the week, I go to the Annual World Breastfeeding Week planning meeting to see what can be done. Women in fancy complets sit at the organizing table. They go over the program, the seating arrangements, and the delegation of responsibilities. Then they get to me. All grins, so well intentioned, they explain how I'll get my women into Ferké, and just when they'll appear in the ceremony. I say, "Is there no room for at least an eleventh? I've gone over each woman's participation so many times, and I still come up with eleven who have done everything right."

The chairwoman glances down at her papers, turns to her neighbor, looks at her papers again. I'm being difficult, I know, but I can't discourage that eleventh woman. She's just on the cusp—her baby was born small and she has no money for nice clothes or talcum powder. Yet she appears in my courtyard occasionally, saying not "Can you fix this cut?" but "I want to help her eat better. What should I give her now?" The chairwoman looks at me over her glasses. "We'd like to," she says, "but ten is really an easier number."

The last criterion is an adequately intelligent response to two questions: Why do you breast-feed? Why do you vaccinate? They are questions too broad to get wrong. One woman says she breast-feeds to "fill him up." A few explain that vaccinations are given to cure illness, as if the baby were inherently sick. It's all a question of words in the right order, though, and most answers can be manipulated into the right one. I refuse to fill in the points or make it a beauty pageant, instead basing the selection on the women's participation in the courses and the weighings over the last few months. Then I hand in my list and leave town.

From a table at a falafel joint in Abidjan, I watch the news for three straight nights, hoping to see my mothers. The fourth night, they're shown, Oumar's mother and her tiny, wide-eyed daughter, Massieta struggling with Drissa. All ten Nambonkaha women in their best pagnes are flashed all over the country. But that night I am far from a television screen and miss the whole thing.

My efforts to detach myself from the contest prove futile in the end. When I return to the village a few days later, the chief comes to my courtyard with a few elders. He shakes my hand for a full minute, thanking me. The women come by to show me their breast-feeding trophies, and Abou and Mandou explain that they were watching it all on the president's new television and they saw Oumar's maman! And his sister! On TV! It seems so stingy of me to check their happiness. Dramane and Sidibé might understand my concern for the larger picture, but no one else bothers to intellectualize it. So I smile a small smile instead of the big grin they're used to and explain that it's the good work of the women and really not me at all that got Nambonkaha on national television.

Course No. 4 begins an hour and a half late. In other words: *early.* We have to send petits to get more benches. It is prime peanut-picking time, but the market terrace is bristling with women. And they are excited. We're talking about home remedies today—teaching mothers to look at familiar things in new ways. Medicinal leaves are prescribed for any illness, but I want to propose other remedies as well. "Who has a sore throat?" we yell out to the women. We pick a volunteer to demonstrate how to mix citron and honey with hot water to make cough syrup. "Who has a bad cut?" A mother hobbles up to the front and presents a nasty slice on her shin. "What do you do with a cut like this?" we ask. *"Put sand in it to stop the bleeding!" "Put hot pepper in it because that stings and kills the bad stuff."* Bakary hands the woman a bar of soap, a bucket of water, and a scrap of clean cloth for a bandage, and she dresses her wound as we instruct the crowd of women craning to see. Volunteers help us demonstrate how to make oral rehydration solution for diarrhea, how to breathe steam for congestion, how to give cold baths for a fever, how to treat pinkeye and thrush, how to soak infected thumbs in hot water.

These are not sexy remedies. But there are sounds of discovery throughout the din, and the mothers are eager. When we check off their carnets at the end of an exhilarating few hours, there are plenty that I've never seen before. Surely some of these strangers have visions of trophies dancing in their heads. But in their quest for the gold, they've learned to make cough syrup and to clean cuts, and that, in the end, is what counts.

15

Boutons

Djeneba comes to the village during planting season. She's got a giant bundle on her head and a tiny baby on her back. That's all she has. She can carry her life with her hands free. She moves in with the young family of Adama le Gros, a man with a *paunch*, of all things—and he's not even thirty yet. He is tall too, one of a handful of villagers over six feet and the only one with more than muscle on his bones. Adama doesn't talk much, but his smile is easy and his movements slow. He plays the huge bass balafon in the village band. The other musicians are wiry—they have to lean back to keep from pitching over from the weight of their instruments. But Adama's shoulders were made to support. When he plays, he hunches forward. His arms move fast; his face doesn't flinch.

Adama le Gros has three young wives, who keep his courtyard swept and the pots bubbling. They like to sit on a plastic mat in the shade of a mango tree and shell peanuts together or braid one another's hair. When I pass by, they're always there, a pocket of happy faces and supple, beckoning voices. The third wife is a cripple with a charmed smile and a foot twisted inward. The second is tall and lithe and laughs at everything. The first is Alimata, the only childbearer of the three.

Alimata has perfect teeth. Wooden chewing sticks are the main instruments of dental hygiene, but the villagers do all right. A few mouths look like old graveyards—some teeth bent forward, some backward, some crumbled and chipped. Most others have creative spaces in their grins, yet the teeth that have made it are sturdy enough to crunch chicken bones. But Alimata's teeth are perfect. When she smiles, they appear straight, strong, white, and bracketed by dimples.

Alimata was second in line the day I began weighing babies. She has come faithfully ever since, as if she has been waiting for some way to prove herself. I'm sure there's a collection of French words that she keeps bound up and dusty in the back of her head, but she never lets even one out. We've become friends over this year through cobbled-together Niarafolo and gestures. Her two older children are in school. Her youngest is a strapping baby girl with a mouthful of a name who thinks I'm Satan.

Djeneba shows up in late June. She is a stranger in the village, but no one seems surprised when she appears. The population here is kinetic: there are always people leaving—to work faraway fields or care for elders. There are always people coming—distant relatives who've hit rough times in the city, or sons come to live off parents. When Djeneba arrives, Adama's third wife moves her pile of pagnes to one side of her hut to share the space. And Djeneba finds a spot on the plastic mat to shell peanuts.

Djeneba, I am told, has come to stay. Her husband died recently in the city. Adama is her dead husband's nephew and also his closest male relative. So, according to tradition, she becomes Adama's fourth wife. This is life insurance, village-style. The community doesn't let anyone fall through the holes. The imam took all his older brother's wives—not in some incestuous, chauvinistic ownership ploy but out of duty. Thus Adama takes Djeneba as his wife. He becomes her breadwinner; he safeguards her future. She's enveloped in family again.

When I first meet Djeneba, she looks up at me through her lashes and extends her hand hesitantly. She's nervous around this white woman—that old, noxious inferiority complex bobs up again, and it's up to me to dissolve it. So I run over to torment Alimata's baby, who can't figure out whether to love me or to be terrified by me. The child grins, then hollers loud. I chat with the crippled wife, who is still convinced that I have a husband hidden away somewhere. Then I pick up a pestle and help Alimata pound corn for a few minutes. It works. The intimidation wears off. Djeneba warms up and brings her child over. "Alimata told me about the contest," she says in soft Niarafolo. "I want to enter Largaton." She holds up a bundle with high cheekbones and a chiseled jaw. He is ecstatically perfect and tiny—like dollhouse furniture or robin's eggs. Yet it's not right for an infant to look like this—he should have chubby arms and folds in his neck. He should be laughing or crying or spitting or *something*. But he just watches us serenely.

How old is he? I ask her. "Four moons." She hands him to me. He's not wrinkled up like malnourished babies; he's scrubbed clean, and his skin is smooth. He's just unbelievably miniature. "What does he eat?" I ask. "I breast-feed him," she says, biting her lip, as if she might have answered wrong. *"Ki chengué,"* I reassure her. That's good, that's good. I'm bewitched, can't stop looking at this child with long lashes and no flesh. He's angelic and so beautiful—it's hard not to cry. And his eyes are bright, serious, wise. He gazes straight up at me with vivid trust. Unblinking. And he makes no sound at all.

Alimata and Djeneba show up at our courses together. Alimata's stubborn little giant jumps all over her mother's back. She cranes to look over Alimata's shoulder, pummels her mother with playful fists. Largaton snuggles up to Djeneba's back and stays still. He watches everything with his old-wise-man eyes.

When I tell Djeneba that since Largaton is a little small, she should probably come to weigh him every week, she nods eagerly. And every market day she's among the first in line, shoulders squared and smiling as she unties Largaton from her back. She's so proud to be doing the right thing! Just keep breast-feeding, we tell her. Don't give him water or sugar or rice. Just breast milk and the right vaccinations and everything will be okay.

The line on Alimata's daughter's growth chart soars along the top of the optimal range. She walks with confidence by now, eating rice and sauce and even fish! Alimata assures me. Alimata decks her out in bright frilly dresses. Largaton's line wobbles near the bottom for a while. Then it flattens. Then it points downhill.

One market day, Djeneba comes before we've finished setting up the station. Largaton feels hot, she says, pulling him around to her front. His eyes shine as if the moon were behind them. His tiny body burns. Cold baths do nothing. Trips to Sidibé for medicine do nothing. For days, little Largaton is on fire.

A few weeks later, Djeneba flags me down as I'm heading back home from the market. The wives under the mango tree greet me, but their laughter is muted. *"Largaton, wo wi weh,"* says Djeneba. Literally, this means "He doesn't exist anymore"; day-to-day it is used to say "He's not well." I stride right up to the baby, but I'm scared of what I might find. Largaton's eyelids are laced with yellow crust; his long eyelashes are tangled. My heartbeat slows. Nothing more than pink eye. I show Djeneba how to put hot compresses on his eyes and tell her not to let the other kids touch him. I tell her it should go away in days.

In a few days, his eyes have cleared. But mysterious little bumps have cropped up on his chest, on his head. *Boutons,* or "buttons," is the blanket term that applies to any skin ailment—from abscesses and boils to chicken pox and minor rashes. They are a constant and mostly benign plague among children. Some are caused by allergic reactions, others from insect bites or contact with animals. Unless the child complains of pain, boutons remain unexplained and largely ignored.

But Largaton's boutons can't be ignored. They don't burst; they don't fester; they don't grow. They spread. To his belly, to his arms, to his legs. Largaton's boutons are sinister, as if something evil is trying to get out of that tiny body. As I look at him, his delicate brow crumples and his eyes squeeze up. Tears slide across his cheekbone, pass a hard little bouton by his ear. He's not exactly crying. The sound he makes is a soft mewing, as if he's already grown beyond babyish bawling. Beautiful Largaton weeps.

And then one day when I am on my way to the old man's boutique to pick up some sugar, Djeneba stops me in the middle of the road. Her face looks fragile, just like her son's. She puts her hand on my wrist. *"Largaton, wi kou,"* she says. Largaton is dead. Looking at her face, at her hurt eyes, all the puzzle pieces that I've been fighting to keep separate zoom into place. *Of course.* AIDS rears its head in Nambonkaha. Djeneba's husband succumbed. Djeneba's baby succumbed. Djeneba, looking at me with Largaton's eyes and her mouth pinched, is doomed. And who else?

The future—it churns my stomach. This story has no end. Watch the virus invade my village: the first domino has tipped, and soon they'll all be falling down. Djeneba's story isn't one of wanton promiscuity. Or prostitution. Or carelessness. It's just a tale of tradition—a sweet, old, dependable tradition that keeps widows and children from dereliction and poverty. But when AIDS seeps in, good tradition goes bad. If Adama had known to recognize his uncle's killer as AIDS, would he have kept away from his new wife? No. Because tradition overrides pragmatism. If he didn't consummate the marriage, he'd be insulting his dead uncle and his new wife. Trouble with the spirits weighs heavier than gossamer rumors of modern disease.

What will come of this courtyard? Who will go first? Adama, with his shoulders that can hold up anything? The third wife, who limps around the village at a clip and giggles about my hidden husband? Smiling, shining Alimata? When I come back in a few years, will there be no women laughing under the mango tree? What if these children who run back from school in clean uniforms and plastic shoes are reduced to a handful of urchins in rags without the means to continue their education, let alone eat rice with fish?

Other men will die in other towns and cities. Their wives will appear in Nambonkaha to become wives of their brothers and nephews. And no one will know that their blood is infected, that these shy young widows are poisoning the village. Instead of sealing up the holes in the community, this tradition will invite AIDS in to chew through families and leave a lacy trail of orphans and invalids.

.   .   .

Largaton and his mother are the first AIDS victims I've seen in Nambonkaha. For the moment, most cases in Côte d'Ivoire are restricted to urban areas. In Abidjan it's old news. Some say 12 percent of Abidjan's adults are now HIV positive. In a 1998 study, 50 percent of the prostitutes tested positive. But the villages are teetering on the cusp of disaster. There is no brick wall between urban and rural. Sons and daughters living in Abidjan pass through the village all the time; villagers bike into Ferké daily or weekly. And Ferké is all but lost. It is, in essence, a glorified truck stop, a dusty crossroads where you can pick up rice and sauce and a quick lay. Truck drivers are notorious: they breeze into towns and villages along their routes, search out a girl for the night, and move on in the morning. They stop in Nambonkaha only if an axle breaks or a tire bursts along our stretch of road. And usually there's already a girl from Ferké sitting next to them in the cab. They don't often bother the girls from Nambonkaha. But the prospects for promiscuous girls in Ferké look bleak.

And when a Nambonkaha youth with a little money in his pocket bikes into Ferké, it's often those girls that he's hoping to find. He won't say he's paying for sex. He might even call them girlfriends for a little while. They're not *really* prostitutes, since they don't hang out by the brothel, right? They're just girls who will have sex if you make it worth their while.

The *boutiquier*'s son used to be a successful local transporter. He was the only villager with an automobile—a low-riding pickup truck that he kept with him in Ferké for commissioned errands. He moved back to Nambonkaha permanently sometime last February. And now he just squats. He squats day and night on the stoop outside the boutique door, complaining vaguely of incessant diarrhea and disintegrating slowly underneath his faded boubou.

Sidibé and I bite our lips and throw each other wide-eyed glances. Babies die all the time. Largaton's eerie death blends in with the rest without seeming too suspicious—sorcerers have all kinds of tricks when it comes to babies. But a healthy adult just wasting away is peculiar in the village. We should say *something,* shouldn't we? But it's not that easy. As health workers we can proselytize all we want about the dangers of HIV and AIDS and the importance of wearing condoms. Yet when it comes to concrete cases, we are bound and gagged. In a village this small, to associate any invalid with the label "AIDS" is a damning accusation. To hold up anyone as an example is to hex his or her whole family. Behind closed doors at the infirmary or in meetings with Bakary and Dramane, it can be whispered that Djeneba's baby had AIDS, that the *boutiquier's* son is dying of it. It is *never* said in public.

There is a fear that once someone is known to be stricken with the virus, family members and communities will abandon them, not only afraid for their own health but nervous about the implicit danger of sorcery that lingers over the sickbed. If you can get away without admitting that this feared disease is present, there is less reason for abandonment. The community sticks together with the glue of forced ignorance.

Wailing wafts over from the boutique one day in July. The *boutiquier's* son squats no more. We fill up the courtyard between two old concrete houses to mourn. It could be my imagination, but it seems there's a silent ache in the air, a realization that this death is bigger than the loss of a father and son. It seems that the truth is here, in the young people's eyes at least, but it refuses to slip down to their tongues. The dead man's daughter is a clever girl in third grade. His son is about to start first grade. The dead man's wife sits with blank eyes in the corner of her dark house while the vieilles splash the body. When the men carry the shroud to the cemetery, two older women pull a rectangle of thin foam—a mattress—out of the house and scrub it with soap and water. I've never seen this practice before. Maybe the deceased didn't have mattresses at past death ceremonies I've attended. Or maybe they're trying to scour out the pestilence. Washing is usually done with a bounce in the hips and a stream of chatter. These women work with hard rhythm. Their faces are grim and still. Their hands roll and knead and thrash that mattress. Suds fly. Nambonkaha is silent but for the slosh and spray. That mattress will be clean again. If only AIDS were washable—a good scrub with strong hands and market soap might save this family, save this village.

Abi is ladling deep-fried chicken into a bowl one evening when the lamplight etches a lanky silhouette out of the darkness. When the mayor's face moves into the light, Sidibé lets out a pleased laugh. He says, *"Ça fait deux jours!"* which means not that it's been two days since I've seen you, but ages! Abi pulls a chair out as if she had been expecting the mayor all along and plunks down a bowl. The mayor has been spending much of his time in Ferké of late. Sidibé and I have speculated that he's been avoiding the humiliation of the embezzlement scandal, but others have said that he's picked up a new mistress in town.

The wind blows in gusts tonight. We sit on the porch because the air smells like rain. The mayor rolls up a sleeve and reaches for a chicken wing. "I'm thinking of taking my third wife into town to get a sonogram," he says, chewing. "Then we can find out what's not right in her stomach—why she won't get pregnant." He says it nonchalantly, as if it were completely normal for an illiterate planter to know all about medical technology.

"A dozen kids isn't enough?" I laugh. He chuckles and shakes his head. The mayor hasn't talked about struggles with his wives in a long time. Last year's brouhaha has settled into quiet discontent. And since he's not around as much, the three women seem to get along better.

Raindrops spatter the courtyard. The mayor looks off to the west, draws his knees up to his chest, and holds himself in his arms. Surely it's the breeze that makes him cold, but curled up that way he looks small and scared. "Women used to be good," he says. "Kinafou—eh! When her husband was sick, she bathed and fed him and stayed with him all the time. Till the day he died. Nowadays, the first sign you're sick and *pof!*" He claps, "Women assume it's AIDS and take off."

He said *the word*. Wind riffles through the mango tree next door and swoops past our faces, sweet, cool. No one says anything. But that word still ricochets. Was that a plea for help? Does he think he's sick? Words seem to twist in the air between us, but none of us can pick out the right ones. The mayor has said for months that his guts have gone all wrong, that he suffers diarrhea much more than he used to. I've wondered, haven't I? But I don't ask for clarification, don't ask for truths or confessions. This is the village way. I'm bound by it too. No one wants the unhappy stories.

Sidibé coughs an awkward chuckle to break the silence and starts talking about the rain. His daughter scurries out with a broom to clean the floor after the meal. All the unpretty questions just get swept out with the chicken bones.

I have wondered. And I've found myself looking for signs— in the mayor, in people on the streets of Ferké, in educated sons back from Abidjan. It's a terrible habit, to look for death in people's faces. But it's beginning to come naturally. Not out of paranoia, not out of fear. I guess I'm just trying to comprehend the devastation that lies ahead. It's all in the eyes. They go hollow. The skin tightens around them; the skull sticks out on either side; the brows sharpen. The virus sucks away crow's-feet and laugh lines first, then leaves the eyes sunken, haunted, laughterless.

The mayor's eyes are all right. It's just speculation in the end. Just my own fear of the worst. But he's a flagrant philanderer— the worst is a distinct possibility. And he brought it up. If he did have an inkling that he was infected, would that change his ways? Would he start using condoms? Would he stop chasing women? Would the specter of his large family languishing without parents influence him? I doubt it. Not because he's careless or evil. It's just an unfortunate extension of the Now philosophy. It's hard to change behavior today when the consequences are so distant and the precautions are so intrusive. The mayor and the rest of the villagers as well are caught between "It will never happen to me" and "It will definitely happen to me," and neither encourages preventive behavior today.

Bakary and Dramane will talk bluntly about HIV and AIDS.

They have learned all about it since junior high, and we can intelligently discuss the inherent problems in educating the villagers. They can explain how it's transmitted; they can rattle off the symptoms. When I ask how it's prevented, Dramane will say, "Stay faithful to your wives" and Bakary will chime in with "Always use a condom." With minimal fanfare, we've added condoms to the selection of items for sale at the weighing station. I secured a small stash from an NGO in Abidjan, but it's taken weeks to sell just five of them. I can't figure out if no one buys them because it's too embarrassing or because they just don't care. I've gotten in the habit of handing them out as *cadeaux*. Most young men blush under dark skin and bluster, *"Non! Non! Vraiment! Ça va!* I don't need that!" But if I push hard enough, they'll stick one slyly in their pocket. I tell my assistants that it's up to them to talk about condoms to their peers, that clearly no lusty teenager will listen to a *woman* telling him to protect himself. Dramane nods encouragingly, though I don't know if he'd actually evangelize. Bakary just scoffs. He purses his lips when I hold up the little condom package and says, right after explaining how to prevent the disease, "No way, I'm not wearing that."

You need to set the example! I tell him. You're a health worker, too! People will look to you as a model! But Bakary just steps back, wagging a finger and laughing derisively until I grab his shirt and stuff the damn thing in his breast pocket. I laugh too, because showing frustration would get me nowhere, but it's not funny. I have to muster all the sinister threat into my eyes to convince him that this is no joke. I say *"Tu vas voir,"* you'll see, a hundred times. He just chuckles.

When will he get it? When his best friend or brother dies? When no one is left to work the fields or make healthy babies? And the others—the ones who aren't privileged like Bakary, who didn't learn about AIDS, who aren't working as health assistants—will they only get it even further down the road?

To a frightening extent, the villagers don't believe that their behavior has anything to do with getting the virus. They might have heard that unprotected sex leads to HIV infection, but fatalism and sorcery dictate that there is absolutely nothing to be done. If they're going to be infected, by Allah's will or sorcerer's magic, they're going to be infected. End of story. AIDS fits perfectly into the sorcery scheme. Malaria picks off children and is considered routine sacrifice among witches. AIDS signifies a more serious breach of ancestral loyalties or spiritual contracts. Whole *families* fall under the curse. So when a husband dies, and then a baby, and then a mother, the villagers step back and say, Someone must have really done something wrong in that family! They might accept the medical realities of AIDS, but in the end they will attribute the wasting away of their fellow villagers to incorrigible acts of sorcery.

Most of the educated youths understand that AIDS is an epidemic. Like Bakary and Dramane, many have heard how you get it, how you prevent it. This doesn't necessarily mean they write off the curse explanation, but they understand the personal responsibility involved in protecting themselves and others. And still nothing changes. Like Bakary, many choose instant gratification over long-term guarantees.

The American Baptists in their fortresslike hospital in Ferké hold frequent prayer meetings. Their machine runs full throttle, teaching Africans about Jesus, converting Muslims to Christianity. They offer AIDS education only to the converted. They test for the virus during routine bloodwork, but when they find a sample that tests positive, they don't tell unless specifically asked. No one asks. It's easier not to know. But what if the Baptists are passing up the greatest service they could ever do this society? When asked what reason *they* have for not telling, the young missionary who had come to conduct a study on AIDS replied, "It's impolite."

But what about *my* responsibility? I realized too late that Adama's new wife will die of AIDS. I realized too late that AIDS is what made the *boutiquier*'s son squat all day long. So when the mayor scattered hints on Sidibé's porch, why didn't I catch all those unsaid words in the wind and say, "*Monsieur le Maire,* maybe you should go get tested"? Maybe *I'm* afraid of being impolite. Maybe we're all just tied up in our own private taboos.

Sidibé says that, for the most part, his outlook on Africa is optimistic—economics and the political systems are maybe, in the long run, looking up. Africans, he says, are sick of bungling leaders and the old systems. "But AIDS! AIDS!" His voice goes slack. "AIDS might ruin it all." We're sitting on his velour-covered couch after lunch. Snowy footage of the national news rolls off the television screen in stripes. "The one sure way to devastate Africa is to let loose a lethal disease that's transmitted by sex," he says. "Because no matter how you teach, no matter how you plead, Africans love sex, and they're not willing to compromise it with fidelity or condoms." Sidibé slumps. "We always say you can't eat a banana with the peel on."

Even the ones who try to use condoms run into barriers. "In Ferké," Sidibé says, "prostitutes will charge a thousand francs for sex. For sex with a condom, they charge twelve hundred. They say they don't like the way it feels." He sits up straight again and looks at me with his eyebrows pitched down. "And many girls get offended if a man wants to wear a condom. They look at it as a sign that the man thinks they are dirty, or cheap, or already infected."

Government ministers at some meeting appear on the television in gray ribbons; their images climb the screen, their smiles flashing over and over. "It's because of poverty," Sidibé says. "That's one reason AIDS spreads so fast here. A man will offer a young girl some money for sex and she has nothing, so she'll *saut à l'occasion.*" That's not it, though. Prostitutes exacerbate the situation, but the problem is pervasive even without them.

Sidibé speaks of a friend, Pascale, who slept with at least four different women every day. He chuckles and hits his knee as he remembers. "*Pascale était en forme!* All the girls wanted him. He would go to work in the morning and then come home with one girl at ten A.M. There'd be another one waiting for him at lunch, and then a different one at the end of his siesta. Oh! *C'était un homme, deh!* We were all jealous, though he took it too far sometimes. At one point, he slept with a mother, daughter, and niece of the same family." Sidibé shakes his head with a bitter smile and looks out the window. Chickens squabble outside. He gets up and flicks off the television. "And in the end," he continues, "big, manly Pascale was hardly recognizable. I honestly didn't know who he was the last time I saw him. And all those women—he brought many down. *Il a mangé la vie, et la vie l'a mangé.*" He ate life, and life ate him.

There's another story: when a teacher in Sidibé's hometown got infected, he wanted revenge. So he slept with a slew of his students—all girls in their early teens. "I'm ashamed to tell you of him," says Sidibé. "It's a black, black picture, and so many only think of themselves. So few will try to change it."

On a trip to the town of Korhogo, I ran into a friend from Ferké who had come to the hospital to watch her mother die of AIDS. I had never met Bintou's mother before that day, but Bintou says she used to be a *vraie tantie,* the big kind you dread on transport because they smush you up against the window and pile your lap with bags and babies. I never would have guessed it. This woman was thin, bones smooth under her skin. She looked just like Bintou, maybe five years older. Bintou is just past twenty. She stopped school in third grade and has no real vocation. She just wants to be a good wife and a good mother. That day she lolled on a mat on the grass outside her mother's sickroom, and said casually, "The day we brought her, I thought for sure she'd die here." She said that in the ten days since they arrived, two people died in the room—just stopped breathing, life whisked out before their eyes. One old woman lay there dead on the next bed for hours before they took her away to the morgue.

Bintou's mother was released with a hospital bill and no lease on life. She went home and died a few weeks later. Bintou's stepfather died six days before her. She told me they all knew he had the virus ages ago. "But Maman would not believe it. Even when he got sick." In a week Bintou was an orphan; in a week she became responsible for her six siblings.

AIDS education is infiltrating the schools and the public health system and even reaching out to bush communities. NGOs and government programs sponsor skits and education fairs. They publish comic books, posters, pamphlets. There are bumper stickers with slogans: *"Le SIDA ne viendra pas chez moi!"* And T-shirts, visors, television programs, teary pop songs.

AIDS education is a mandatory part of school curriculum, starting in junior high. But it's a sad twist of irony that the ones teaching are among the hardest hit. The schoolteachers are succumbing in record numbers. And even the head of reproductive medicine at the Ferké health base is now a rack of skin and bones.

Sidibé leans forward on his elbows. "I would say that the situation might improve if the economy got better. But there are always those without. There would just be more men with money to spend on women, and always enough women who can be bought. I would say education helps, but look at all the educated ones who are dying. Treating people does nothing to slow infection rates. There is only one way that Africa can rise out of this disaster: an AIDS vaccine. Until that comes, *on est foutu.*" We are screwed.

We are three. Dramane, Sidibé, and me. Three with enough respect among the villagers, enough face time with the world outside, enough health experience to break the silence surrounding AIDS in Nambonkaha. Three and a half, if you count Bakary, who'll talk the talk but leaves the action to others. Everyone else is squeezing their eyes shut.

So what the hell should we do? We can be honest. Lay out all the facts, emphasize personal responsibility, start a dialogue. We can say, Yes, indeed, AIDS has hit the village. And it's going to spread. Don't be scared—just be careful. We can be persistent. Lay out all the facts again. And again. Sell condoms at the market but also at the boutique, at the clinic, and at Dramane's house, where people might be less ashamed to pick them up.

We can work *with* sorcery—accept that it is interpreted as the source of all misfortune and use it instead of fighting it. This might be the work of witches, but don't give up! You can protect yourself. You don't need indigenous stews and magic shells: a small piece of latex can help block the hex, can save others from being cursed.

They might listen, or they might just hear. They might take us seriously, but indifference is so much easier. It might take years for their behavior to change. Some will never change at all. At this point, this is about the best our little team can do to save Nambonkaha from the virus. The rest is up to the villagers.

First, it's time for a formal introduction. Dramane and Bakary and I start drawing up plans for an AIDS Awareness Day—a "SIDA fête," as they're known—in Nambonkaha. Calling it an AIDS *party* sounds absurd, but the villagers won't swallow ugliness without a spoonful of sugar. No one wants harsh truths dredged up.

Dramane is excited about doing a theater piece. Bakary says, "We'll have trivia contests, right? With prizes like they have in SIDA fêtes on TV?" The international NGO responsible for those popular, publicized AIDS events has just opened its first branch in northern Côte d'Ivoire, so I pay a visit to their new office in Korhogo. It's spare but organized, complete with cartoon posters and condom advertisements. My contact man, Issa, is small and all business. He sketches on his calendar as I tell him all our ideas. He says, "Okay, SIDA fête, Nambonkaha, September fourth. Ten A.M." Then he scoots back his chair. "Wait!" I say. That was too easy. There must be more to it. "What should *we* do?" He looks at me quizzically. "Why, nothing. Just find a good spot and hang a white piece of cloth to use as a screen, get a generator for the slide projector, and we'll take care of the rest."

But if they take care of the rest, our SIDA fête will be nothing more than a traveling show. Nambonkaha needs to have a stake in the event; the villagers need a role, or else all the information will leave with Issa and his team when they drive off at the end. So I rush home and call a meeting with Bakary and Dramane to organize some homegrown activities. They won't even talk about it. Not until I've gotten permission from the chief. This must be residue from the last spat—they can't risk another power struggle, so they've fatalistically accepted that this project probably won't pass the chief's inspection. "This is a touchy subject, Guiss," Dramane says. "You must make the plan, and then go over every single step with the chief." He holds up a finger. "And remember that you need to *hint* that you want us to work with you, and then he'll select us as if it were his idea."

"In your country people always want others' plans to succeed," Bakary mutters. "Here they just want to spoil them."

When I visit the chief with the president and Sidibé, it is night already. He invites us into a dark room, and we sit on a woven plastic bench where, I imagine, he sleeps. His ailing battery-run cuckoo clock yodels several times. As I explain everything I want to do, he listens without a word, looking down at his hands. The globe of lamplight barely reaches our faces, but it bathes his hands. He is not a large man, yet his hands are mammoth. He rubs them together, slowly. I can hear the scrape of his callused skin. His palms are cracked and wide; it looks like he could knock down a hut with one blow. The nail of one thumb is a broad, yellowed square, flat and smooth like an ancient tablet. He studies it as if wisdom were etched there.

When I'm done with my petition, he looks up. The only thing I can read in his one good eye is the flame of the lantern dancing. His reply goes first to the president, who rocks forward, then spins it into Dioula for Sidibé. His voice is subdued. I brace myself for rejection. But when Sidibé turns to me, I know we're good: there's victory fighting to keep still in his eyebrows. The chief has spoken for many minutes, but the heart of what he's said is this: "You ask all the time for permission to do your work. You ask for my cooperation, and I try to give it. What you bring has always been good for Nambonkaha. Make your plans as you wish. I trust you."

I'm stunned. It's like being knighted: a few small words of appreciation mean everything coming from the chief. They mean that he sanctions my efforts to improve health in the village even if it involves changing habits or tradition. He has given me free rein.

For our theater piece, we glean actors from the regular crew of young village men and high school boys home on vacation. A few nights before the fête, I summon the cast for our first rehearsal. Half the male population shows up. Without electricity, quiet little Nambonkaha thirsts for nightlife. On moonlit nights, they hang out on the main road. But tonight there's a mission instead of a moon. Everyone wants to be involved. We gather around lanterns in Angélique's courtyard. Her eldest, sixteen-year-old Filomène, has primly agreed to play the sensible girl in our story. Since she isn't allowed out of her courtyard at night, all the men have come to her.

There are two scripts in the running. Mine is a skeleton to be fleshed out by this excited crew. The plot line is simple, and the language, pure *villageois* French, must be translated into Niarafolo. The other script is offered by Dramane's Abidjanais friend Yakou, the computer science student. By tracing the life of a family within its community, it touches on every single issue related to AIDS in Africa. It's brilliant. But far too complex.

So we bushwhack through my script, adding jokes here and clarifications there. The play follows the fortunes of two young men: the careless philanderer *"l'Infidèle"* and *"le Fidèle,"* the prudent one-woman man who always uses condoms. *L'Infidèle,* of course, gets strangely sick, visits the nurse, finds out he has AIDS, and dies. *Le Fidèle* lives happily ever after in blissful monogamy.

The imam's nephew Américain is the Infidèle. Dramane plays his disapproving villager father. *Le Fidèle* is played by an easygoing seventeen-year-old student who makes sure we clarify that it is *unprotected* sex that is dangerous, not just sex. We go over the improved script. Most with lines can read them, but we have to recite them a few times for Américain. He thinks over each one and then nods for the next. He and Dramane fall right into their roles as if they've been waiting for the opportunity to flex their dramatic muscles forever. The first run-through takes an hour—everyone has a stage direction to recommend or a nuance to suggest. Femme Claire's husband's eyebrows keep popping up when he thinks of staging tips. He tells Américain, "When the nurse lists diarrhea as a symptom of AIDS, clutch your stomach and go rushing off! People won't forget that!"

Sidibé's assistant, Issouf, will play the nurse, but he's in Ferké tonight. So Sidibé steps in to help create the dialogue. When we get to the part where the nurse gives the patient his diagnosis, my script reads: "Frankly, *Monsieur l'Infidèle,* you have AIDS." Sidibé says, "No! A nurse would never say how bad it is. That would ruin the patient's life. They'd say, *'Ça va aller.'"* It will be all right. This is interesting. So there's no such thing as terminal illness? I ask. No one is ever dying, they're just taking a long time getting better?

"Sidibé!" I laugh. "We don't *want* the audience to think that '*ça va aller*'! We have to be dramatic or they'll never get how serious it is." Dramane can do drama. He says, "My friend, you are going to *die*," in the voice of a horror-movie announcer. Américain, toothy and sparkling, buckles with imaginary stomach pains, swaggers like a stud with his arm around different "girls" played by boys. The dark night around us sings with energy. We are *creating*, schooled and unschooled alike, men of authority and teenage boys and girls. We are bubbling with talent and purpose.

Filomène is being an extremely good sport. Aside from me—and I don't really count—she is our only female in the cast and crew. The rest of the village girls refuse to put themselves in the limelight. But *l'Infidèle* is a ladies' man, and we need some ladies. Bakary and I bike to a neighboring village to audition. There are a handful of teenage girls pounding corn when we arrive with our offer. It's not hard, we tell them—all you have to do is flirt with one character in the play. They finally accept, but on the day of the rehearsal, they send their younger sisters, ten-year-olds in lacy dresses. Not exactly what we had in mind for the role of seductresses.

The day before the fête, a beautiful young woman from Abidjan comes visiting with her family. She's coy at first, but you can tell she finds the idea of joining the company flattering. A city girl among villagers, she'll relish the chance to strut and preen in front of her village sisters and, of course, all the boys.

The height of rainy season in this slice of savanna means passing thunderstorms several times a week. On the day of the fête I wake up to a steady shower. Not worried! I assure myself. These things dry out by noon as a rule. I run to the school grounds to see how the awning for the guests and elders is holding up. There's not a soul in sight, not a pole set up. I trek back across the village to Bakary's hut. "Can you rally the *jeunes* to set up the awning?

They were supposed to do it last night." "We've already told them to do it," he yawns. "They'll do it." That's not the answer I want. Rain is splattering the mud, spilling off the roof, dashing down the roads. But I refuse to give up faith in the sun. I slosh over to the chief and ask if he could please get the delinquent *jeunes* in order.

The sky is that dreary gray where the clouds look like they'd rather walk than fly, and they sink ever closer to the earth. The *jeunes* finally show up around ten-thirty. But it's raining too hard to lift the awning. It droops in the middle and slides off the poles.

We make a last-minute executive decision to move the whole fête into the derelict school canteen, a one-room structure with a few tables and chairs and resident bats. The floor is carpeted with every kind of dropping known in the village. Abi orders ten girls to start sweeping. Sidibé runs in with a giant bottle of air freshener and sprays till the acrid urine stink mingles with the scent of cheap perfume. Everyone is ordered to find a bench or a chair and bring it now. In the middle of all the fracas, the deputy doctor shows up. What's this? He's only an hour late? How dare he come so early the only time we're not ready? Abi no doubt sees the terror in my face and beckons him to her house for a meal. She glances back at me, my boubou bedraggled, my hair dripping, and says, "Why don't you come too, Guiss?" But villagers are streaming in from the campements. There are clusters on the main road, greeting one another and asking why the fête hasn't started yet. *"Wasn't it supposed to be at nine? Well, it's nearly twelve."* Yet nothing will start till the deputy is good and full and the NGO team arrives. I down a bowl of *riz gras* to prevent collapse and return to supervise the stuffing of all the mothers and elders into the tiny canteen. The elder hierarchy relegates the *jeunes,* our target audience, to the standing space along the walls. Others crowd at each of the window openings, craning in to see what exactly makes an AIDS party.

The room is packed and humid. It quiets as soon as the deputy arrives and takes his spot in the front row. Issa and the NGO team still haven't arrived. A bat slap-slap-slaps over the crowd. I grab Dramane's sleeve and whisper, "I think we can do it on our own." I've made up games and activities just in case we have extra time. "Let's get the opening remarks started." Dramane translates as I introduce the deputy, who delivers a short speech that's mostly about me and not AIDS education. Then he turns and says, "I'm afraid I can't stay longer; I have a meeting in Ferké." This is the first happy news of the day. Ceremonies are about the *grands types,* and this one really needs to be about villagers.

So here we are, my health assistants and I, standing before a sweltering crowd expecting a great fête. The room is silent except for our muttering about how to start from scratch. And then, finally, behind the staccato rain, comes loud modern music. Four hours late, the NGO team swings up in a shiny Peugeot, music blaring, as if they had just come from a tailgate party. They just might have—the big burly one stinks of alcohol. Issa is unapologetic. "We just had to eat lunch before we came," he explains. And then he strides in to set up.

The others linger outside. They're astounded by the size of the crowd. Eh! How did you rally up so many? they ask. There must be at least five hundred! Yes, that's five hundred waiting for *you,* I say, shepherding them inside. The big one greets the audience as if he's a movie star and blurts out, "We brought lots of *cadeaux* for you! Key chains, T-shirts, hats." Issa claps for quiet and bursts into his spiel in brisk Dioula. Dramane translates.

They flick on the slide projector. A fuzzy photograph splashes across the wall—a man's torso scabby and stained. Villagers squint and look sideways and finally relate to one another what exactly it is. The next: a woman's face eaten by dermatitis. Then a skeletal baby lifeless on a cloth. Issa hollers his information above the beating rain. Dramane hollers it in Niarafolo. Then Issa drops his voice and speaks to the elders in the front. He's asking "pardon" in advance, getting the sanction of the elders, because the next images are pretty graphic. I wonder what they're expecting. The next slide shows a chancred penis. Then a festering vagina.

The room crackles with gasps and murmurs. The elders purse

their lips as close-ups of diseased genitalia parade in front of us. Poor Dramane! Issa at least is a stranger, but Dramane is village-grown, and not expected to fill his mouth with these unsaid words.

Is this AIDS education? It seems more like shock therapy. What happened to clarifying the facts? It's not so hard to succinctly and simply explain HIV and AIDS. Where's the part when the villagers learn about prevention and symptoms? If this disfigurement is how they are expected to recognize AIDS, then anyone who looks healthy will be presumed healthy. These scare tactics are misleading.

I want to disappear inside my boubou. I have brought this ghastly porn show to my villagers. I called it a party! They must be terribly offended. Dramane must be so upset. And considering the lack of substance, it might not be worth it at all.

When the slide show ends, Issa pulls out a wooden phallus and demonstrates how to put on a condom. My shoulders relax—this is more what I had in mind: practical knowledge. Issa invites a girl and then a boy to the front of the room to practice. A little giggling embarrassment is refreshing. The awkwardness slides slowly out of the room.

Then he moves on to the trivia portion of his presentation. "There are *cadeaux!*" he says before the questions start. "Lots!" I fight an urge to leap from my chair and tackle him to the ground. He's already redefined HIV/AIDS as a visible disease. He's emphasized the extremes of the illness and not prevention measures. And now he's drawing attention to the gifts and not the answers. This is the grassroots effort of a renowned international NGO? These events are supposed to be well-orchestrated information sessions, not scandalous game shows. Ironically, they even fall short in *cadeaux.* After all the hype, it turns out they only have one T-shirt and one baseball cap. They do, however, have plenty of bumper stickers for this mostly illiterate crowd, and a slew of bottle openers for my Muslim, bottleless village.

The rain slows to a drizzle and then stops. Issa declares that he's finished, and mothers, youths, elders burst out of the stuffy room. "Wait! We're not done!" I shout above the ruckus. Dramane and Bakary send out envoys to rope everyone back. The NGO team thanks me for bringing such an impressive crowd. I can't fake it. I say, "You didn't need to give out anything except condoms, but you gave no condoms at all. I've heard that at most fêtes hundreds are handed out." They slap me on the back as if we go back years. "Of course! We forgot!" They offer me two boxes of ten packets each. "You hand them out, okay?" Then they jump into their car and crank up the music.

The clouds have lifted and left bits of fuzz across the sky. We move the masses next to the school across the field and set up our stage in the mud. The actors are exhilarated, and it's contagious despite my disappointment.

Nambonkaha's theatrical debut begins as dusk seeps in. Peering out the window of the schoolroom that serves as a backstage, I can barely hear the Niarafolo. But I can see just fine. Our Abidjanaise actress wears tight jeans and lipstick, but she speaks too softly. *L'Infidèle* exits too soon in one scene and has to come sauntering back in. *Le Fidèle,* it turns out is almost *fidèle:* there's an improvised episode with another woman, but before he disappears behind the curtain that symbolizes sex, he waves a condom in front of the audience and declares that he doesn't want to get SIDA. I suppose it's more realistic that way. Otherwise, the play glides as if we'd practiced for months. Américain struts as the smooth ladies' man and then huffs indignantly as the AIDS patient. Issouf explains in a clear, loud voice how *L'Infidèle* might have gotten the disease. While he lists all the symptoms, Américain ails hysterically. It must be true that every actor yearns to die on stage—amateur Américain staggers and moans and shudders on his back before falling still.

The audience eats it up. They jump up and down, they're so pleased. Dramane's eyes brim with triumph. "I think it went really well!" he says breathlessly. "It did!" I tell him. "They loved it!" After a miserable day in a hot room staring at hideous photographs and trying to win nonexistent *cadeaux,* the villagers are thrilled by the antics of their own actors and leave in high spirits. Granted, high spirits aren't exactly what we're after with our

AIDS party, but the villagers are far more likely to remember the details if they enjoyed them.

Dramane and Bakary walk toward the village center with me, wired with success. I ask them what they thought of all those horrid pictures. To my surprise, they dismiss my worries. "The villagers don't know any better what to expect from a SIDA fête. They'd never been exposed to the information before. It was awkward, but it was a start." "I'm sorry you had to translate all that graphic stuff," I say. "It's okay," Dramane answers. "As long as they all know those weren't my words, it doesn't matter that they came from my mouth."

Abi catches up to us on the main road. "You're eating with us tonight," she declares in her no-arguing voice. Bathed and bone-tired, I show up early for dinner. She and a visiting niece are sitting close to the fire, grilling fish. I pull up a stool next to them, drop my head to my knees, and sigh. Abi smiles at me and says, "Your day was a success." But I've had a chance to review the afternoon, and, aside from the play, I'm quite certain it wasn't a success.

"How could they just show a bunch of diseased body parts?" I ask. "What has that got to do with preventing AIDS? They did their little condom demonstration, but they didn't explain anything important. I can promise you, very few left that meeting understanding how AIDS is transmitted or how to prevent it. All they're talking about, I'm sure, is those terrible pictures."

Abi's niece is studying to be a midwife. She and Abi glance at each other. Abi says, "Guiss, I really think it was a good thing." Her niece chimes in, "People are too ashamed to see a doctor or tell anyone if there's something wrong with their sex organs. This way they know that it happens to a lot of people. And they learned that sexually transmitted diseases are sometimes linked to AIDS. They know to take them seriously."

Abi's low voice sounds like the earth. "No one ever talks about bodies in the village," she says. "Everyone has sex, but no one ever mentions anything below the waist. Village men don't know the first thing about women's bodies. They go to them in the dark. They don't see anything, and they don't understand anything." She fans the fire with a metal plate. "Today, for the first time, people stopped and thought about each other's bodies and their own too. They saw those pictures together, so they'll talk about them later, even if just in private. You forced them to break a taboo. Maybe they don't know everything about AIDS just yet, but you've knocked down an obstacle to teaching more."

She flips a fish onto a plate, piles on cucumbers, tomatoes, and hot pepper sauce, and hands it to me with a bowl of attiéké. There is nothing better. Tension seeps out my toes. All that rain has left the night cool. The earth smells green. Scorpio stretches across the sky, clawing toward the moon. The Southern Cross has gotten unhinged and slipped sideways behind the mango tree next door. I scoop up a handful of attiéké and cock my head to see the Southern Cross straight. Perspective is all.

16

Tonic

I have scheduled the last course in our healthy-baby contest for this morning at nine. Today I hope to convince the women that family planning can make their lives better. Except that I'm stuck in Ferké, and they're in the village. They know there's a meeting—I sent the message out days ago. The ones from the campements will trickle in and pool in friends' courtyards. And the ones in the village will continue their pounding, pumping, chopping, and washing and wait for somebody to round them up. That's usually my job. But I'm not there. Today we are having guests—illustrious guests whom I am slated to meet at the Shell station in Ferké at eight-thirty to escort back to the village. They are representatives from a small family-planning NGO who are driving two hours just to educate the women of Nambonkaha. I have worked with them before, and been impressed by their professionalism and their motivation. So I'm somewhat petrified by the idea that I'll drag them all the way to the village and find the women scattered.

I have one option. As the morning sun peers sleepily into Ferké, I stop by the shack that serves as the station for all transport north. The token itinerants have arrived early. One flops in a chair; others perch on benches. I scrawl a note that says, "Get the women to the market terrace fast!" and hand it to a familiar one in an envelope marked "Dramane," asking him to drop it off when the next badjan passes through Nambonkaha. As long as time is of no essence, the bush telegraph is a gratifying, efficient system.

But time, today, is essential. "How full is the badjan?" I ask the men, looking around for a vehicle and finding none. The one in a "Surf Naked" T-shirt gnaws a kola nut and then spits the fibers on the ground. "Five seats taken." That means seventeen plus to go before my message can be sent. This badjan might not go anywhere till noon. No choice but to squelch a pang of panic and run back to the Shell station.

The brand-new Shell station store is a squeaky-white air-conditioned oasis where you can buy Snickers, Pringles, Energizer batteries, and champagne. I pace the scrubbed tile floor for two hours, waiting for the family-planning brigade. Two hours to ponder the probability of my women deciding for sure that there's no meeting since I'm not there yet. Finally the brigade arrives in a Land Rover, wearing matching T-shirts. Michel, the head educator, opens the door with a smile and beckons me in. It's like entering an advertisement for African development. There are four in the car, a woman and three men. And they are all talking. Importantly. They pause to greet me, then resume their debate. The topic is how to co-opt traditional men into family planning.

The woman sits in the front passenger seat and gesticulates to the windshield. "You have to approach them with the economic benefits. Less children means fewer mouths to feed, fewer vaccinations, fewer schoolbooks. When you concentrate your earnings on four instead of ten, those four are much more likely to succeed, and be able to support their parents in the end. And you can save money to build a concrete house, to buy television, motorcycle, medicine, *quoi quoi quoi*." The driver says, "It seems so obvious." We slow at the checkpoint, and the gendarme waves us by.

The conversation distracts me a bit from the potential embarrassment of finding an empty village. As we hit the eighth hill, I start to silently fret. Up the last grade, past the baobabs, my eyes pinch shut. Then open just a sliver. Then snap wide open. From the road we can see the splayed sheets of the market terrace roof and, underneath, a beautiful sight: rows upon rows of women's backs. The rush of love is nearly too much to handle; it inflates my lungs, pushes my heart against my ribs, unties my eyebrows, tickles my mouth into a grin. They are *so good*. My women are so good.

Michel and I hop out of the car. The rest are continuing on to the frontier town of Ouangolodougou to check up on birth-control suppliers. "I didn't expect this many," Michel murmurs as we climb up the road bank to the terrace. Seventy women sit quietly in a wide circle. Dramane and Bakary are perched nonchalantly on a table in front, as if punctuality and organization were old tricks for the villagers of Nambonkaha.

Michel begins slowly. He sets up a flip chart and turns the page to a drawing of a bedraggled mother with a herd of emaciated, dirty children clinging to her arms and sitting at her feet. He strolls silently around the empty space at the center of the women. He's tall, well built, magnetic. The women can't take their eyes off him. When he flings a hand toward the picture, they follow the movement as if hypnotized.

With Dramane translating, Michel launches into a methodical report on the life of a mother. "*D'abord,* you have the first pregnancy, which is often hard because your body's not used to it. Maybe you're circumcised, so the birth is very difficult because the skin where the baby comes out has gotten tough." (Here there are gasps throughout the audience.) "But you recover okay. Your stomach goes back to normal mostly, your scars heal, and you're still strong." He turns on his heel and walks directly to a woman in the front row. "How many children do you have?" She looks down bashfully. "Three." "Will you have more?" She nods with a nervous laugh. He looks up again.

"You have your second pregnancy, and maybe your third comes right after, before your body has healed. So all your insides are just repairing themselves, and—*pof!*—here comes another baby to rip them up even more." His audience is rapt. "And after a few more babies, your back sways in because it's used to supporting the weight of a child in your stomach. And your belly gets all stretched out and saggy like an old soccer ball with all the air gone out." (The women throw each other astonished glances.) "Your legs ache, your feet ache, and you just feel tired out like an old woman. It would be nice if you could rest now, but you have eight children and a husband to take care of and the courtyard to clean." (*Hai!* they breathe.) "Your grown daughters might help you, but it takes a lot of work to pump enough water, chop enough wood, and pound enough corn for such a big family."

In the pause before his next point, an older woman stands up in the front row. She plants her hands on her hips and cocks her head. "The way you are talking, I think you are a woman too! How do *you* know how it is for us?"

He smiles, stops his pacing, and walks to the flip chart. "You can tell by looking. Look at an old woman who has no children and then look at one who's had ten. Their bodies look different. Your body can recover from three or four babies. But if you start when you're too young, or keep having them when you're too old, or have many, your body suffers. Look at the woman in this picture. She works hard, but there are too many mouths to feed. They are poor, they don't have enough to eat, they can't go to school. She can't even take care of herself. She is like a field planted with cotton too many years in a row. It can't produce like it used to; all the vitamins have gone out of the soil.

"So how do you save your bodies all the pain and the work?" They stare at him like baby birds waiting for the worm. No one answers. A man who wants them to pay attention to their own needs? This is all too bizarre! "You space your children," he says casually. "Instead of having ten, you have four. You wait a few years between each one to let your body rest." He flips through a few more pictures, showing how you wait till one child can talk before having another. Then he lands on a picture of a smiling family, complete with father, schoolbooks and furniture, and four kids.

A woman from the campements bursts up from her seat. When her year-old son recently died, she sadly returned his defunct carnet to say he could no longer be in the contest. She points to

her stomach, swollen again with child, and says with exasperation, "You say space children. But *how* do we do that when we
just get pregnant all the time?"

It's as if he planted her in the audience. "How *do* you do
that?" he asks them. No one responds, but the audience is crackling. They've forgotten their timidity around this strange man.
Maybe it's his frank manner, maybe it's the fact that he appears
to know all their secrets already, but their shyness has shrugged
right off. The pitch rises. He baits them further: "Nobody knows
a good way to space babies?" Alimata stands up with her neighbor. They bend forward and wag their fingers at him wildly.
Alimata's teeth shine through her grin. Her eyes glitter, but she
wants an end to the teasing. "We *don't* know! Not at all! You
must tell us!"

It's all I can do not to run victory laps around the crowd.
They are bold, they are excited, and we are about to unveil a
miracle. These women, amazingly, have not heard of modern
birth control. And we are the lucky ones who get to open the
door to the knowledge and the power.

Michel lets their voices reach a climax and then says in a low
voice, "*Avec contraceptifs.*" Dramane works out a good translation
since there's no word for "contraceptive" in Niarafolo, and the
women lean in closer. Michel explains natural ways of avoiding
pregnancy, but they no doubt know of those already and have discovered their unreliability the hard way. "But there are more efficient ways too." The next dozen pages of the flip chart depict all
kinds of birth control available in northern Côte d'Ivoire. You can
get an IUD for two thousand CFA—a little over three dollars—
but you have to go to Korhogo to get it. There are suppository
tablets, condoms, diaphragms, a shot in your arm, a capsule in
your shoulder, and several kinds of pills for 10 cents a packet.
He explains how much each costs and how it is used, unbashfully,
methodically. The women titter at the details, but their fascination overrides embarrassment.

"Remember," says Michel, snapping the flip chart shut, "this
is family planning. Not *mother* planning, not *father* planning, but
family planning. Go home and tell your husbands what you

learned today. Discuss with them what is best for your family. Make decisions together. But, please, don't use birth control without their consent—that is only an invitation for disaster."

A few women snort; others shake their heads. Defeat flashes across several faces. Now comes the hard part. Men are the decision makers, not the women. It will not be easy to detach the brood mentality from fathers hoping to prove their manhood. But some women in the mix already have nine children, and more childbearing years in front of them. And others have husbands who might be responsive to modern trends and give this one a try. They're by no means the majority, but they're a start.

The women file out past me, singing out, *"An y che! Guissongui-yo!"* as they always do. But this time there's the thrill of conspiracy in their eyes. We share a secret—a big one—about how women can take charge of their womanhood. A mother who speaks a little French walks by, balancing a bench with an infant on her back. "Yeh!" she laughs. "A *médicament* to cure you of babies!"

Sidibé invites Michel to come to his house for a round of tea. This is a northern, Muslim ritual. Michel is southern and Christian. He's fascinated, wants to know all about the process. "I hear some people make it with milk," he says. "Or mint? How do you know how much sugar to put in?" Sidibé's quick to expound on his favorite tradition; he goes through the ritual with a detailed explanation, emphasizing that the key step is pouring the tea into glasses from far above to make thick foam on top. They're just talking about tea, but their voices are animated and cheerful. Energy bounces and zings around them, and I feel like I'm watching the reunion of long-lost brothers. Michel leans back in the special guest chair with his shot of sugared tea and a look of absolute contentment on his face. When his ride finally appears, we all walk him to the car, shake hands once, twice, and then one last time. We wave until the car turns the corner.

Abi sits back down at the fire to clean and cut meat to be smoked. She knows all about birth control—she's been on the pill since her youngest was born. Sidibé makes sure of it. *"Vraiment,* Guissongui," she says, looking me in the eye when I come to join her, "what happened today was important. Maybe you have changed some women's lives. But to convince the others to stop having so many children, that will be hard work, deh! Sidibé's sisters-in-law, for instance. Sidibé sends pills to them for free. They have nine children each, but the babies are getting big, so now they want another. As if they're dolls! Hah!" Her voice begins to bellow, and she calls across to Sidibé: "I forgot to tell you, *che,*" she says, "your brother's wives want to stop taking the pill."

Sidibé kicks his chair with his heels. "*C'est pas vrai!*" he mutters. "He can't even support what he's got already." Then he nods vigorously, "*C'est bon! C'est bon!* He should have as many as he wants. It's not my choice. But if one more kid comes out of those wives, my charity stops." Abi grins at him. She wiggles her shoulders and bats her eyelashes and coos, "Me, I want to make a national soccer team!" There's a pause while she stops to count. She counts her four kids, the nieces and nephews who sleep under her roof, Tenen the helper. Then she looks up with a helpless laugh. "Eh! We've already got one!"

A week later, I'm scurrying across the village with my basket of market purchases on my head. Roll upon roll of black clouds have trudged in from the east. One of my model mothers calls to me from her courtyard. Assiatou must be in her mid-thirties. She is a stellar baby weigher and has come to every course early and eagerly. Her brood begins with a brawny twenty-something son we all call Tyson, though he seems quite pacifist, and runs through at least seven others before ending with a two-year-old girl.

We exchange greetings, and I tell her that I'm heading home before the sky opens. But she steps up close. She has doelike eyes that barely mask vulnerability or some old sadness. She looks at me shiftily and then whispers right at my cheek. "Guiss, I want the medicine."

The medicine? These are words I usually dread; after all this time I still occasionally have to direct people to Sidibé, insisting that I am not a pharmacist. My confusion catches her off guard. She wants me to understand something but scrambles for the right words. "You know. What you said before." Frustration knots her voice. She nods quick and leans in again. "*Pilé tibé,*" she breathes. "Baby medicine." For a brilliant second as the sky boils above us, Assiatou and I are bonded by our breakthrough. I think we might just glow.

At the market, we've stocked our weighing station with those little blue pill packets just as a reminder, knowing few will be brazen enough to make a purchase in public. Sidibé has the real supply, as well as the tools to gauge a woman's fitness for birth control. "We'll go see Sidibé in the morning," I tell her as the wind spins around us and thunder splinters the clouds. "He has the medicine. He will tell you how to take it." Assiatou clasps my wrist with a little squeeze. With her big shiny eyes, she looks straight into mine, then dashes off before the squall.

17

Boy

Tall grasses swallow Oumar and Moussa a few feet ahead of me. We are winding through the bush—the three of us with Nick— to get to Oumar's fields. Oumar has been raving about them all week. Since school got out in late July, he has worked the fields daily. He is wearing a baseball cap and a blue T-shirt that shows the faded outlines of beach equipment. "Play in the Sun," it says, and that's just what we're doing. He's all pride and dimples as we cut through the last grasses and come upon the first row of corn stalks.

Last week I visited the mayor's fields and found hectares upon hectares of cotton, peanuts, yams, and corn, striping the earth in even lines as far as the eye could see. They were weeded, pruned, and alive with busy wives and children. But nature has been too much for Oumar's family's fields this year. A few days ago a mighty storm broke the nearby dam and swelled the stream into a brown sea. Fields disappeared seven meters under, and just the tallest treetops floated on the surface.

The evidence of the inundation is visible all over Oumar's low-lying fields. Corn stalks lie scraggly and slain. Parts of the rice fields are silty and flattened, as if someone had tried to brush them down. Oumar is unfazed. His voice is high and sweet as he points out the different crops. He snaps one of the downed corn plants, strips the stem to its core, and gives it to me to chew. It's sweet and spongy, like sugar cane. "Birds like to eat the corn," he says, sucking his teeth. "They ruin it. That's why we think it's okay to shoot them with our slingshots."

We sink into mud ruts along the rice fields. Nick bounds over peanut plants, chasing birds and field mice. The boys run through the rice stalks with their hands out. "It's nice to look at, isn't it, Guiss?" Oumar's face bobs just above the brilliant green spears. Moussa appears in dark slivers as he moves. There's clarity in a rice field: light gets bound up in there and turns the whole world bright and beautiful. The sky is heart-stopping blue. "Who works the fields now?" I ask. "Me," Oumar says with a fast grin. "What about your mother?" "*Mon maman,*" he says, confusing her grammatical gender as usual, "comes sometimes too when she's finished cooking. But Papa has to stay home because his head hurts too much."

We cut north in a big loop to find the path home and come across a giant tree cracked by the wind, its trunk fallen parallel to the path. Spots of white seep from the bark. Oumar hops on and scratches at the white stuff with a twig. "It's like chewing gum," he says, pronouncing it "shingum," since the French haven't come up with a better word. "Try it." It tastes like nothing and squeaks a bit, but it does feel like gum. I'm chewing pure latex. In the south, rubber trees are one of the most lucrative crops, thanks to this pricey plastic that dribbles out. Here they scrape it out with twigs and use it as glue or gum. Pockets crammed with tomatoes, arms full of corncobs, chewing tiny bits of rubber, we head back to the village.

They'd like to draw, they say, so I unfurl my orange mat under the mango tree and bring out scrap paper and colored pencils. Oumar has cracked open their artistic horizons by drawing, instead of just squarish stick figures playing soccer, things he sees: a pen, a chicken, a hoe. He and Moussa both concentrate hard on depicting my mango tree from underneath it. I'm cleaning house. My little pail of noncompostable trash fills only every few weeks. I usually dump it in a shallow pit outside my courtyard and set it on fire. Routinely, children come running, no matter how empty the village seems. Today Moussa and Oumar are fire-side in a flash. They eye the prospects eagerly as flames start to lick the edges of envelopes and old rags. Then Moussa swoops in for a used-up Scotch tape dispenser, an empty saline bottle. "*Mais! Mais!* How could you!" he scolds. He ferrets them away with a righteous glance.

Within minutes, little feet thump in from every direction. A hundred small hands dodge flames to retrieve derelict treasures: scrolled toothpaste tubes, fuzzy photographs, empty matchboxes. They retreat proudly with their booty. Moussa is curled around his drawing when I come back with my empty pail. He gathers his collection of loot and unloads it on my table with an air of triumph: Look what you would have tossed if it weren't for me! "Please put these in my bag," he says, referring to the ragged Ziploc that holds his crumpled pages of alphabet practice and his pen. He keeps all of his prized possessions at my house for safeguarding from his brothers. Thus, the clutter I was happy to be done with finds its way back into the house. I'm such a sucker.

Oumar agrees hesitantly to come back after dinner for lessons like he used to before Nick bit him. He shows up at nightfall with his sputtering old lantern. I run a two-ring circus, alternately reading with Oumar and teaching basic words to Moussa and Abou. The latter have been coming every other night to practice writing their names, although Abou still hasn't figured out what his last name is. "Go home and ask your mother!" I've told him nightly. He nods eagerly each time and returns the next day smacking his forehead with his hand. "I forgot again!" Moussa, on the other hand, has decided his last name is Yéo, even though his older brother Mandou goes by Ouattara. Oumar reads steadily, but he's just started fourth grade, and his new book is much harder than the last. We crawl through tonight's story, his voice like soft chimes, his expression serious.

The lamplight bronzes their faces, their small hands, cracked and dry. They are laughing and happy, and I don't really want them to go when the lessons are done. I put Oumar's corn on the flame to roast and toss them a magazine. It's a *New Yorker*. Not much in the way of glossy photos and bright colors, but they're content with all those words crammed together and the funny-looking scribbles. "What is that?" they ask, pointing to a cartoon. They've seen the pictures I've drawn for my health activities. They've seen the true-to-life drawings in their textbooks. But these sketches baffle them. "It's a drawing, just like you draw," I say. "See that's a woman, and that's a man, and they're sitting at a table, talking." Their eyes go bright and that precious sound of comprehension comes from all three at once: "Aaaanhaaaaa!" They've got it. But then they peer closer at the potato-shaped heads with dotted eyes and no necks. "Are there really people who look like that?" they want to know. "Not really," I say. "They're drawn that way to look funny, to make people laugh." "Is that his nose?" Moussa giggles. I nod. Pages ruffle by—*look at all the noses!* They slam their fingers down on fat ones, pointy ones, ski-jump ones, declaring, *"Fonana! Fonana! Fonana!"* at each one. Nose! Nose! Nose! Then they come to a sketch of a rocket. "What's this, Guissongui? An airplane?"

"It's a special airplane that can go way above the clouds, all the way to where the moon and the stars are." Moussa sits up straighter, says, "Haï!" Oumar's eyes are wide and incredulous. He studies the picture again and then looks up at me. His voice lilts on soft night air. He asks me, "Guiss, when they go up there, do they see God?"

Abou comes to lessons alone tonight. He appears first as just a dark smudge outside my door. *"Bon soir, Abou,"* I say, but he doesn't respond. There's a crackle of paper, then a white scrap flattened against the screen. *"Regarde,"* he says, so I squint at it with the lantern held up. His mouth twitches in the gold light. In penciled cursive, floating a little toward the end, the word "Sékongo" is written. Abou's last name. He's awfully proud. Abou petitioned hard to join our lessons, but in the end what he wants is the power to write his name and the ability to copy words. Meanings, reading he has no patience for. And why should he? The only person he ever sees reading for pleasure is me. One of the only written words in the village is on the sign that says, "Nambonkaha." And he can recognize that now. He doesn't care about the rest.

He sits on my mat and plays the syllable-matching card game I've made. "Where's Moussa?" I ask him. "Oh, he's up there." That means he's hanging out with the boys on the other end of the village, near the butcher stall. "And Oumar?" He shuffles the paper syllables around. "He's sick. You know, his legs hurt."

It's nothing new—another episode in Oumar's struggle with his own joints. The pains seem to come every couple of months, making him limp more than usual. But in the morning, his little sister walks by with her little sister tied onto her back. "How's Oumar?" I ask. "He's so sick," she says. Her cheerful little face turns serious and adult. "He can't even walk." So I start running.

Oumar lies on a pocked foam mattress, skinny, all black angles as my eyes adjust to the dark room. I sit next to him and his mother kneels above, eager to hear what I have to say. She is trusting, so sure that I can save him, but too modest for any request. Oumar sleeps, but when I put a hand on his hot body, he wakes up. His voice catches in his throat. My guts plummet. He sounds deathly weak. But it's just sleep playing in his airways. He clears his throat and tells me what hurts, though it's obvious. His knee and his elbow are burning, hard, swollen. They're thicker than my own, but stuck on brittle legs and arms. His ribs bow out, his eyelids droop. Still, he looks at me with eyes bright with pain, and he smiles a helpless, hopeless small smile.

"*Eh, mon petit mari!*" I whisper into the dark. His mother breathes a laugh. She won't speak French, but she understands most of what I say. I run my hand from his knee to his ankle. His shin is covered with rows of chalky white circles. Sidibé, man of modern medicine, has told me incredulously of traditional healers fixing broken bones in seconds, chasing away long-term illnesses with secret concoctions. But Oumar's dots of kaolin, some pink, some white, have gotten him nowhere. He can't stand, can't walk; he can't even begin to bend his right leg.

In the early days I made rules for myself about playing bene-factor. No giving out medicine. No paying for doctor's visits. No lending money. They were self-preservation measures. I knew that if I started out looking like a moneylender, I'd have trouble living it down. But those rules have crumbled. Everything has grown so much bigger than righteous principle. The village is no longer my stage; it's my home. And this sad, suffering boy is my brother. There is not a second guess anywhere in my head or heart. I say, Get him ready. I'm taking him to the Baptists.

And I have faith, so much faith in Western medicine. I'm confident, when it comes down to it, that the Baptists will be able to reap some miracle upon Oumar and fix his joints for good. I've read through my health manual a hundred times and decided the disease must be arthritis of some sort—not curable even in New York City. But I'm still convinced that this boy can be helped with a dose of modern medicine.

When I get back to their courtyard an hour or two later, Oumar is dressed in his best shirt and clean khaki pants. But he is still prostrate. He lifts his shoulders, but his elbow won't support his weight, and neither will his legs. His uncle has come in from the campements. He is young and tall and looks just like Oumar's beautiful mother. Without saying a word, he lifts Oumar—that smiling mouth all twisted—high in the air and seats him on one shoulder. They cut a strange, sad figure: one strong and healthy, the other frail and crooked, together as tall as the thatch roofs. Oumar's father pulls on his overcoat, whose slightly puffed sleeves indicate that its first owner was female, and our sad parade winds to the road.

The benches on the terrace of the Baptist hospital are cluttered with slumped bodies and dour faces. Oumar lies amid suffering elders and screeching babies. He's brave, resigned. And when they finally call him in, the Nigerian doctor can't hide his dismay. "It's infected," he tells me in English. "It must have gotten into his blood." They plunk Oumar down in a chair and unsheathe a four-inch needle. Oumar scrunches his eyes but says nothing as the needle disappears into his knee. Muddy pus wells into the tube, filling it slowly. Oumar's fragile father stands beside him, and repeats, "Ça va, Oumar, ça va?" I hold his hands from the back, and say, "Pinch me hard when it hurts—that way we'll share the pain." But he never does. He just holds my hand tight and swallows gasps. The doctor rubs his knee. That long needle sucks out six syringes' worth of poison. Oumar's face screws up, but he stays quiet. They take blood, hook him up to an IV, and set him up in a bed in a room with a few other children. "He'll be here till we get the results back," the doctor tells me. And once he's left, I realize we have come completely unprepared. Most hospitals are do-it-yourself facilities. The family has to take up temporary residence to take care of their patients. Relatives sleep, cook, and wash in the courtyard. Only Oumar's father has come. Not imagining they might be here days, I've forgotten to tell him to bring a change of clothes, a mat to sleep on, pagnes to use as towels, pots to cook with. And I'm not sure where my responsibility ends: has Oumar's father got any money of his own, or will I be feeding both?

I ask Oumar what he would like for lunch. "Meat!" he says in a weak but determined voice. Meat? How I take things for granted! I've always bypassed the butchers who grill gristled beef kebobs right next to the cows' heads in the market. Even when they offer me one for free I refuse. And yet a whole meal of meat is the biggest treat Oumar can think of. When I return with a greasy paper full of meat, he sits up with a grin and eats like a champion. His chiming voice is back. *"Merci, Guissongui, c'est très, très, très gentille!"*

But whatever it was that dissolved the pain wears off in midafternoon. He writhes on the bed, and then the sound barrier breaks. He whimpers quietly. Then tears burst from his eyes and he lets out a scratchy, gut-wrenching cry. *"Ya yohhhh! Ya yohhhh!"* Again and again. I've never heard anything like it. He must be calling for his mother, *"ya."* All that pain gangs up behind the words to push them out: *"Ya yohhhh!"* I run for a nurse, who comes in within minutes with yet another needle. It just takes seconds. Oumar sleeps, artificially serene. My throat hurts from swallowing so much pain.

I leave him there after dinner and sleep at a friend's house in town, expecting naively that my patient will be discharged in the morning. I hope to see one of the American doctors, who might get to the bottom of this with me. But in the morning the Nigerian doctor tells me it'll be at least four days while they wait for blood work. Oumar is weak and chilled, wrapped up in a pagne. I give him the tank top I wore the day before. He beams and shrugs it on like a piece of home; the armholes gape at his lower ribs; the back pools behind him on the bed.

Some villagers who happen to be in town stop by to see how we're doing. We're easy to find; they just ask anyone for the little boy who came with the *toubabou mouso,* and everyone seems to know. They stand looking at Oumar forlornly, and, embarrassingly, they heap praise on me.

For six days I make a pilgrimage into town, bearing grilled meat, alloco, fruit, cookies. If I were African, I would tote in my fire rocks and cook rice and sauce for him. I explain that I'm no good at that, hoping he understands, and hand him another greasy bag of beef. His father sits, day and night, by his side. He sleeps curled on a borrowed mat on the floor at the foot of the bed. But when I ask him if he wants anything from the village, he can think of nothing except an extra pagne.

At the end of six days, when the doctor finally unplugs Oumar from his drip, we are short a remedy. His face is rounder—not chubby, exactly, it's just that he has cheeks where before he had only cheekbones. I assume at first it must be from the medicine, but maybe all the grease and protein have finally put some weight on him. The Nigerian doctor surmises that the disease is juvenile arthritis, a permanent condition prone to infections. I want more information. But this is not a doctor's office, it's a busy hospital, and the Baptist doctors whom I've endowed with all the touchy-feeliness of family practitioners all seem to be on vacation. I get only bare advice when I ask. And a little traditional fatalism: really, there's not much you can do, except catch the infections early. We stock up on painkillers and anti-inflammatories and hobble home. After a week of treatment, Oumar can hardly put weight on his left leg, and his right elbow remains too swollen to bend. When our taxi pulls up as close to Oumar's courtyard as the paths will allow, we're welcomed as if we've just brought a POW back from the war. His mother laughs, "You've gotten fatter!" His little sister, with the littler one on her back, dances in circles around him. But I can only feel a pang of disappointment that, despite all the drugs, he cannot dance with her.

I leave Oumar sitting like an elder with a cane at his side. Abou walks ahead of me on the path to my house. He had come to check on the arrival and caught me helping Oumar limp home, explaining the medications. Abou pivots on the path and looks at my feet. *"Tu as bien fait, hein?"* he says in a clear and earnest voice. You've done good. Then he turns and walks on. All the gushing of the adults has just embarrassed me. But this quick, simple approval from a twelve-year-old means everything.

I stop by Oumar's house day after day, to make sure he's taking the medicine right, to show him how to exercise his joints. School is out of the question; fields are forgotten. He just sits in a chair with his puffed-up knee sticking out in front of him, covered again with rows of kaolin as a backup to the pills. And slowly, slowly Oumar starts to walk stiffly with a cane, then fast enough to hobble after his friends. The knee shrinks a little, but never enough. And I wonder, What's in there? What won't go away? Too much blood? Some kind of cartilage? Pus from the old infection? I imagine that Oumar's knee is crowded with curses, all twisted up and calcified, a lifetime supply of pain.

18

Cadeaux

After the fiasco of the AIDS fête planning, the whole village has pitched in on the preparations for the healthy-baby awards ceremony in October. Early in the morning, the awning is up on the school field, the *grand type* armchairs are in place, and stacks of plastic chairs are arriving from the campements on the backs of mopeds. A crew of older women has set up a winding line of fire rocks by the school director's house, and they're busy sloshing water and rice in giant calabashes.

It seems like a storybook beginning, but it's not—quite. The women insisted on four liters of oil for the sauce, and maybe that's a fair estimate, but *four?* Eh, Allah! Oil is expensive! Donations from merchants in town have covered the majority of the cost of food and prizes, but I've put up at least fifty dollars. (A paltry sum till you consider it's a quarter of my monthly stipend.) And Abi, preparing for the onslaught of *grands types* eating at her house, expropriates nearly half the Maggi cubes, though surely they won't *all* be going into this meal. Then Sidibé drives up in the early morning with his son looking peaked on the back of his moped. "I think Tidiane might have typhoid," his says, his voice ringing with apology and desperation. "I have to take him to the hospital in Ferké, and I don't know if I'll be back in time for the fête. Pardon, Guiss." Please don't worry! I tell him *Allez-y!* Help your son! May Allah protect you! But there's a major player out for the count.

At the last women's meeting, I called for volunteers to help out with the award ceremony. Thirty hands went up, but I asked just ten to meet me this morning. Dramane and I pull them into a circle under a mango tree hours before the fête. "This contest is all about you," we tell them. "It's about being good mothers and knowing how to keep children healthy. So that everyone understands what you've accomplished, we want you to participate in the activities. We'd like you to present what you've learned during our courses."

They swing their heads to look at one another, murmuring, "*Haï!*" I feel like I need to give them a way out. "I know the first course was six months ago, so we'll help you with what to say. Just try to remember what we talked about."

I have come with a list of key points from each of the six courses, just in case they draw blanks. These women couldn't take notes, and they're not used to memorizing—how can we really expect them to have retained the information? I'll nudge their memories, but I'm prepared for no more than halting answers.

"Okay, let's start with the course on nutrition and weaning," says Dramane. I hold my breath. This is the litmus test of the whole contest, of half a year of work. "Who remembers something about it?"

The women look down at their feet, shift in their chairs. A cluster of sheep sidles noisily up to scavenge the last of the fallen mangos. Three women simultaneously pick up pebbles to hurl at them. Still no one says a word. This is okay, really; I didn't expect them to remember from that long ago. I'm sure they paid attention, but maybe they just didn't understand. They never went to school, probably couldn't discern my drawings. Excuses reel through my head—to reassure them, to reassure myself. It's all too quiet under the mango tree.

Then Alimata looks up from her hands and straight at me. She says, "You should give breast milk and nothing else till your baby has five moons."

Eh! Dieu merci! Relief nearly catapults me onto her lap. The other women lean in a little, recognition spreading on their faces, as if they just needed her cue to unlock their tongues. Bakary's sister-in-law says, "Babies when they start to walk should eat lots of sauce with meat in it and not just kabato, or else they won't grow fat."

Moussa's mother, Massieta, says, "That water stuff that comes out instead of milk when the baby is just born is good for him to drink." Another adds, "Then milk will come after a few days."

It's a conversation. No one's scrounging for ideas—they're interrupting one another, responding, finishing each other's sentences. All of them have something to say! About every topic! They regurgitate details I'd just assumed were casualties of time. They can list the best ways to keep away malaria-toting mosquitoes. They can recount the price of every single kind of contraception Michel named. They can explain the basics of how AIDS is transmitted and how it's prevented. Granted, we have to snip some responses, straighten out some others, expand on most for reinforcement's sake. But all the lessons planned, all the hours of discouraged waiting for women to show up, all the battles with planting season and NGOs have paid off! Ten illiterate women have learned and understood. And if they have, many of the others might have too. I jump up to clasp every woman's hand with both of mine, to grin and say, *An y che, an y che, an y che, mi luoh, an y che!* Thank you, my sister! But I what I really want to do is dance for them as they do for me, to bend low and move my feet in a blur, to crouch at their knees till they recognize my appreciation and touch my shoulder.

We're right on schedule: two hours late. Hundreds of villagers hunker down on benches and chairs under the awning and the nearby mango tree. Our plush seats fill with all stripes of *grand type:* the deputy doctor, looking importantly bored; Dominique and his NGO team, who nearly ruined this moment with their own contest; the village cadre Siaka, up from the capital. Fluffy speeches ensue; each guest and several elders ramble through exhaustive praise and thanks. Clustered together in our blue weighing uniforms, Dramane, Bakary, and I stand before the crowd. I explain the structure of the fête. And then these ten women leave their Niarafolo timidity in their seats and assemble in a line of jumbled colors in front of the crowd. Dramane steps forward to translate their speeches for the non-Niarafolo members of the audience. But Siaka, dashing in a boubou so white it zings, jumps up with his hand raised.

"You're their teacher, Dramane," he says, facing the audience, "so you know all the right answers. How will we know if you're changing what the women say?" He speaks in rapid French and ends most sentences with a shrug and a laugh. "*Tu vois?* Without even meaning to, you might adjust their words to make them sound more correct. We want to see what they really know, so how about I translate?" He gets the audience's sanction and Dramane steps back, amused. There's nothing belittling in Siaka's tone—with a few sentences he's made the ceremony dynamic, drawn together the program, the villagers, and the guests. It's as if he were written into our script.

Assiatou, who asked me for "baby medicine," is the first up. Her topic is nutrition and weaning. Beads of sweat spring up on her forehead. I realize at the last minute I forgot to give them pointers on how to speak in front of a crowd. But Assiatou needs no pointers. She takes a shallow breath and belts out the information. Halfway through, her baby notices everyone watching and starts bawling. In a perfect visual aid, Assiatou flips a breast out of her neckline and continues her speech while nursing.

Siaka translates with great seriousness, as if he's never heard these ideas before. "I just want to make sure I got it right," he says, leaning forward before Assiatou can move back in line. "You say you should start giving porridge at about five moons? What kind of porridge was that again? Are you sure eggs won't turn children into bandits?" The tension in her face bursts into a bashful grin. She knows the answers. It would be so easy for him to mock these women with a touch of sarcasm, but instead he's mocking himself. He's playing the dummy because everyone knows he's not. He relays Assiatou's answers to the deputy doctor, to Dominique and his team. They nod and throw in a few extra facts. This is incredible. These *grands types* have abandoned their patently dulled expressions—they're playing along!

Assiatou steps back into the line of women, breathing audibly. Massieta unrolls the illustration of a dirty courtyard that I drew for the hygiene course. She points out the unkempt, distracted mother at the center of the picture. "This is Drianchen." She even remembered the name I used four months ago! "She doesn't take care of her courtyard. See, the goat is eating from her mortar. There are flies on the rice she prepared. Her baby is going to the bathroom in the courtyard."

Siaka notes what she's skipped over. "What about the puddle next to the house? Is that okay?" And spunky Massieta laughs and says, "No, that's where bugs make their babies."

Here is a highly respected, educated man completely involved in what the women are saying, accepting their messages, challenging them for more, and treating humble mothers as equals, as teachers. Nambonkaha men do not relate to wives this way, especially in public. They're listening, I'm certain, but without Siaka's regurgitation they might not have taken the women's words as seriously. The ceremony is cutting edge for most of these traditional villagers. Siaka has legitimized the women's speeches, reaffirmed their progress.

The president's third wife stands to talk about HIV and AIDS. She turns her face toward the sky and hollers out the basic facts with her eyes cast down. In two minutes flat, she's torn through all sorts of taboos: a woman openly discussing sex in front of all those men and elders! Outrageous! Except that Siaka doesn't seem to think it's all that weird, and the *grands types* don't either, so maybe . . . they're on to something. Maybe it's okay.

Behind her Dramane and I wave boxes of condoms and remind the audience that they can be purchased at Dramane's house, the market, and the infirmary. But Siaka wants to talk about them a little more. He hops up to our table again, and with feigned puzzlement, he says, "Can I see one of those things?" I hand him a packet. "So this is a *capote?*" He unravels a string of condom pouches. And then he turns to the audience and explains exactly how to put one on. They heard this during the frenzied demonstration with a wooden phallus during our AIDS fête, but this is no stranger who can drive off and leave shame behind. This is their own distinguished uncle, brother, son playing the compromising role of sex educator. Perhaps this is how people will start to change their behavior: by listening to the wisdom of a respected, modern village son.

Alimata steps forward and explains birth control, reiterating the exact prices of each method. Siaka's eyebrows shoot up, and he glances at the *grands types* to see if they've registered her accuracy. My women are teaching their husbands, their fathers, their elders, and Siaka even! They have strength, *so much strength*—it breathes and has many facets to it. I stand to the side, with Siaka and the women at center stage. And I bite my lip to keep in the joy, tangle my fingers so my arms won't fling out and send me twirling in the sunshine. There is little better than this.

The next part of the fête might not be so blissful. We've come to the meting out of gifts. There's a chance that squabbling and opportunism will erupt, and I'd rather not be the responsible party. Américain and other weighing-table regulars are on hand to bring the prizes out of the classroom. Bit by bit, the grass before our audience fills with rows of shiny buckets, big plastic cups used as potties, and drinking cups, each stuffed with some combination of T-shirts, talcum powder donated by Sidibé and Abi, soap, bibs, toothbrushes, powdered milk, tubes of lotion, dishcloths, and more. The crowd whispers at first, but as the gifts keep coming, the pitch rises.

The rows stretch out, bright strings of promise. And I realize, looking over the rainbow-colored field, that these *cadeaux* are no longer carrots, no longer lures. The women deserve them. Today's spoils exceed any obligation to the contest, yet, for once, I'm not worried about excess.

I'm giving without any tightness in my chest that it might skew my reputation in the village. I am finally loaded down with *cadeaux for* them instead of *from* them.

Kinafou, the president of the women, strides over to the buckets to get a better look. She cocks her head, gasps "Yeh!" and bites her knuckle. We have compensated everyone who came to at least one course. Twenty-four women have met all the requirements: they weighed regularly, followed the vaccination program, and attended our courses every month. The buckets stuffed with prizes will go to them. Eighteen missed just one vaccination or course. Sixteen mothers joined late or gave birth during the contest and signed up afterward. They'll get the plastic potties.

Only twenty-two have done a below-average job of meeting our criteria. A few were admittedly latch-ons fishing for gifts after seeing the windfall from the breast-feeding fête. Their cups contain powdered milk and Maggi cubes. (Mariam the Burkinabe, for all her promises, is, I'm sad to say, among the twenty-two.)

Our *grands types* take turns presenting the prizes as I call out the names. "Sékongo Pétidjumatchen! Soro Kadiolossori! Ouattara Siengbelegnon!" The women's faces are sober as they shake the *grand type*'s hands. When they get to me, they're swallowing laughter. Maybe it's the way their names roll off my tongue— there are little inflections I still get wrong. But it could be that their smiles have nowhere to go but out. Aside from painful wedding nights, they've never been the stars of the show before. It's like graduation, the way they pass through to shake our hands and then move off to a chair set up in front of the school to have their picture taken. And if there are squabbles, maybe from those twenty-two, who looked a wee bit sheepish collecting their cups, I never hear a word of it.

The woman who wanted to enter her wrinkled, malnourished infant at the beginning of the contest shows up again with a chubby boy on her hip. My assistants, stunned into silence when they saw the child months ago, jabber about how fat he's gotten. Sidibé putters in with Tidiane smiling behind him, just in time to hand out the last prizes. Siaka sends a petit to fetch bottles of orange Fanta, chilling mysteriously somewhere in this unelectrified village, and offers them to our guests. The ceremony ends with a dance contest arranged by Dramane to "*animer le coin.*" Our crew of *grands types* becomes a panel of judges. They've gone from formally haughty to guardedly affable to raucous and weeping with laughter at the modern-dance moves of villagers used to balafons.

The villagers devour huge bowls of *riz gras*. The *grands types* mosey down to Sidibé's house for *riz gras* with the good chunks of meat, finagled by Abi from the fête goat, though I'd hoped the women might get some. When Dramane, Bakary, and I finally make sure the mass consumption at the party grounds is under control and appear at Sidibé's for our share, the *grands types* are lined up in chairs in the courtyard, stuffed and stretched out, shifting occasionally like a row of sunbathing walruses.

Usually women leave soon after the ceremonies to get home to start cooking. We've scheduled a soccer game just in case a few want to stay. Matches happen all the time, and the only ones watching are wistful men who've gotten too old to keep up. But the women—nearly all of them—haul their benches around to the field, take their spots, backs straight in their complets, and watch avidly. They want to wring every drop from this day. The players wear tattered shorts or old pants cut off at the knee. Their feet are bare or falling out of plastic shoes. They play excellently, lithe, strong, sliding and careening across the field, punting the ball with bare toes. The referee wears no stripes among these motley players, but it's hard to miss him. He's decked out in shining teal silk pajamas. Anything goes.

I have asked the chief to order the balafon band to play after the fête, expecting an hour or two of halfhearted, prescribed dancing. But at dusk, no one seems ready to go home. Siaka dashes off to Ferké in his car and returns with a generator. All the chairs are moved from the school grounds to the middle of the village. The generator coughs on, and a corner of the night lights up so that the festivities can last till dawn.

I dance for them for hours, circling with the mothers, whose winning babies bob sleepily on their backs. They dance for me, hold up my arms to honor me, crouch at my knees when I sit. Siaka and Sidibé take chairs right next to the dancers. They say, "Eh! Guiss! *Viens t'asseoir!* You must be tired!" I'm too exhilarated to stop for long. But I do stop, just to say thank you again for the light. Thank you for the sodas. Thank you for abolishing hierarchy for a day. Thank you for turning good words into lessons for everybody. Thank you for being the grandest kind of *type:* open-minded, forward-thinking, and so good for this village.

Past midnight, sleep is oozing into my feet, turning my steps into shuffles. I don't want to leave this good night, but it's starry and clear away from the bulbs, and silence feels good on my ears. I sleep long, deep, dreaming to the beat of the balafon. The women keep on till morning, elbows pumping, shoulders switching, feet hammering the ground. Their babies dance in their sleep.

●

19

Rising

For most villagers, even Abidjan is too far away to count. They follow the political situation in the country like a show that's only minimally entertaining, watched on a television with bad reception. So when a government budget cut sparks months of countrywide student strikes that paralyze the educational system, Nambonkaha's classrooms remain full. And when international aid organizations withdraw their support after the disappearance of a $26 million European Union loan to the Health Ministry, the few villagers who hear just smirk. What else can they do? President Bédié feigns outrage, fires his health minister, and turns select members of his herd into scapegoats. He declares that the perpetrators will reimburse their countrymen, and he hikes up gas prices. Taxi drivers raise their fares, and transport everywhere gets more expensive. Except on the road to Ferké: our badjan fare stays put. The villagers gripe about the extra ten cents they have to surrender for a bottle of gas for their mopeds. Nambonkaha is otherwise unfazed.

President Bédié pays a visit to the north in late October. Smooth black pavement is slapped down on every road he travels, like a red carpet rolled out to hide the northern dust. It is the first obvious infrastructure improvement to hit the north in ages. Some villagers, including Dramane, wear T-shirts with Bédié's face at the welcoming rally in Ferké. "You're a Bédié man?" I ask him. He hedges. "Not exactly." The whole "candidate" idea still sits a little funny here. Multipartyism is just a decade old; everyone is used to having only one choice: the ruling PDCI (Parti Démocratique de la Côte d'Ivoire). The number of political parties is growing, but they are distinguished less by platform and more by religion and tribe. In the most passive way possible, Nambonkaha villagers support the opposition candidate, Alassane Ouattara, a Muslim from the north. No matter—when the president comes, they go just to see him. They listen to his toothy promises and come back without much criticism, or much to say about it at all.

A few weeks after his visit, Bédié arrests an assortment of opposition leaders for organizing demonstrations. Elections are approaching in 2000, and Ouattara is gaining popularity in the north. With unmasked desperation, Bédié searches for a reason to disqualify his rival. He lands on the question of citizenship. Ouattara, he declares, is not an Ivorian but actually hails from Burkina Faso. Bédié and his cohorts dig up an old study-abroad application in which Ouattara listed himself as Burkinabe. Somehow it trumps his passport and identity cards, which claim that he's Ivorian. Meanwhile, the criteria for being Ivorian become more and more narrow.

At issue is the definition of "Ivoirité," a jingoistic term roughly translated as Ivoirianness. Côte d'Ivoire is a country of immigrants—almost all of its sixty-four tribes have roots elsewhere, and a third of its population are foreigners who have ambled in since the economic boom in the 1970s. Bédié declares that for one to qualify as an Ivorian, one's parents must have been born in the country. Yet the country was not even established until 1960; the ruling puts most of the population beyond the pale. It even disqualifies beloved former president Houphouët-Boigny, who had to go to Ghana to bury his father. At the time, he was revered for showing respect to his elders. No one focused on the fact that his family came from Ghana. Somehow the same concessions don't apply to Ouattara.

Ouattara's supporters throughout the country are outraged by the ruling. In Korhogo they chase the *sous-préfet* from his house, beat up a gendarme, and get socked with tear gas. In Ferké, youths take to the streets—dozens maybe, not hundreds—but enough to burn tires on the main road and set fire to the government general store, which is, ironically, the only spot where opposition papers were sold. The fonctionnaires and a few young men ride into town to gawk at the black rubber scars and the rubble. The rest of the villagers go to the fields. There's cotton to pick.

Two weeks before school starts, the Education Ministry reaches in and plucks Alidou, our third- and fourth-grade teacher. He's transferred to a school far in the eastern part of the country. Forty-five kids are without a master. The director tells me he's petitioned the superintendent in Ferké, but it doesn't look promising. There's a teacher shortage anyway, and Nambonkaha is not a priority.

This year enrollment is so high that the first- and second-grade teacher, Ibrahim, and the director examine each prospective first-grader and tell the smallest ones to come back next year. On the first day of school there are three first-graders to a desk, and the overflow sit elbow-to-elbow on tables imported from the canteen. I count seventy-five little bodies in the classroom. Ibrahim just shakes his head. "To take care of them, plus all the ones next door, it's just not possible."

But the director is not about to watch his school fail, and neither are the villagers. Dramane steps up to the plate. It's been two and half years since he failed the exams to get into eleventh grade. But he's a good reader, a committed worker, and willing to volunteer. The director spends a night preparing him, and the next morning Dramane arrives in the classroom, an instant teacher for the third and fourth grades. It seems like he's found the best of both worlds: he can stay with his family in the village and still have a respected job. He's happy—but hesitant. "You see, Guiss," he tells me as we're shucking dried corn with his family one day, "I am a teacher now, and a health assistant and baby weigher, and I help with vaccinations. I manage the tractor, and I'm the secretary for the cotton cooperative. I'm involved in everything. But it's scary. People get angry when one person does too many good things, or becomes too popular. They're liable to put a curse on me if I do better than other villagers."

The sky is blue, but harmattan dust encroaches on its edges. We're sitting on mats with a growing pile of corn between us. I don't respond immediately. I haven't figured this one out. "Even if I were to earn money," Dramane continues, "and share it among my family and my friends and the chief, some people would still be angry that I earned it in the first place. That's why it's better not to stand out, even if it's for good things."

Night after night, Dramane sits at the table in the director's courtyard, grading papers, asking questions, drawing up charts in his notebooks to keep his students' work straight. He wants so much to use his head, to help his people. And day after day, Dramane appears for work in a brown plaid shirt, holding a thermos full of his new wife's sweet coffee, standing in for a faulty ministry, standing up for a village, and wondering if he's been cursed yet.

Sidibé comes back from Ferké one afternoon small and sad. For each of the past two years he's dedicated the early months of the rainy season to studying for an exam that could propel him out of the nursing circuit. He's been a nurse for going on eleven years, and though he likes it, he thinks he's cut out for more specialized work. He wants to be an emergency medic. He wants to save lives. But it's more than a calling. One afternoon, he pulls a piece of computer paper from the cabinet in his salon and thrusts it at me. It's a pay stub from 1992. "See that figure?" he asks indignantly. "It hasn't changed since the day I became a nurse." The figure is roughly equivalent to two hundred dollars. That's as much as I make. But I'm called a volunteer, and he's called the breadwinner of an extended family.

When I'd first arrived in the village, Sidibé had had a row of clay pots filled with brackish water and leaves lined up against one wall of his house. "What is all that?" I had asked, and he'd told me it was medicine for his head. "I drink some, I wash my head with it, and it makes my head better." Do you have migraines? I'd asked. "No. There's tightness in the middle of my head. I'm tired of thinking so much."

"You mean stress?" I asked. "Stress," he'd repeated, rolling the syllable in his throat pensively. It's a word that's so foreign to village life, but he knew it. "Yes, stress. I always think of it as something for people in the big city, but me, I live in a village, and I am stressed." His textbooks were crammed with confusing diagrams of human organs and systems. "I have to know all of them by heart," he'd said, looking at a digestive system drawn in brown, with dotted lines and slashes. It seemed like a foolproof way to narrow the applicant pool: make everything unnecessarily inscrutable, and maybe only a few will guess correctly. I'd copied his diagrams into multicolored, clear sketches so he could learn them better.

When he came back from taking the test last June he said, "It was long. It was hard. I didn't pass," even though he wouldn't receive his scores for months. But this June, he returned from Abidjan with two woven fans for me and sweet yogurt for his whole brood. "I don't know," he told me. "I won't say anything. But this time I feel good."

The grading process is held up by October's political scuffles. At the end of November, Sidibé rides his moped into Ferké every afternoon to check his mailbox. And when he comes back defeated at dusk one day, I know his news isn't good. Big, bellowing Abi stays quiet. She cooks alloco and everything he loves best and brings each plate to him with softness in her face. Salif Keita sings sorrowfully on one of Sidibé's suicidal stereos. My friend lies back on his long bamboo chair, looks up at the sky all prickled with stars. His hands are jumpy. So are his shoulders. He sits up again. "Even if I passed," he says, thumping his chair, "Even if my score was good enough, I can't pass. Because I don't know anyone in Abidjan. I don't know anyone in the ministry— don't have any relatives there. And I am a Muslim from the north. There aren't many spots, and the ones who get them aren't always the ones who do best; they're the ones who can pay off a friend or an uncle on the inside. Why would I want to work hard if I know it will never get me anywhere? How can I continue to enjoy helping others when I myself am stuck?"

In the morning there are clay pots lined up against the wall.

One day in October, I come back from a short trip south to find wooden streetlight poles studding the village's dirt lanes. Massieta has packed burning embers around the roots of the giant mango tree in her courtyard behind my house. "Current is coming," she says. "We have to take down the tree to make way for current." I wonder how she defines electricity. Is it light? Is it black wires between poles? What will she turn on when it comes? There are no fixtures in her mud hut, no appliances waiting for a socket. But electricity, nonetheless, means that Nambonkaha has made it.

A year or two before my arrival, the national electric company alerted the village that electricity would come by the end of 1998. They ordered the chief to realign the village into a grid, and to chop down a dozen trees that would interfere with the power lines. Wayward mud huts were razed; granaries that strayed too far into proposed lanes were destroyed or relocated. But the electric company never came back. The préfet came, yet he wouldn't say anything about Nambonkaha getting light. Electric poles sped north on either side of us—along the road, along the train tracks—but Nambonkaha stayed dark.

And now, after a flurry of activity, we are all set to be electrified. By the end of October, the poles are strung with ugly black cord, and the lightbulbs are all in place. This kind of speediness in a government project is phenomenal. I'm not so excited, however. Biking in from Ferké over the ninth hill, what you see first now is the wavy frame of wires and poles that hangs over the grass roofs. It makes Nambonkaha look short and small, breaks up its connection with the sky.

There's one saving grace, at least for me. The lights don't come on. The poles stand dark, snickering at our expectations, through November, far into December. And then one day at three they flicker on, tiny orange lights whining against the harmattan haze.

Kids dance. Elders stand under the lights and stare up, baffled. But it's just a tease, a cameo appearance. They're dark again in an hour. Our afternoon is well lit up, and by night we rely on the moon again. "They won't go on for good until some government *grand type* comes to declare that Nambonkaha has electricity," Sidibé tells me. "They want to make it political, make us support them, so they'll need a ceremony. We'll just wait with our lanterns lit." At night, darkness comes on; the streetlamps remain black.

The moon appears in a bright shard, swung down like a bowl among the stars. Everyone knows Ramadan has begun. For weeks it's been debated whether that infant moon will appear on Tuesday or Wednesday. When it comes, the imams announce it over the radio. But Sidibé and the mayor, sitting in the courtyard around the fire, have already squinted at the sky and decided the ritual has begun. Sidibé, as usual, will fast. The mayor, as usual, will fast only the first day.

Me, I'm cheating. I have a week till a vacation in Mali over Christmas, and I want to spend it fasting in solidarity with Sidibé and Abi and the other villagers. But I've got the first inkling of a cold, and I'd rather not bring it with me to Timbuktu. So I've dictated my own fasting rules. The others won't let anything pass their lips till the sun sets. They are stoic and determined and uncomplaining. I am, too, but I wash down my hunger with a dozen liters of water. Of course, giving up food for the day is just a question of refocusing your thoughts. Giving up water, in a season that sucks the saliva right out of your mouth, is a torture whose only balm is devotion. But I'm not trying to prove anything to Allah.

Just as the roosters get their cue, in the quiet clarity of dawn, the prayer caller sings. It happens every single day, but I am usually still asleep. He has no tower, no loudspeaker. He stands outside the little mosque and sings away the darkness. The prayer wafts over sleeping huts, stirs life into the village.

The dawn air is chill and moist in December. The sun burns

off any winter aspirations as soon as it rises, but dawn is deliciously cold. I dig out socks and jeans from the bottom of my basket and milk these frosty minutes for all they're worth. I boil oatmeal and coffee, sit back in my wooden armchair, and listen to the village awaken. My last spoonfuls are finished before five-thirty. And then there's just the rest of the day to not think about food.

It's not too hard to skip eating: there's nothing on the shelf I can just munch on without a fair amount of preparation. Even peanuts take shelling, roasting, skinning, and salting. I can fast easily just by enforcing laziness on myself. Market day, on the other hand, is crowded with temptation and nonpracticing Muslims. The woman who comes in from Ferké fries up just as many fish as always, fills bowl after bowl with handfuls of attiéké and hot peppers. The girl from town whom Bakary pesters every week sashays through the lanes of women with bags of bisap and yogurt stacked high on her head. Angélique is Catholic. She arrives with fresh sweet bread exploding from the top of her basin, and the scent seems to linger behind her like a wavering cartoon curl.

But Abi and I are unflinching. I forgo my weekly chapalo date with Angélique and Femme Claire, I decline my habitual bag of bisap. I glug my water as if it's the last in the well. Abi drinks nothing. She sells her soap and Maggi cubes. I weigh a long line of babies. The sun inches, so slowly, through the trees.

Dramane and Sidibé's assistant, Issouf, are not fasting. They sit on a bench next to me, doing improv for anyone watching. An Ivorian comedian has recently come out with a cassette on which he mocks gendarmes, the government, villagers, and everything in between. Dramane and Issouf, inspired by the health aspect of our baby-weighing station, are extemporizing the contraception skit. Issouf holds a packet of birth-control pills. "Every morning my girlfriend drinks down one of these so she won't get pregnant. And then I take one too, just to make sure." Dramane inspects a pack of Prudence condoms with feigned puzzlement. Issouf assumes a nasal ignorant *villageois* voice and explains to Dramane: "It's medicine against adultery."

Dramane tells of a SIDA fête he attended near Korhogo while he was in high school. The educating team came from Abidjan, did their spiel in mostly French and Dioula, and tossed condoms into the crowd. There was a scramble to pick them up, because free anything is worth having. The Senoufo women mused over the little packets, then ripped open the foil and stuck the condoms in their mouths. They chewed and chewed, but the condoms never got softer. Finally one woman asked, "What's wrong with this chewing gum?"

Bakary buys beignets and thrusts the bowl between us. The men descend on them. I drink some water and walk over to Abi to commiserate. Fasting has rubbed out her edges. She says, in a gentle voice, "Whenever you want to, Guissongui, come break the fast with us." I don't dither. "How about tonight?"

The sun packs up the day's dry heat and carries it over the horizon. It leaves no dramatic light show in the west; night shunts in without fanfare. Abi has dragged a few tree trunks to the center of the courtyard, and these harmattan nights we huddle around the slow burning circle of flame. In other parts of the world, kids are lining up to sit on Santa's lap, holiday songs are wheedling from every speaker. We sit on a mat on the ground, all wrapped up in the huge savanna sky and the glow of embers. Abi ladles out rice porridge, which is just old rice cooked till it's thick and mixed with sugar. We eat slowly, silently. Rice porridge, and it tastes like the best thing I've ever eaten.

Must be the stars, must be the warmth of the fire in this harmattan cold, must be Sidibé, relaxed again, or Abi, lolling on the mat, a scarf draped lazily around her face. Must be the children, darting around in the dark outside the firelight. I feel like I'm eating joy. And I just get fuller and fuller. Abi's two-year-old climbs onto my lap and leaps at her reclining mother. There is so much easiness in the air, so much peace. I scrape out the last bite of porridge. Night sinks down on our little bunch lit up by the fire, and really, truly—carolless, Santaless, tinselless—it feels like Christmas.

·　　·　　·

The first coup d'état in Côte d'Ivoire's history happens in the thick of Ramadan, on Christmas Eve. I'm at the foot of a steep slope of huts in Mali, drinking a warm beer after dinner. Our plates are pushed to the center of the table and a tall, thin man in a basketball shirt is telling us about his favorite music. A great cleft of rock towers black above us, abridging the speckled sky. The man takes a swig and says, nonchalantly, "So, what do you think about what happened in your country today?" Today, my brother and two Peace Corps friends and I have been hiking the escarpment, cut off from everything except isolated Dogon villages. We haven't a clue what's happened in "our country." "In America, you mean?" "No, no," he laughs, "in Côte d'Ivoire." He settles back and pulls out a pack of Excellence cigarettes. "Well, what happened?" we ask. He shakes out a cigarette, fumbles for matches, and finally gets up to light it from the cooking fire. "They chased out the president." All four of us jump in our chairs. "Who chased him out?" "I don't know, the military, I guess." So it was a coup? He shrugs, cocking his head to the side, and nods.

Maybe we should have seen it coming. There was so much discontent, so many scandals. But Côte d'Ivoire is the rock of West Africa—stable and supposedly democratic for decades. When all you've known is the status quo, it's hard to imagine it turned on its head. "*En tout cas,* Bédié's out of there," says the Malian. "They say he's in Togo, but he's going to go to France." There's a moment of silence while we all try to swallow the information. Then stand up and clink our bottles. Bédié's out. Merry Christmas, deh!

We are toasting a military takeover. How did it come to that? Perhaps we've been influenced by our counterparts: Sidibé's discussion of the opposition leader Ouattara has gone from respectful to effusive since October's nationality muddle. Maybe we recognize the dire need for change in Ivorian politics and will naively accept whatever form it takes. When we finally find a youth with a radio, French BBC tells us the coup was bloodless. They also report that the temporary leader, Robert Guéi, has taken office only in order to pave the way for fair elections. The history of West Africa is cluttered with coups. Only a handful have fostered democracy. But a few countries away in Nigeria, interim leader General Abdulsalam Abubakar is shepherding in elections, as Guéi has promised. We are operating in a political system that is far distant from our own. We want to believe that democracy and justice will prevail, that General Guéi will merely sweep out the mess and leave the room. So we do.

We travel by boat, bus, and skeletal Peugeot to get from Timbuktu back to Côte d'Ivoire. It takes five days. In that time, my initial euphoria evaporates. The party that has led since independence in 1960 has been catapulted out of power. The country is, for all practical purposes, a military dictatorship. What will it mean? More checkpoints? More bribes? A crackdown on free speech, basic rights? Everything might have changed in the weeks I have been gone.

The same guards man the border. They sprawl in chairs amid a collection of beer bottles emptied already at ten in the morning. Transport costs the same, and is predictably unpredictable. We're stopped by gendarmes and detained for an hour while the bags of some unfortunate passenger are emptied into the dirt and inspected. That's nothing new. When they dump me off in my dusty village, the vieilles are crouched in the scant shade of their firewood stacks. Massieta and her daughter pound corn. A few men roll off to Ferké on creaking bikes. The Peuls laze under thatch at the butcher's stall. Sidibé treats a snakebite. The first-grade class is singing about a lost handkerchief.

The old government lies in tattered ruins! The military has claimed the radio and television stations in Abidjan! There are tanks in the capital! The earth has quaked in Côte d'Ivoire, but hardly a tremor is felt in Nambonkaha.

Except in Sidibé's eyes. They dance. "This is it!" he says in a voice energized despite his fasting. "We've thrown out *les faux types,* the bad guys! This is Côte d'Ivoire's revolution!" But it's the military, not the people, who have overthrown the government, I point out. "Yes," he says, "but the people wanted change.

They had no means to bring it about themselves. The military has accomplished it—Guéi is our hero. People are calling him Father Christmas!"

Who is Guéi? I ask. "A general from the west," says Sidibé. "He's doesn't claim a political party, and the whole coup idea probably wasn't even his. The military chose him. Many of the Western ethnicities have strong alliances with the northern ones, so he has wide support. Plus, he and Ouattara worked together in Houphouët's government. He'll be the one to let Ouattara run in the elections!" The forgotten north, with its rutted roads and dark villages, will finally count! Sidibé has so much faith. I say, "But Sidibé, what if he doesn't usher in elections? What if he just sticks around like Mobutu or Abacha?" He shakes his head. After a pause, he resumes with a little less energy. "It could happen. But I don't think it will." I can see I've brought a little rain to his spirits. Then he stands abruptly, and declares, *"Maintenant, ça va aller. Ça va aller."* He fills his plastic teapot with water for his ablutions, still saying, *"Ça va aller, ça va aller."* It will be okay. I wonder which one of us he's trying to convince.

On the last day of Ramadan, the space next to the mosque fills with lines of bright, patterned backs. At lunch, Abi serves a giant bowl of *riz gras,* covered in stewed vegetables and chunks of meat. The president, the mayor, the school director (an honorary Muslim today), Femme Claire's husband Ibrahim the schoolteacher, and I (an honorary male most days) devour it. Usually we'd sit back and talk about the weather. Now there are more pressing topics.

Sidibé and Femme Claire's husband beam. They're focusing on the fact that Bédié is gone—this holiday there is something extra to celebrate. The director, more taciturn, doesn't nod or smile much. Either he supported the ruling party or he's looking ahead, as most are not, and is concerned. The mayor gestures all over the place. He says that now maybe we'll get electricity. Now there's someone who will listen to the north, who won't forget the Muslims in this country. The president leans on an elbow, one hand framing his jaw: *C'est ça qui est là. Vraiment!*

Elsewhere in the village, there isn't much talk about the coup.

For most of the people of Nambonkaha, the patriarch is their president, the chief their prime minister, and the elders are his reliable cabinet. And the laws that must be followed are ordained by Allah and the ancestors. They have no use for the charades in Abidjan.

Siaka's mother-in-law died during Ramadan. So instead of dancing for Allah in the chief's courtyard after the holiday meal, the whole village travels to Ferké to dance at her funeral. The country is in a state of flux, the military reigns! But the talk is of cotton returns and how much meat Siaka has put in the sauce. We dance all night, and when the sun rises, a straggling group dances still, their movements smooth and taut after all these hours. After dawn, Siaka insists on giving me a ride home. We zip past the shell of the burned government store, glaring in the early light, a lone beacon of unrest. The gendarmes wave us by. We rise and swoop over nine quiet hills. Brilliant yellow flowers tumble from the acacia trees. Baobabs dangle with velvety pods of fruit. Everything else is harmattan dead. The teak trees are leafless. The tall grasses have browned and broken. The earth is stained in splotches with ashes from bush fires. The sky is hazy and flat. Along this road, nothing changes but the seasons.

20

Reach

Siwatoun stumbles over the word "conjunctivitis." His shoulders are braced and his long nose is bent toward a glossy, hardcover health manual. He reads like an elementary school student, nervously, mechanically, thrusting out each word with equal emphasis. It's quite possible that he hasn't been asked to read since leaving sixth grade, over seven years ago. He's memorized chunks of the text—that's expected of students in grade school. Those parts he repeats looking at the floor, and they come out all bunched up. But we're not in grade school; we're training to be community health workers. And I'm trying to dissolve the pass/fail, master/student dynamic that has dominated all the classroom experience of the five trainees. Siwatoun, a twenty-something farmer from a far campement, is leading the discussion of this week's assignment.

The books have been donated by the Rotary Club to bring health education to barely literate villagers. The illustrations feature everyday African villagers: watercolor women give birth, men clutch ribs rattling with heart attacks, children scratch their chicken pox. The ailments and their cures are summarized in simple charts and a few straightforward sentences. Dramane and Bakary dither over the Niarafolo translation for each malady. The other students, Samadou and Adama, wince along with Siwatoun, mouthing the words as he goes. They are nervous, but they are also motivated and proud. They are preparing to attend a formal health-worker training in Korhogo.

Our group of Peace Corps volunteers based around Korhogo has put together an elaborate training program to produce health workers, or *agents de santé communautaire* (ASCs) with a solid base of knowledge about everything from wound care and vaccinations to family planning and AIDS. Ideally, the workers will control a three-ringed health initiative. First, they will be the extra eyes and ears of the nurse, encouraging women to weigh and vaccinate their babies and looking out for polio cases or meningitis outbreaks. Second, they will administer basic health care with the help of wooden "pharmacy boxes" stocked with aspirin, antacids, malaria pills, wooden phalluses for condom demonstrations, and wound-care supplies. Finally, they will be responsible for teaching their fellow villagers about improving health. They're becoming backwoods health consultants.

Adama, a conscientious man from a campement a few kilometers to the north, wears thick, black-framed glasses on his moonish face. When I ask what his vision's like, he says, It's just fine, why do you ask? He finished elementary school two decades ago and has since been occupied with two wives and nine children. He came to me one day to say that he'd seen Dramane's shiny new book and he'd like one too. I told him the book came with the role of health worker. If he wanted one, he had to be the other. He considered this an even better offer.

Samadou, or Sam, always wears a biker hat with the bill turned up. He might be in his forties, since his mustache and sideburns are graying. He's no taller than me and always stands akimbo to increase his presence. Sam is a member of the budget committee for the infirmary—a cotreasurer—and he's worked on the vaccination campaign for five years, he tells me proudly. He used to be an ASC years ago, and Sidibé begged me to ask him to be one again.

Sam comes from the nearest campement, Adama and Bakary from just a ways down the road, and Dramane lives in Nambonkaha itself. When it was just these four in the outreach program, we weren't reaching far. I wanted someone distant, from Midjiri, the largest and furthest campement. When a Midjiri woman is sick, she gets a bumpy ride on the back of a bike or moped if she's lucky, or walks if she's not, all seventeen kilometers to Sidibé to get medication. If a Midjiri child is sick, it's easier to rely on indigenous medicine rather than bring him all the way to the infirmary. Midjiri is clean, motivated, organized, and completely stymied when it comes to health. Dramane and Bakary put out a few feelers to their friends in Midjiri, and in pedaled Siwatoun. In a sense, he is the test of the whole project. If he does well at the training, Siwatoun will be *the* health source in a fairly wide stretch of bush.

There's one hitch. Two, really: a pretest before the training and another test afterward. Mostly they will measure the success of our classes. To a lesser extent, they will weed out those who haven't been able to step beyond square one. But these five men, all of whom were forced to stop their schooling by failed exams, are convinced they won't pass. They're certain that our pretraining classes will be all for naught. They barely speak of the training—to do so would only jinx their chances of attending.

We trudge through symptoms of whooping cough and typhoid, how to treat snake and scorpion bites, toothaches, headaches, backaches, stomachaches, how to splint a broken bone. But when we get to the AIDS chapter, I say, Skip over this one. I don't want it to blend in with the rest. I've typed up a basic fact sheet, describing the causes, the symptoms, and the progression of the virus. On the back, I've included a long list of terrifying statistics. I want to blow them away. The AIDS fête last rainy season was an important introduction that whittled away taboos and inspired frank discussion. But did it change behavior in any significant way? Doubtful.

For the rest of the villagers, a sugarcoated message still works the best. But these five have adopted health as their agenda, and they need to know the worst. I save this discussion for the last class and lead the meeting myself. We start out reading the manual, following the fate of a painted couple that first frolics in the dark, then wastes away in lonely agony. It's easy to laugh at the caricatures, but I snap the book shut and hand out my page of horrors. "Who will read this sentence about two thousand Ivorians dying a week? Siwatoun? Bakary, how about the next about the drastic reduction in life expectancy? Or the one that details the economic repercussions of such a severe blow to the fifteen-to-thirty-nine-year-old population?"

Every line is poisonous; we pick through them gingerly. Dramane is businesslike and precise. He seeks clarification and facts. Bakary and Samadou cluck their tongues and mutter, "*Mais!*" and "*Eh, Allah!*" but not much else. Siwatoun's face twists with innocent discomfort. But Adama, Adama doesn't hold back. He looks up at me from this miserable list, and behind his glasses his magnified eyes are filled with despair. "What are we to do?" His throat strangles his voice. "*We're all going to die! C'est fini!*"

Seeing him so devastated, I realize it's time to break through the taboos. "Remember the *boutiquier*'s son?" I flip open the book to a picture that looks eerily like our lost neighbor. "Look at this. What do you think killed him?" I take a deep breath and plow on— I'm just telling the truth but to vocalize the AIDS sentence seems as good as a curse. "Remember Adama le Gros's dead uncle? That little baby died, and now his wife Djeneba is sick, too. What do you think that is? It's AIDS. Adama le Gros and his other wives might be sick, but they don't know it yet. You must protect yourself even if you're just following tradition."

"But our wives, who's to say they're not cheating on us?" Adama cries.

Bakary shakes his head. "Come on, you know that it's mostly men who have girlfriends. Most women here don't sleep around once they're married."

Dramane adds, "It's still early enough to teach your family about it. Go home and explain it to your wives."

Adama won't be assuaged. His elbows splay on the crooked desk, and he holds his head in his hands.

Bakary wearing his orange vaccination T-shirt, is conscientious about reading the numbers right. "Two thousand Ivorians will contract AIDS each week in the year 2000." His voice is clear when he discusses the disease, and encouraging when he's comforting Adama. But when I direct a comment about condoms to him, he looks out the window with an angelic smile and shakes his head. "Jamais." Never. What more will it take?

The training in Korhogo is a six-day event. As expected, Bakary passes the preexam with a good score, Adama's is middling, and Siwatoun and Sam drag up the rear. They're horrified, but I'm not. They're familiar with much of the information; it's the reading that stumps them. And Dramane is a schoolmaster now—his advantage over the others is nearly absolute. He sails through the exam, ranking premier, though we're not really counting.

For six days, thirty men and five women listen to experts discussing hygiene and female circumcision, act in skits about effective teaching methods, and treat nonexistent wounds. Aside from a chubby woman who stares vacantly during classtime and sleeps her way through many of the male trainees in the evenings, a hospital-employed trainer who treats the villagers like dunces, and two clowns who only now admit they never got past first grade, the training goes swimmingly. Dramane tells me that every night they return to their rooms and study until it's late.

Dramane gets one wrong on the postexam. Adama does even better than Bakary's good mark; Siwatoun doubles the score he got on the pretest; Sam barely musters ten points more than the first go. But all have demonstrated the competence and knowledge to become ASCs. We deck ourselves out in uniforms made especially for the occasion. Sidibé appears in a shiny boubou for our closing ceremony, having driven seventy kilometers by moped to surprise us. Nambonkaha's new ASCs grin even wider when they see him—his presence legitimizes their new role.

The *grands types* of Korhogo, or at least their stand-ins, come to speak about what these men and women have accomplished. All but the two ex-first-graders receive a diploma and a varnished pharmacy box filled with medicines (paid for in part by their communities). We stand in a large blur of blue lattice fabric and take all combinations of photographs. When we return to the village, we are proud, intoxicated by our mission.

. . .

Our weekly meetings in the village continue after the training. We are no longer bumbling through health lessons; we are discussing real issues. I have always had frank discussions with Sidibé, but our candid conversations rarely made it past his courtyard. As a nurse, he feels he has to sweeten prognoses for the sick or else they won't seek his help. But the ASCs are dealing with disease prevention. They want to be blunt so that villagers will understand why it's important to keep their courtyards clean, to wash their hands, to get vaccinated, to use condoms. We meet every two weeks in the dim school classroom, scoot the desks into a circle, and hunker down to discuss how to approach educating the people of Nambonkaha.

Dramane brings up female circumcision before I do. At the training, the family-planning expert spent a whole afternoon explaining how the practice is medically dangerous. Last year, Dramane did nothing to stop his own wife's circumcision. It's obviously an issue that makes him uneasy.

The true obstacle, of course, is sorcery. The vieilles say that Nambonkaha has been cursed, that children of uncircumcised mothers will not live. I have pulled a dead baby from the womb of an uncircumcised woman. Who's to say that meant nothing? Few are willing take risks when spirits are involved. How do you sneak past sorcery? Is there any way to spin rituals so that the spirits won't find out? I throw out some ideas. The ASCs bat down each one. "Why can't they list all the men the girl has slept with but change the actual procedure? What if there was just a pinprick or a little stab instead cutting out the entire clitoris?"

Adama says, "Because the woman has to be scared into naming past lovers. If the operation was less painful, maybe she would treat the ritual less seriously."

"Why won't it just die out after today's older generations are gone? You have learned about the dangers of female circumcision. When you are the generation in charge, don't you think you can overturn the curse? Won't people be more likely to listen to educated leaders?"

"Most educated villagers believe in sorcery too," says Dramane. "And even if they don't, there will always be enough of the unschooled population to keep the curse alive. Anyway, sorcery isn't just a phase, Guiss. Even if we were to somehow get rid of this curse, another could come to take its place. As long as people are scared, they won't take any chances. The women themselves want to be fertile wives. They'll accept circumcision if that's what it takes to keep their babies alive."

"But how do they know it's a curse that's killing their babies? Why won't they accept that it's just malaria or dehydration or a genuine miscarriage?"

Dramane pitches forward. "Those are all tools of sorcery. That's what we believe. Why are people sure there's heaven? Why do people think God can hear when they're praying? Sorcery is what we've always believed in. There's no way to prove that we've been wrong all this time."

This is a lopsided battle: I'm standing up for women who don't even think circumcision is worth fighting. I have one last card. It's a push, but I try it anyway. "You struggled against the colonists and won. You struggled against Bédié and won. Why can't you struggle against the sorcerers? What if every young woman stood together and defied the curse as one force? Surely not all women would become barren or miscarry. At most, a few babies would die, and the curse would buckle."

Dramane looks at me incredulously as if to say, *Are you listening to what you're saying?* "What woman would do that? Maybe standing up to witches and genies will only bring a worse curse. No one would risk that."

"The only way to combat it," says Bakary, "is with modern laws." Modern laws exist already. In Mali and even in Abidjan old women have been jailed as an example to vieilles everywhere. Officials have announced that Korhogo has finally defeated the tradition. I don't believe a word of it. "The minister of justice is the only one who can enforce the laws," Bakary continues. "If someone comes in and arrests the vieilles of Nambonkaha, *that* might stop the practice. Otherwise, there's nothing we can do."

· · ·

We are just waiting. Abi, Femme Claire, and I are perched on the raised walkway of the maternity clinic shell. Femme Claire is making tea. The hot stream arcs through the air, swishes into the glass. "Has the money come in yet?" she asks, looking up at the unfinished structure around us. No. Not yet.

I paint a cement billboard for the dispensary along the paved road. I paint a boy sign and a girl sign on the new school latrines. I paint the word "Nambonkaha" on thirty plastic chairs that the village youth group will rent out for funerals and fêtes. I'm biding time. Sidibé and I sit on his terrace, dunking fingerfuls of yam foutou into eggplant sauce. He glances across at the cement skeleton of the maternity clinic. "Have you heard anything about the check yet?" No. Not yet.

The village *grand type* Benoît rolls up from Abidjan in a surprisingly humble BMW. I know he's coming before he even enters my courtyard—his cologne unfurls before him. He yanks a baby mango off my tree on his way in. He's a university professor of French in Abidjan. He has a grand way of speaking, even when not saying much. He asks after my family and smiles a glassy smile. Then he says casually, "And the check? Has it come yet?" No. Not yet.

Last May, Benoît and Siaka asked me for help finishing the village maternity clinic. Eight months later, my grant has been written and accepted, fund-raising letters have been sent out, and responses, mostly from my family and friends, have trickled in and filled our request. In late January, our check for $12,000 has yet to be cut. I'll be leaving Nambonkaha in mid-April. I'm running out of time. "I'm going to Abidjan," I tell Benoît. "Maybe I can get things moving." At the office in Abidjan, I secure an advance of a quarter of the funds. Benoît picks me up within the hour.

The lumberyard where he drives me is behind a junkyard beside a busy road. From the outside, there is nothing to see but crooked car frames, flattened tires, and long stretches of rusty tin roofs. On the inside there are rows and rows of wood beams in all sizes. Benoît seems to know all the merchants. He says they'll give us great deals.

We spend an hour testing all kinds of wood. Then Benoît realizes that it will cost more to try to transport so much wood the six hundred kilometers to Nambonkaha. We buy only what will fit in his car: thin pieces of metal roofing for the overhang. "Look!" he says, grinning. "Only ninety thousand CFA. That stuff is usually much more expensive, Guissongui!" He speaks as if humoring me; my youth and femaleness would discredit me completely if it weren't for the money in my bag. But, Benoît, I say. That wasn't in the budget. You never mentioned that we'd need that. The car, with its trunk full of metal, thumps over ruts in the dirt as we pull out of the junkyard. "We'll buy the rest in Ferké," he says. "I know some people there." The air is sharp with his cologne. I breathe into my sleeve.

"We can't actually buy the corrugated tin till we get the rest of the money," he tells me when he shows up in the village a week later. Well, let's at least start with the wood beams, right? "I've already got them ordered," he says. That's promising. "Now I just need this much money," he adds, handing me a receipt. It has my Lebanese hardware vendor's logo on it, and his signature too. "See this?" Benoît says, "Where it says, 'minus twenty-five thousand?' I got a huge discount!" But the sum is still a bit over the budget. He orders Américain to drive the tractor into Ferké and pick up the beams. "*Tu vois,* Ferké is a much better place to get our supplies," he says in a singsong voice. "We have our own transport to bring everything back to the village."

To his credit, workers arrive the day after the wood comes. The storage room at the infirmary fills up with wood scraps and dozens of boxes of nails. From that corner of the village, the sound of hammering can be heard from early morning to late afternoon, with only a break for siesta. It's sharp and staccato behind the thump of pestles on corn. To me, it's music. How many stories have I heard about construction projects that never get off their feet, about cornerstones left derelict in the dirt? In

Nambonkaha, they're on a mission to get the work done. The chief and Benoît are the force behind the momentum. "We want you to see this finished," says Benoît, with his inscrutable smile, "so we will work without stopping till it is complete."

The two carpenters finish the frame for the ceiling and roof of the maternity clinic in three days. Then they climb right up the walls of the midwife's house and start building that frame too. "Benoît!" I run up to him as he's revving his BMW for the long drive back to Abidjan. "They're working on the midwife's house! We didn't plan for that! There's no way we can afford it."

He just chuckles. "Sure we did. The budget is for two structures. Don't worry, Guissongui!" His wheels spin up a cloud of dust. Two structures? There's his copy of the budget, scrawled in pencil on grid paper. There's my copy, printed out in an Excel graph, in English and in French. He has studied both. I have studied both. Nowhere on either is the midwife's house mentioned. In fact, in our conversation last May, I specifically recall asking about it, and being told that it would be built later on.

But walking back to the building site, it occurs to me that maybe this is not such a bad idea. It might actually work better than the first plan. As a civil servant, a midwife requires her own lodging. We could build a flawless maternity clinic and it would only remain unstaffed until the house was completed. This way, at least, both structures will develop together.

So the wooden beams are banged into place over the midwife's house. For the better part of a month, I borrow Sidibé's moped and drone into town every two days to call Abidjan to see if the check has come in. For the better part of a month, the wooden beams hold up only sky.

When the check finally arrives in late February, it turns out the deflated CFA has padded an extra thousand dollars onto our fund. I cash it all in Abidjan—banks here aren't equipped for transfers. The highest denomination of CFA is a ten-thousand-franc bill, roughly seventeen dollars. The teller hands me thick stacks of bills, one after another, after another, after another. I feel like I should have a briefcase handcuffed to my wrist. I call up Benoît. He says,

Meet me in Adjamé. Adjamé is the bus station and market district where roughly one out of two foreigners passing through gets robbed. I'm carrying over six million CFA in cash. I don't have any of those nifty traveler money packs. I strap the funds in a pagne around my waist, tuck it under the elastic of my bra, and put the rest in an old rice sack under some pagnes. Even ratty old backpacks get snatched. I step out of the taxi on the main street of Adjamé. Every nerve jangles.

Benoît has changed his mind again. He wants to discuss transporting roofing tin to the village. It's so much cheaper down here, he says, it might be worth the cost of getting it up to Nambonkaha. He leads me down the crowded street, through back alleys, into dark shops, looking for the best deal. I pull the rice sack over my shoulder, trying not to clutch it obviously. I cross my arms over the wads against my torso; I pull on my shirt to cover my belly, bulging with cash. It makes me giddy—it's so surreal to be strolling through a den of bandits strapped with bundles of money. Benoît doesn't even know. We just keep walking. "This next guy is my good friend," he says about two or three of them. But none of his good friends has a good deal to offer. "I guess we'll have to buy it all in Ferké," he says after an hour. Another blow to the budget. Our estimate had been based on Abidjan prices.

Siaka's car is parked outside the patriarch's courtyard when I get back to the village the next afternoon. Before I can peel all the cash off the various parts of my body, he's bounding through my courtyard entrance. "Guiss!" He grins, clasping my hand in both of his. "Benoît called to say you got the money, so I came right up. Before we do anything, we have to present the gift to the elders. Not the cash, just the sum. They're waiting for us now."

They sit in dusty boubous, munching kola nuts and grunting during the spaces in Siaka's explanation to show they're listening. The elders have not seen the budget, and they can't read all those numbers anyway. They have heard that money is coming, but since they haven't seen hard cash, I imagine they never believed it. In any case, high expectations only invite disappointment. It takes Siaka a full minute to say the total sum in Niarafolo:

8,696,000 CFA. There's no word for "million" in the language—you have to add several other numbers to get the idea across. As each word sounds, the elders move in closer. But they're not smiling. When he finishes, there's fidgeting silence. The elders look perplexed, almost troubled. The chief rests his forearms on his knees and clears his throat. "How will we pay it back?" They're leaning in anxiously. When we explain that they don't have to, it's like a cord snapping; they tilt back, bring their hands together, and let out all those clucks and snorts of approval that make an elder an elder. The chief pops out of his chair with a twinkle in his good eye and shakes my hand. Then the owner of my house, the patriarch, and the imam line up to shake my hand, to bless me, to thank me. And I keep saying, I sought the money because *you* began the project, because Nambonkaha was motivated enough to bring about change on its own. I want to help you because you want to help yourselves.

Dramane stops by in the evening as I'm chopping vegetables. He sits back in my chair and plays with my shortwave. Casually, he says, "Can I ask you something Guiss? Did you take any of the money?" I spin around to look at him. "Of course not!" I bluster, "That's the money of my friends and my family for the village, not for me." He nods "You didn't? Not any? It's okay if you did. Here, it's just understood that if you bring in a lot of money, you get to keep a little for yourself. No one would be angry."

"I'd be angry at myself though," I say emphatically. "And my parents and their friends would be angry too. Plus, I want this money to go as far as possible. If I took some, we wouldn't be able to complete the maternity clinic." At first, it throws me off that my closest village friend would condone embezzlement. It's so easy to forget that corruption is not always seen as deviance, just as an inherent part of economic life.

The village tractor drags in shiny stacks of tin days later. The carpenters come back and cover up the sky within a week and a half. Benoît and I visit the wood sellers of Ferké and order supplies for the ceiling. We have plenty budgeted for the plywood, but the thin joining beams aren't in the budget at all. Why not?

Benoît told me he had done this sort of thing before, said he had consulted with carpenters and builders before drawing up the budget. Clearly I should have reviewed more than just prices. I should have consulted my own carpenters and builders. But my impulse had been trust—to assume that Benoît and Siaka had been thorough in their research.

The tractor pulls up with our piles of plywood, and the ceilings of each building are in place after two weeks. Benoît is getting slippery, hard to pin down. He shows up in the village without warning, disappears without saying when he'll be back. I say, Let's go get the next round of supplies together. He says, Okay, but I'm picking them up in Korhogo and I'm not sure when I'm going. And then he leaves. He has a car. I have a bike. He hands me estimates and I hand him cash, in increments, because it seems I don't have a choice. He buys things every time he goes anywhere. I should insist, I should go everywhere with him, but I have only weeks left in the village, and so much to do to make sure my work is complete and my programs will carry on. And anyway, Benoît seems good with receipts—he brings them all to me, returns with change. It all adds up.

Villagers passing by stop to watch the new buildings take shape. They visit my house to say, *An y che, Guissongui-yo!* A Peul woman with a cataract in one eye grabs me one day as I cut through her courtyard. She points through a space between the huts, to the men hammering away at the maternity clinic. "Your house!" she says. "It's almost finished!" I'll chalk it up to her ethnicity, to her distance from the other women, that she thinks after all this time, just weeks before my departure, my work as a midwife is just beginning.

"I have a nephew making the doors and windows in Korhogo," Benoît tells me. The work takes longer than planned, but in the meantime, the electrician comes and digs channels in the walls for wiring. Benoît and the electrician purchase coils of cords and heap them in the chief's back room. Américain and others haul in tractorfuls of sand and deposit them in dunes next to the clinic, to be mixed with cement to face the buildings. Then come the doors, with locks and dead bolts, and the windows, with surprise antiburglary bars (not included in the budget) to ward off all those who might want to steal a speculum.

There are things we can pitch from the budget. Like plumbing, for instance. It's taken three years to *not* bring electricity to the village. Running water is not even on the agenda. We're not so bad off, considering we've nearly completed two buildings with money meant for one, in just over a month. All that's left are floor and wall tiles, cement facing, and paint—and Benoît swears he has seven buckets from a French NGO waiting at home.

I paste the receipts in my budget book, write down each cost in my accounting book. But a few things are off—the receipt for the dead bolt, for instance, is at least triple the price I've paid in the past. Most receipts are from the government hardware store in Korhogo. I ask Benoît why the locks were so expensive, and he says, "It's a special kind of lock. . . . Maybe I don't know the right place to get them. . . . Must be more expensive there." There's a stutter in his voice that I haven't heard before. My heart sinks. I stick the receipts in my backpack and jump on a badjan to Korhogo.

All the locks sold by the government store are spread out on the counter. I've told the clerk my friend recently bought a lock for seventy-five hundred CFA. The clerk shoves one forward. "This is the most expensive one, and it's only four thousand." "I think this is the one she bought," I say, pointing to the kind that's soldered onto the clinic doors. "That's one's only twenty-five hundred. Madame, your friend got swindled." It's a piddling difference of eight dollars—but what if it's just the tip of the iceberg? I've bought enough wood and hardware for other projects to know that many of the prices on Benoît's receipts are correct. But what about the ones I don't know? And what about the fact that the inflated price is on a legitimate government-store receipt? What if one of Benoît's many "friends" stands behind the counter here? I'm up against a juggernaut.

What do you do when your collaborator is nibbling at your funds? Confront him? He was appointed by the chief. It's too late to open rifts in our operation—I'm nearly gone, and I don't want to leave this village with bad blood spilled. In any case, if I confront him, my complaint will last only as long as the rest of my stay here. As soon as I leave, his responsibility to me will dissolve. The plaintiff needs to come from the village.

Before I can call Siaka, he calls me. "Can you please photocopy all the receipts and send them to me, Guiss? I know Benoît has copies, but I'd like my own." His voice is cheery; there's not a hint in it that he has any suspicions. But this is my chance. "Siaka," I say, "I'm confused about some of Benoît's prices and receipts. There are a few discrepancies." I list four or five examples of duplicate receipts or exaggerated prices I've found in recent purchases. "I expected as much," he says, "and I've asked the man in charge of the village accounts to review the budget books. If we find inconsistencies, we'll bring Benoît before the chief."

Sidibé says, "I'm not really surprised. He's been known to skim funds in other projects." He tries to reassure me: "*Ce qui est sûr:* he won't take that much. If the village realizes he's deprived them of a maternity clinic, they won't let him get away with it." Siaka shines his broad smile on me days before I go. "Don't worry, Guiss. We'll get it back, we'll finish the clinic. The village is willing to put up funds too. We've done the biggest part." Benoît speaks in his brittle voice, looking over the unfinished maternity clinic. "If we run out of funds, it's no problem at all. I have a French NGO lined up to cover the rest of the expenses."

But I'm disheartened nevertheless. How, *how,* could this man have skimmed our funds, knowing, first, that they were destined to help his village, and, second, that they had come directly from my friends and family? It's underhanded, it's selfish—it's betrayal.

Isn't it? Or is it what my honest friend Dramane would do if he were in charge? Didn't he expect me to "take some for myself"? Is it what the mayor would have done if he were managing the work? He was quickly forgiven for depriving fifty farmers of part of their income. Would Sidibé? Maybe it's just an expected perk of doing work for your community. You choose your commission. If only I had known this was just part of the breakdown—I could have included a skimming fund under the miscellaneous expenses in the budget. Everyday *bouff*ing is tacitly accepted. It's a system, that's all. Not efficient, not progressive, but a system that nonetheless works if you know how to work in it. "Integrity" has a different definition here.

21

Tournée

Massieta is Moussa and Mandou's mother. When I return from a funeral in Abidjan, she is cramped over with her back against the side of her hut. Massieta grimaces; her belly is stretched round with child again, despite her forty-odd years, despite her six boys and one girl, despite her husband's lack of income. This is too much.

I drop my bags and crouch in front of her. "What's wrong?" I ask. *"Lala na mi ya,"* she mutters. My stomach hurts. But, damn it, that phrase means everything and nothing in this language: I feel nauseous, I have diarrhea, I have cramps, I'm in labor. It could be anything. Is it the baby? I ask, and she just shrugs.

Massieta is too old and tired out to handle a tenth pregnancy. The way she's squatting, holding her stomach, breathing in sharply—I don't know, it looks ominous. Her stomach is hot; her head is hot. I am bone-tired; I can't make any brilliant decisions. But I can't leave her suffering. Moussa and Mandou, clowns, philosophers, rascals every other day, say nothing now. They linger around us and twist their fingers, peering at their crumpled mother, staring at the ground.

I find Sidibé at the school director's house. "It's probably diarrhea," he says. But when I ask again, "Are you sure it's not a miscarriage?" he swallows his own opinion and defers to mine. "If you're going to the hospital, Angélique will be there too," says the school director, nodding over at his wife. "Her brother is very sick." She's pounding corn, throwing her whole body into the motion. "I'm going soon," she breathes, dumping the crushed corn into a screen to sift it. "I just need to finish making dinner." She is more distressed than I've ever seen her. On the way back across the village, I pick up Bakary. "I'm going to take them to the Baptists," I tell him, "but I think there should be a lesson in this." We corner Massieta's husband and remind of his responsibility for the health of his wife and the well-being of his children. "This is the deal," I say. "I will take her to the hospital if you allow her to use birth control." He nods with his head bent to the side, grunting his approval a little too readily. I don't believe this one lecture will send him scurrying for the pill, but it's worth a shot. I pack Massieta and her husband into a badjan, reassure my boys with faces drawn tight that their mother will be fine, and hurtle back to Ferké, back to the Baptists, to establish what ails Massieta.

It is night when we get there. The badjan driver can't be bothered to enter the property, so we hobble up the darkened driveway on foot. In the hospital courtyard, women bend over fires with babies on their backs, girls scrub dishes under a spigot. It's like a makeshift village—the hush of low voices and the soft clank of pots is comforting and warm. You almost forget why they're all here.

The benches on the hospital terrace are stacked in a corner. There are just two outside the door marked C, where we have been told to wait. An old man pushes a mop in slow circles on the floor. Only three other patients wait with us. But we wait and wait, watching the mop slop across the cement. Massieta is quiet, her forehead knotted. Her husband smiles at me like a sycophant, bending crookedly at the waist every so often, in a strange half bow. He speaks less French than his wife or his eight-year-old son. Around me, he rarely speaks at all.

When door C opens finally, a nurse invites us in. She is tall and young and attractive, and, surprisingly, Niarafolo. Most Niarafolo women I know are corn pounders. She brings Massieta behind a curtain and, with a quick probe that elicits a cry of scandalized shock, determines that the pregnancy is untroubled and the pains come from elsewhere. Then we're strung along through a variety of lab tests and deposited, exhausted, on a bench in a pool of sterile fluorescent light to await the results.

I leave them there and go off to find Angélique. The court-yards are peopled with shadows. Haunted eyes follow me as I walk. I forget sometimes that I'm a different color. They must think I'm a Baptist, a doctor, but I'm just looking for my friend. Angélique's older brother is a successful boutique owner in his village. I look for him in the private rooms. Angélique must hear the mumble of *toubabou* before she sees me. She pushes past her sisters through the screen door, grabs my hand, and brings me into the room. Her arm entwines around mine and she speaks in a low voice. "Look at him, Guissongui. He started with just a small store. But he's a good businessman, and he's kind, and so his store became the biggest one in the village. He gives out loans to people all the time. He sends money to all his relatives. Just look at him! He is so good, Guissongui, *il est tellement bon.*" But his success and his goodness lie heaped in a corner with his clothes. He is just a man struggling to hold on to life. He is thin and writhing, unclothed but for a pagne loose around his hips. His arms flail perpendicular to his body. He looks eerily like Christ.

Angélique speaks to him in a raised voice. "This is Guissongui, who lives in our village." Her brother focuses on me for a second, manages a smile, and attempts to start the greetings. Oh God, I think, don't waste your scant breath on me. His arms move vaguely forward as if reaching for invisible hands to help him up; his body clenches. His jaw works in circles. His eyes are clear, but they won't stop rolling. Angélique shakes beside me, clutches my hand.

My own patient suffers, too, across the black whispering yard. When Angélique's brother has calmed, I return to Massieta. She is not dying. Dysentery, it turns out, is ripping up her guts. It can't be good for the baby, but she is not dying. Sidibé was right. We pick up medicines and shuffle back down the driveway to the road to catch a taxi home. It's past eleven. Every taxi that stops refuses to take us so far. We stand defeated, drenched in the orange fuzz of the streetlight. Sickness and sadness seem to hover just outside in the blackness. In Africa there's always some-one walking alongside the road. Tonight there's no one. Only a few trucks pass, groaning, squeaking, crooked on their axles. And then there are slaps on the pavement, and Angélique runs out of the shadows into the orange. "He stopped breathing," she cries. I hand Massieta's husband enough money for the ride home and hurry back up the hill. My friend gasps explanation at my side, half-running past rows of bodies asleep on mats in the dust. Her hand tightens around my wrist, as if seeking a pulse.

I am struck first that there is no wailing; wailing is part of the soundtrack of this hospital ground. Angélique's brother lies in his pagne. The muscles that strung his neck in desperation are flat; his brow is smooth. His wife and sisters stand horrified, numb. Angélique thrusts herself outside and crumples to the ground. She starts talking in a broken voice. "There are so many children." She rises, faces the room. "And look at that woman in there. She has lost everything. She has nine children to feed and send to school. How will they survive?" She stands and pushes her head against my shoulder. "How will they live? So many like that?" Then she paces, throwing her arms out as if to shake her hands free of death. It's a gesture so hopeless, so filled with utter despair. It sends prickles of revelation rushing across my skin: this is me, this is what I do, this is how death hits me too—in the hands. I'd heard the news two weeks ago that my close friend, a fellow Peace Corps volunteer, had died on the road to Boun-diali. We'd lost a brilliant soul; we'd lost our comedian, our *grand frère*, who had warmth enough for everyone. And all I could do at the news was throw my arms down, shake my hands, again and again, uselessly, unconsciously trying to fling reality from my fin-gers. I did not recognize it in myself until I saw it in Angélique.

There are so many times when difference is all that's in focus. When you're forced to accept that despite all you love, there will always be rifts that can't be bridged. These women want stability, reliability, community, and enough money to have nice clothes made and buy meat for the sauce, maybe some new pots. I have the liberty to be an idealist, a romantic. I'm stuck on all those Western clichés: happiness, love, adventure, fulfillment. I'm here to suck the marrow out of life, but I have the luxury to leave when I wish. In the village I represent freedom and rare opportunity: to support myself, to be well educated, to travel, to never stop learning. Friends at home tell me I'm brave, of all things! They are lawyers or bankers or executive vice presidents. They say they wish they had followed their hearts too. The village women, I'm not sure they envy me at all. We wear life in such different ways.

And death? So many people say, Well, death is different in Africa. They're healthy about death in Africa. They greet it with dance, music, celebration. But it's not so simple as all that, and it is not so foreign. Largaton died slowly, evilly of AIDS. Grinning Ali died of neglect. Abi's mother just died. Angélique's brother had a twisted-up heart. My beautiful friend was crushed behind the wheel, snapped out like a flame. There are so many ways to exit—each has quality, drama, horror of its own. Each society has its own meaning to attach to the exit, to make it less final, to make it more tangible. The dead linger on Earth as ancestors; they come back as kings or beetles; they traipse around in heavens that look different to everyone. But in spite of so many differences, some deep thread runs through it all, ties us all together. It's spun from life's constants, but maybe from death more than anything else. And it is somehow such a beautiful, tragic thing, standing in the dark that smells like smoke and antiseptic with the trembling shadow of Angélique throwing death off her hands as I have, to feel the singular pulse of a disparate humanity throbbing, throbbing. We are sisters, despite all; we are the same.

Assiatou beckons me from the mortar where she is pounding the husks off rice. She smiles at me a little breathlessly, and it sounds like she's about to tell me something important. But it's just *"Fochanganan,"* good day. How that used to drive me mad—if they had something to say, why didn't they come to me? Now

I just take the pestle from her to pummel the rice. As she steps into her kitchen to get the winnowing basket, I notice a dark wobbly line ringing her hut about halfway up. My eye follows the stripe to the next hut and then the next—the line continues at the same level around every hut in her courtyard. "What's that?" I ask her. She smiles sheepishly and says, "Manure." When I ask her why it's there, she winces and shrugs.

The next day, the huts in the imam's courtyard are ringed too. Then Oumar's courtyard, and Dramane's. And then they all are. It's like yellow ribbons or Christmas lights—the whole village has been galvanized. But for what?

Dramane steps in as the designated unraveler of all mysteries. "You know genies live in trees, right? Not all trees, just certain ones. Obviously, those trees can never be cut down. Most people know which ones not to touch, but in a village near Ferké, a woman chopped down a genie's tree for firewood. By accident, she killed the genie's son."

"The genie's son? Is that a living person?"

"No, no. He's a spirit too. *En tout cas,* the genie was very angry. She swore that she would kill every child she saw to revenge her son's death. She communicates through seers and fetisheurs. They're the ones who heard about her revenge, and they're also the ones who determined the only way to escape it. If you circle your house with a line of manure, she cannot hurt your children."

Within days the word has poured over the countryside, seeping into every settlement, every courtyard, so that even a week later, when I ride over an hour into the bush to an isolated campement, I find it banded by the same stripe of manure. Belief is so powerful! If only our Western aid organizations, if only those dedicated NGOs had ridden its coattails! Because it seems to me, watching every corner of the savanna streak itself with dung in some bush version of Passover, that there's tremendous potential for modern enlightenment in animism. Maybe if, in the beginning, health organizations had worked *with* sorcery instead of scorning it, AIDS would be an entirely different issue. What if they had accepted that villagers thought AIDS a curse and had introduced condoms, with the help of chiefs and féticheurs, as the only fetish that can stave off the magic?

Sidibé's house remains unringed. So do the houses of the other fonctionnaires. But it's an edgy state of limbo. They chuckle sometimes at the idiosyncrasies of Niarafolo ways. They pride themselves on being modern thinkers in a traditional village. But there's a twinge of anxiety about sorcery that peeks out on occasion.

All the fonctionnaires are stretched out under grand trees in Angélique and the school director's native village. Her brother's funeral—just a brief church service outside; he was too young for dancing—is over. So is the meal. We are talking about everything except death. Around us, all the structures are banded with manure. "They're so silly," says Angélique's husband. The others grunt their agreement. I'm not surprised by his derisive tone. He's a teacher who once hoped to become a Catholic priest. "All this business about manure lines . . ." He shakes his head with a smirk. He seems to be speaking with my old voice. I've been so intrigued by the issue, I've forgotten my own skepticism. Then he continues, peering up into the branches above us. "Why didn't they just build their villages away from the genies' trees? That way they'd never have to worry about which tree to chop."

For a minute there it had sounded like revolution. Nope, it's just belief again, battle-worn but strong as ever.

Jogging back from the ancestors' bridge as dusk approaches, I find Oumar's father, small and frail in his frayed woman's overcoat, clearing burned weeds on the outskirts of the village. What are you doing? I ask him. He rights himself and says with a resigned smile, "I'm building a courtyard." What about the other one? He shakes his head. "We can't live there anymore. The owner's son came back." He bends again, holding closed his jacket, raking up blackened grasses with his fingers. The spot he's been offered is the furthest corner of the village, close to the train tracks. There are small piles of trash scattered around it; the nearest neighbors have used the area as a dump for years. I jog on into Sidibé's courtyard. He is walking from the dispensary in his white coat. "Why is Oumar's family moving to a dump?" I ask.

Sidibé sucks his teeth. "Oumar's father has rented that courtyard for ten years from a man who lives in the campements. It's like your situation. The man only shows up once in a while, and stays in one of the rooms. So Oumar's father fixed it up. He built a hut for a kitchen and a little bathing room, and faced the whole house with cement.

"But all of a sudden, the owner's son has come back from the city and wants the courtyard for himself. Oumar's father tried to make a deal. First he offered him two rooms. Then he said, 'Since I've built here, I'll help you find another courtyard.' But the son from the city wouldn't accept. So Oumar's papa said, okay, he'll create another courtyard if only the man will help cover the building costs. Again the man said no."

Oumar's father has asked the chief to demand pardon, to ask for mercy from the city man. All it's gotten him so far is a few weeks' respite to start building. It seems so miserly, so un-African. What happened to community, to not letting anyone slip through the cracks? Oumar's father is crippled with migraines. Oumar is crippled with arthritis. And now the family is homeless, on top of moneyless and healthless. The villagers will pitch in to help him build; that's a given. But it's such a pathetic sight: this fragile, misplaced man who can barely tend his fields, digging for a home amid ashes and trash on the fringe of the village.

For a few months last year, Djeneba joined the frying brigade at the market. It spreads out just in front of the weighing station, a tightly fitted mosaic of women, fire rocks, spitting woks, and hot piles of fried everything. Djeneba sold fish. And I was proud of her. After AIDS had killed her son, Largaton, she had avoided social gatherings. Instead she'd chopped wood in the bush with her cowives or washed clothes at the pond. Frying fish at the market was her first step out. It lifted her spirits and seemed a sign of better health. I rarely buy fish at the market. I bought her fish every time.

Djeneba's frying days are over. She has returned to the court-yard. To a different mat than the one on which her cowives braid each other's hair. She needs more space; she needs to lie down sometimes. She is not ostracized, as far as I can tell, not mistreated. The other wives cook for her, draw water for her. Since no one has uttered the word "AIDS," they just treat her like a dying elder. Her dimples become wrinkles, her soft jaw turns square and sharp, dullness swallows the gleam in her eyes. Djeneba watches the mangos grow plump and her nephew-husband Adama le Gros grow rounder. And she just melts away.

Taking inventory of my papers one day, I come across a stack of photograph doubles I meant to give away. I bring them to the weighing station one day to show my health workers and our faithful groupies. There's one shot of the interior of a plane. "See? It's a little like a bus, with all the seats, only it's not as crowded. And there aren't any chickens." Adama picks this one out of the stack. He takes his glasses off and squints at it. He puts them back on and holds it at arm's length. His face is grave. Then he lets out a loud laugh, shaking his head in relief.

What's so funny? I ask. He points to the photograph. "That's not at all like a sorcerer's airplane. For a minute I thought you might have traveled in a sorcerer's airplane. But that can't be what they look like." "What exactly is a sorcerer's airplane, Adama?" I ask him.

The others are listening, but not intrigued—they must know about this aspect of aviation already. Adama says in a comfortable voice absolutely devoid of humor, "They can be as small as a cup. But a hundred people can fit in at a time. They can go all the way to Abidjan at night and be back in the village by morning. They travel almost instantly. That's how they harm their relatives who are outside of the village. They fly in and destroy their work or make them sick, and then they fly right out again and no one knows they were there."

I guess that if we can have broomsticks, they can have bottomless cups of witches. But it's curious that sorcery, entrenched so anciently, has adapted to modern times. Certainly they didn't ride in eight-ounce airplanes a century ago. Dramane flashes a conspiratorial smile at me. It's so easy to forget that he believes it too, that the conspiracy in his expression is not that we're thinking the same thing but that he knows what I'm thinking.

Oumar leans his elbows on the crossbar of my screen door. We've studied already and he's gone outside, but he doesn't quite want to leave yet. We are talking about school. He has finally gone back after three months of recuperation. He says he has a lot of catching up to do. He walks with a stick still, but his knee is gaining strength and flexibility.

Usually I eat dinner with the shortwave on, but tonight I've turned it off. The silence always zings when the radio goes off, as if it's rushing to applaud the end of the noise. The night is so black, all I see of Oumar is the white stripe up the side of his sweatpants and the glint of lamplight in his eyes, on his teeth.

Earlier this evening, I found his father holding his head on a mat in the courtyard from which he's been chased. "How many weeks till you go," he asked, "*ou bien* it's too many to count?" Oh yes, I can count, though I'm trying my damnedest not to. "*Même pas chekbul sin,*" I said, and they all gasped. Not even two. Oumar's five-year-old sister ran her arms around my legs and grabbed my hand on the other side. And I looked down at the little braids sprouting from her head and thought, Maybe just stay.

Tonight Oumar stands at my screen pensively. He's gone through his happy routine of ranking niceness: *Beel Cleenton est très gentille. Mon maman est très, très gentille. Guissongui est très, très, très gentille!* The room fills up with silence. There's nothing but peace and the lone knock of a pestle. Oumar coughs a little. In a voice as clear and beautiful as his eyes, as this night, he says, "*Est-ce que je peux venir avec toi, Guissongui?*" Can I come with you?

Oh, child, do you know what you're asking? If you left this peace, abandoned who you are, your dream would only become your sacrifice. So I put down my plate and crouch by the screen, and breathing deep so that my throat will not choke my words and my tears will stay put behind my eyes, I say, "You know, Oumar, you might not be so happy in the world I come from. It's big out there. It's hard. I wish you could come with me. I wish you could. But I don't even know where I'm going."

At exactly six-forty one night a week to the day before I leave, the lights of Nambonkaha blink on. There is a moment of stunned silence, and then a babbling din rises, accented by hoots and yells. Life as Nambonkaha knows it is revolutionized in the space of a second.

Outside my bedroom window, Moussa and his neighbors skip and dance in the pool of orange light. The lamppost is right above his hut. I can see everything down to the expression on Massieta's face as she bends over the fire. And maybe they can see me watching them from inside. On my first night in this house, I sat on this floor while a wedding buzzed outside and shadows of heads sauntered across my wall, thrown there by generator-powered lights. Tonight, the light floods my room again, falls in slats on the opposite wall, dyes everything orange. You can't turn it off. Ever.

We've been stripped naked by streetlights. The electric company hasn't spared us a shred of decency. They've crammed in as many lampposts as possible and cut out many of the interfering trees that could have given us the respite of shadow. They've elbowed out the dark: each circle of light bleeds into the next. The whole village glows. Night and day become indistinguishable. I knew I would rue this day, and only now do I know why.

Darkness was delicious. We survived in little islands of light defined by our flame. My house was a spot of radiance in the night. Abi's harmattan fire was a glittering harbor. To venture from your own island to another, you had to cut through a sea of black, slashing your way with a flashlight or trusting your feet. It made every visit, every encounter an event. You speak, you eat together, and then you get swallowed up into the night again. It was cozy, intimate. At home, with the muffled comfort of darkness against my windows, my doorway, there was a precious sense of community. The night was silent; the village asleep. You could see nobody, but you knew they were all there.

And moonlight—moonlight was joy gone silver. Moonlight was children dancing in bare feet, songs lilting on the air, laughter deep into the night. Moonlight made infinity smaller; it made the sky personal. It made nature safe and graspable.

This night there is no mystery, no modesty, no privacy. No need for a flashlight. Nambonkaha glares at the night, a little rectangle of manufactured light in the rolling dark savanna. The stars are switched off; the moon is irrelevant. The night has no fringes: dusk is as orange as midnight. That snooping streetlamp enters my room more than the sun does, even at three in the morning. We might as well just have day the whole time. I have to close the metal shutters to pretend it's night. I never close the shutters. It means shutting out the morning, the *tok tok*, the village.

For now it's just streetlights. It will take months for specific courtyards to get wired. But as electricity expands in Nambonkaha, it will carve lines between those who can exploit it and those who can't. I don't imagine the village will cleave along class divisions. Yet certain families will get televisions, and probably the same ones will get refrigerators and fans, and poverty, which everyone till now seemed to share benevolently, will become more obvious. Maybe Moussa and Sita will grow up addicted to the latest soap opera from South America, and maybe the roads of the village will be scattered with plastic bags from chilled bisap and yogurt. Electricity brings a happy village that much closer to the estrangement of tradition and modernity that perplexes the rest of the country.

Needless to say, the villagers are ecstatic. Kids stand under the lamps at dusk, as if they're waiting for a bus. The littler ones fall asleep in the dust, but the others play and dance, glancing up. When the magic hits, at six-forty on the dot, they stamp and cheer and kick their siblings awake so they don't miss out. It's easier to sweep the courtyard at night with the lights on, easier to wash the dishes. Dramane raves that he can grade papers until late. Abi doesn't mind that night in her courtyard now includes the maternity clinic, the dispensary, and a few neighboring court-yards. Américain struts around, saying, "*Vraiment,* this is going to animate this village." I don't say anything because I feel so selfish.

But me, I miss the stars.

Little fingers twist my hair; small black hands splay on my palms. We are huddled, me and my kids—on chairs, stools, the ground—in blessed leafy shadow amid patches of streetlight on my stoop. Maimouna's dusty belly bumps and squishes against my knees. Oumar's little sister lays her head in my lap and beams up at me sideways. We've popped the last of the popcorn, eaten the remainder of my peanuts, ecstatically roasted marshmallows sent from home. I've handed out old T-shirts that will fall to their knees for years still. I've given them little photograph albums, pictures from an old calendar, deodorant tubes with the parts emptied out to use as piggy banks. I want to give them everything, since I can't give them me. Oumar and his sister will safeguard their spoils in a corner. Moussa's and Mandou's will doubtless lie tattered in the dust of their courtyard tomorrow. But something, I hope, will weather the years and stand for me when their memories grow dim.

It's late. Moussa is pulling mango boughs low till the darkness swallows up his head. Mandou sits on my stoop in a T-shirt he's cut into ribbons along the bottom. The dancing is over, the feasts have finished; the formalities will wait for tomorrow, when the pickup truck comes to take me down the road. We're just talking. It's late, but don't go. My life in Nambonkaha is drawing its last breath. Let's just keep talking.

Yesterday I was summoned to a long table set up outside

Sidibé's courtyard, and seated before a giant bowl of rice and a deep red well of eggplant sauce. Two dozen men and I stuffed ourselves and scooted back our chairs to relax. I was thinking that it was an awfully nice gesture to make a big feast for me, so I got up to thank Abi and Femme Claire for cooking. And then around the corner came the women with their heads piled high, and a couple of the men rummaged around in rice sacks, and all of a sudden everyone was heaping gifts in front of me, as if these two years' worth of market *cadeaux* and gift chickens hadn't been enough. They laid each one on the table solemnly, like an offering, till the surface was cluttered: calabashes, clay pots, traditional pagnes, a twig broom, a sauce stirrer, a winnowing basket, a cotton spinning stick. Kinafou, the president of the women, waved her hand over the table and said, "These are from the women, so you'll know that we remember you, and you can remember us. We want you to take our traditions back to America with you." Then the men stepped up to add to the pile: a teapot and shot glasses, woven blankets, a boubou, a tablecloth, a robe, a shirt (all woven locally), forty guinea fowl eggs to somehow consume in the next forty hours. I stood dumbfounded, breathless. As if I could pack away the village in my old mouse-eaten duffel bag and re-create my charmed life here back home. If only they could wrap up the *tok tok* of pestles, girls singing in the moonlight, Moussa humming balafon songs, their laughing eyes.

They shoved the table back, and the balafon band appeared around the corner. I had to laugh a little that it all happened on cue. *My* efforts at village choreography had always gotten bungled. There under the mango tree, the women pulled me out of my seat and clapped and sang, all folds of bright fabric and dazzling faces. One after another they grabbed my arms to hold them up, appearing before my eyes like a slide show, like a documentary of these two sweet years, the closing images as the credits roll. Kinafou, who slapped mosquitoes off me one long night while we waited for childbirth. Assiatou, who got up the courage to ask about birth control. Alimata, who made motherhood her best work. The imam's fifth wife, who never stopped laughing at me. Mariam, whose baby I helped deliver. Dramane, whom I believed in. Oumar's beautiful mother, who won respect in our contests, whose son I fed meat till his face grew round. Mendjeta, whose placenta I yanked out. My health workers, who strut through the village with words like "hygiene" and "contraception" flipping off their tongues. My Ya, my old shirtless neighbor who sang songs about the white girl who would bring her gifts. Angélique, who ran to get me first when her brother died. One after the other they stepped before me, held my hands high, and danced till I was dizzy and my eyelids burned. And the words that hummed in the back of my head were these: *Maybe I'll never do better than this. Maybe I'll never be this good again.*

Moussa bats at a hanging mango, and the shadow around us shivers. He says, "I'm okay, but I'm not okay." Last night he did laps outside the dancing circle, somehow never making it all the way around, just back and forth in front of me, tiny legs flailing differently than the others'. Sidibé laughed, "Where did he learn to dance like a Rastafarian?" as he threaded back through the dancers to pass me again. Moussa says tonight, "Do you know what my mom says? If it weren't for you she'd be dead. You saved my mother." "No, no, it's not like that," I say. "She wasn't as sick as she seemed." But he brushes away this part. I'm about to disappear, and he wants to believe the miracles.

I went to see Massieta today to count my chickens and remind her to start on the pill once this pregnancy is over. She stood outside her house with her hands limp at her sides and just kept saying, "Thank you, thank you, we have nothing to give." I said, "You gave me your sons, and that's all I wanted. They are many, but *pei chengué*, they are good." Maimouna's mother came by and stood by a tree. Her cheeks were shining. I said, "Are you all right, are you sick?" And Massieta snorted, "She's crying for you, Guissongui." They all say, *Yele sin, na tanri mon na mereban.* You can go for two years and then come back. *Mon na mereban.* You come back.

Last night I couldn't leave Sidibé's. We had tea, two rounds, then three, then four, as night fell around Nambonkaha's orange lights. Abi said, "You don't want to cook now, so just stay to eat." The president came by and the mayor and the school director and Ibrahim the teacher, and Abi unloaded bowls of rice and sauce onto the table. There was a chair for me, too, but I sat on the other side of the courtyard with Abi. She was leaving for Tiébro in the morning. We scrunched up rice with our hands, sitting low by the fire. She gave me greetings for my family—each member has passed through this courtyard and eaten at her table. She told me what she will do when I come back. I'll be collecting things for you, she said, all those things you can't take home this time. Like a really nice mortar and pestle. And a good stool. I'll collect them. And then she muttered, "A sister like you..." into the fire. "A sister like you..." And said nothing more.

They set up chairs in crescents around the middle of the village later on, and Sidibé and Siaka and I sat down on the edge of the dancing circle. Villagers melded into their places: mothers in the middle, girls in the outer ring, feet thumping, shoulders twisting, elbows pumping, between them young men and children spinning. And along the outer edge, just on one side, Moussa in his tiny 49ers sweatshirt dancing Rasta-style for me. My ASCs snaked through the circle in their uniforms, twisting, laughing, a conga line of blue-and-white lattice and grins. I stepped into the line behind Massieta, dancing with a baby on her back and a baby in her stomach. And I danced out the glee, danced out the sorrow, danced out the notion that this end is final, that this dance is the last, that the next ride over the nine hills from Nambonkaha does not turn back.

Femme Claire and Angélique come over after dinner tonight to give me giant calabashes—one for your mother, they say, presenting them with two hands as if the gourds were crystal vases, one for your father, one for your younger brother. The ASCs stop in for one last chat; my house is too crowded, so we move outside. I'm so tired, and I still need to pack all the things I want to do one last time into these few hours. Adama frowns at the ground and says, "So what are the differences between America and Africa?" Adama! All these hours together and you pick the last one! I don't want to talk about *there*, I want to talk about *here*. I flounder for a second and then something happens—I can feel myself retreating from the heart of village life to a more neutral spot. Something clicks—I'm one of a few who can tell them about America in words they'll understand; I'm one of a few who can explain them to America. From my perch on the cusp between cultures, I can really see quite far. I want to tell them everything suddenly, and there's not enough time. So I chatter answers to questions lobbed from all sides: You're sure they're not all white in America? Are there crazy people there too? What do you eat? What are weddings like? What kind of jobs do women have? What are your witches like? We've covered this ground already, but I don't care—let's just talk.

This morning, the whole school stood in a checkered arc before me. The director presented me with an honorary teacher certificate from the Education Ministry, and the CM2 kids sang *"Au Revoir, Cher Ami."* Dramane says tonight he hopes he never hears that song again. "That's when it hit me that you're really leaving. When they were singing that terrible song. It's the first time I really believed it." When the other ASCs have gone tonight, I give him my fancy flashlights and some books, as well as the rest of my paint, so that one day he can paint pictures in his house like I have.

Tonight Mandou says, "Thanks to you we have electricity, a maternity clinic, latrines at the school, a moulin—" "Wait!" I say. "I hardly brought all that." "I know," Mandou says, "but that's what they say." I wonder if we'll go down in each other's histories as only golden, romanticized legends: Guissongui who did everything. Nambonkaha that was my Shangri-la.

Mandou's brother Daouda, so long estranged from me, appeared in my courtyard two days ago with a basin on his head. He looked at the ground and didn't say much, then toppled fourteen giant mangos onto my stoop. Then he hunkered down next to his pile of apology and stayed near me for the rest of the afternoon. I have rice sacks and duffel bags ready to go, and one backpack filled with Daouda's regret mangos and a dozen of my forty guinea fowl eggs, boiled by Abi for the long ride south.

Moussa says, "Ach! We cry or we don't cry, but you're going to go anyway. *Il y a quoi dedans?*" Tough little Moussa cried himself to sleep leaning against my screen. Mandou shoves his hands in the pockets of his prized jeans. He says, "This is why we'll miss you, Guissongui: you came laughing." I tell him I couldn't have laughed so much if the village of Nambonkaha hadn't already been smiling at me. And I wonder if he knows he's a poet.

Tired now, but I don't want to sleep because it just means blowing out this last Nambonkaha night (quiet again despite the lights). I scribble away in my wooden armchair, electric orange bleeding in through the back window but my front room warm with lantern light. So tired, but there must be one last thing before I put down my pen, before I surrender this night. My life here is unfinished but all wrapped up. Why am I leaving? Why do you trade in happiness for uncertainty? What makes you give up a good thing? I have no answers except that there are so many paths that I haven't yet traveled. I'll just keep writing, past midnight, moving on one. My lamplight wavers. For two years it has lit my nights, lit my students crouched around their shivery rows of letters, lit dinner in pots on the stove, lit faces outside my screen. I lift my pen from the page. The fire sputters and stretches, searching for fresh wick. Then with a soft sigh, the flame goes out.

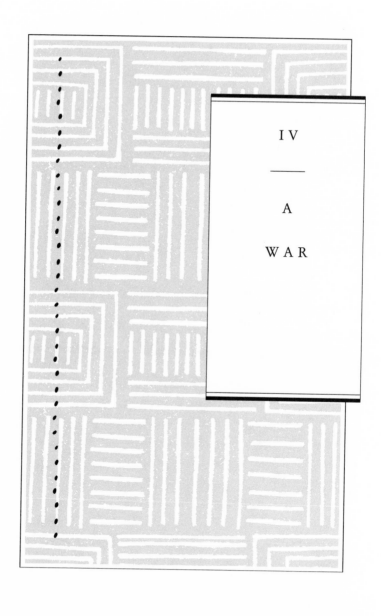

IV

—

A

WAR

August 22, 2001. Dramane writes, "I lost my grandmother, the one you knew well. She had sent greetings to you and thanked you for making me your friend. But Guiss! You should know that my failure at school was also caused by her, it turns out! She was a witch, just like her brother." He tells me that his engagement with his arranged wife, Senata, is over. "Finally my father understands that it was not a good union. We have made an agreement and now she lives with her family, and I live with mine—peacefully." He sends me a photograph of the tiny new daughter his wife delivered not long after I left, dressed in a cloud of pink gauze. He writes, "May God give you lots of money so that you can bring me for a visit to your country before I die." And he wishes me luck on my book about Nambonkaha.

Oumar sends me drawings—pages of them!—and writes, "Sorry I can't draw more for you." Mandou sends already faded and yellowed photos, their backs inky with phrases pressed in hard with a ballpoint pen.

Sidibé sends seven postcards at once, each written in the voice of someone in his courtyard. For Abi, he writes, "Pardon, Guiss—are you going to Ferké like *that*? Can you at least change those ugly pants?" For the older girls: "We've grown a bit now, and so Papa is afraid of boys. But we don't care!" He even writes one from my dog, Nick, who says, "I sleep outside now, and Abi only gives me food if everyone else has eaten. But Sidibé still thinks I'm great." And for himself, Sidibé writes, "I'm embarrassed by my country's politics, so I won't talk to you about that." His postcard shows Côte d'Ivoire's vast basilica, planted improbably amid lilies and palm trees. He says, "Look how my country is beautiful."

We had toasted a coup d'état on Christmas of 1999. There was hope in it—promise of change. But not long after I left Côte d'Ivoire, the old Africa took over, the Africa of tyrants and megalomania that Sidibé had felt sure was fading away. All the hackneyed tricks were played out. The constitution, predictably, was recrafted to exclude all credible opposition from the elections. The elections came months late, in October 2000, and were flawed from the start. Polling stations were set up erratically— mere dozens in the major cities but hundreds in the rural regions, where President Guéi's support was strongest. Less than 40 percent of the population voted, but despite the odds, the majority of those voters supported Laurent Gbagbo, a contender considered too minor to be a threat to Guéi. Guéi tried to strong-arm a victory. But crowds in Belgrade had just pushed out Milosevic, and Ivorians felt empowered to overthrow their dictator as well. Guéi was chased out, and Gbagbo—whom no one had ever thought of as a serious politician—came to power. He started out full of promise, as usual, but lapsed almost immediately into the policies of his predecessors, championing xenophobia and "Ivoirité," and squelching the opposition.

To his credit, he did launch a "Truth and Reconciliation" initiative, which invited all former rulers and opposition leaders to meet and hash out their differences peaceably. And he did not intervene when municipal elections delivered a majority of seats to members of the northern party, the RDR (Rassemblement des Républicains). Foreign-aid packages were approved for the first time since former President Bédié's corruption was unveiled. Arguably, things were looking better for Côte d'Ivoire. But there was ethnic tension broiling beneath the surface. On September 19, 2002, it erupted.

Several hundred mutinying soldiers from the north took over Bouaké and Korhogo. In the fracas, Guéi was assassinated by government troops. There were claims that he was at the helm of the rebellion, on his way to take over communication centers, at the time of his death. But he was killed in civilian clothes, along with his entire family.

The rebels were repulsed from Abidjan, and later from a western cacao-growing capital. But they held their ground in Bouaké, in spite of government attempts to retake the town. The fighting swept over the city and forced thousands to flee, including a group of American missionary kids at a boarding school. The city is now considered the rebel capital.

Perhaps "rebel" is a loaded word. It conjures up images of Sierra Leoneans hacking off limbs, Colombian guerrillas slaughtering whole villages, and Chechens taking hostages. At the beginning, Côte d'Ivoire's rebels numbered just a few hundred soldiers. As they passed through towns and villages in the disenfranchised north, however, popular support for them swelled. The north finally had a voice; the government was finally paying attention. Western newspapers called the rebels "disciplined" and "well organized." Peace Corps volunteers airlifted from the region called them "polite." The northern rebels have killed gendarmes, thieves, and soldiers, but civilians have been mostly left alone. A detail often overlooked in the Western media is that not all the rebels are Muslim: this is more a clash of north and south than a religious conflict.

The rebels are largely from the Dioula and Senoufo tribes—tribes known for diligence and tranquility. It is not surprising that the rest of the world has looked twice at this conflict; instead of condemning it outright as a challenge to an ostensibly democratic government, they have urged compromise and accommodation. This is a clear sign that there are legitimate grievances.

To a certain extent, the rebels' actions have had repercussions on their own people: the uprising has created a de facto siege of the north. Communication lines, cell-phone transmissions, provisions, and mail systems have been severed. The trucks that used to barrel by Nambonkaha to and from Abidjan can no longer get through Bouaké; trade and supplies are cut off.

"It was not good in the north," says an Ivorian friend. "But we did not ask for this." The sentiment is echoed across the north. We believe in the cause, but we did not need this.

In November 2002, rebel groups sprouted up in the west, employing Liberian refugees and mercenaries. Revolution is ripe for opportunists. These rebels are more volatile, less restrained. Skirmishes between the western rebels and government forces broke out, and civilian massacres occurred in several villages. There have been purges in Abidjan. Burkinabes, once more, have been chased out and murdered. Homes have been burned. Government-uniformed squadrons have become a gestapo of sorts, targeting opposition figures in Abidjan. A popular comedian was murdered in his home for his RDR sentiments. Benoît— the *grand type* who worked on Nambonkaha's maternity clinic and skimmed its funds—was assassinated in Abidjan.

On this side of the ocean, we want to believe that these events are no worse than the original Christmas coup, which looked awful in the Western media but was fairly tame on the ground. We hear only scraps of news of villages and friends, but travelers come through and Peace Corps volunteers come out, and everyone says, Yes, the situation is as bad as it looks. If not worse.

A man from the school director's village e-mails me from Abidjan that he still goes to the maquis to eat and drink. The stores are still open, mostly. There are parts of the city, he says, that you just stay out of. They are looking for war, he says. The southerners are looking for war.

However, another Ivorian friend, from the north, seems to want war as much as the southerners do. After peace deals have been signed and dismissed by the president in almost the same breath, he says, "That was the chance, and he lost it. It was a good deal. If we had been southerners, we never would have put up with so much mistreatment." He says, "Guissongui, you know this too." And I do. "Northerners are quick to accept their lot. If we had been southerners, we would have fought long ago. We are sick of this. We are ready to fight. Côte d'Ivoire is just like two different countries now." I tell him that war can't be the answer, that war just means another African disaster, but at the same time there are crowds seething in the south, burning French flags, labeling rebels "terrorists" because that word seems to speak the loudest. The northern rebels stand, unwilling to back down.

All of a sudden it's not so inconceivable that Côte d'Ivoire might become another Sierra Leone, another Congo. I'm reluctant even to put the possibilities to paper, for fear they might become realities—village superstitions seem to linger still. My boys who brought me mangoes and scratched earnest letters by lamplight might get sucked into the vortex of violence and turn into child guerrillas. What else is there for them to do? My well-intentioned women could lose their husbands, their sons, their brothers to war. Sidibé and the fonctionnaires could lose their savings, their livelihoods, the futures of their children. And those nine peaceful hills to Nambonkaha might become a conduit for armies. All of a sudden AIDS and sorcery become trifles. A greater evil has risen, one that can't be controlled or exorcised or protected against: man's own intolerance. It could set this country back a century.

For now though, Nambonkaha ticks on—may it always. These days it ticks like the chief's old cuckoo clock, disregarding the real passage of time and moving ever more sluggishly, as if it were slowly being strangled. Since the mail was cut off, I have heard news only from an American who passed through after the September uprising. Although fonctionnaires all over the country have fled their posts to return to their native villages, Nambonkaha's fonctionnaires, he said, have stayed. The school has closed because no one gets paid anymore, so the school director sits in his courtyard all day and drinks his wife's chapalo. The clinic is slowly running out of medicine, but Sidibé is still there, planning to treat people till all is gone. The pumps are all broken, but the youths are trying to raise funds to repair them. In the meantime, everyone drinks pond water. No one goes to Ferké much anymore. Maybe if the market were still thriving as it did they'd go, but there's not much money, and the trucks don't come, and a village witnessed the execution of a gendarme there anyway, so it just seems better to stay home. The American who passed through arrived on market day. The market was smaller, missing the merchants who used to bike in from elsewhere. But the old women were there, selling their tiny stacks of onions and hot peppers. The men fussed over broken moped parts and chewed kola nuts. And he said they were weighing babies still. The country crumbles, the modern infrastructure is whisked right out of this village, but they'll hold on to what they've got. My team is still there, Dramane no doubt hard at work, Américain in his valet outfit manning the scale, Bakary eyeing the women in the crowd, and a line of mothers snaking back from that meat-hook baby scale. It seems hopeful, optimistic—a challenge, for once, to so much fatalism. I cling to this. As the American left, Mandou, clowning Mandou, passed on a letter to me and some peanuts to go with it. His letter is dictated, dusty, confusing, misspelled. But it sounds just like him. It says, "Really Guiss, if you're in good health, could you at least tell us you're in good health? How are you going to get back to see us? You must do everything possible. *Je te salue beaucoup.*" And I have no choice—when I can, I will.

GLOSSARY

alloco   fried plantain dish

an y bara   "good work" in Dioula

an y che   "thank you" in Niarafolo and Dioula

attiéké   fermented manioc couscous

badjan   bush taxi with twenty-two seats and empty windows

balafon   xylophone-like instrument made of gourds and planks of wood

bisap   sweetened, cold hibiscus tea

bouffer   steal, embezzle

boutique   small general store characterized by chicken wire separating buyer from merchandise

bouton   button, commonly used for rashes and spots

brousse   bush, wilderness

cadeau   gift

cadre   educated urban professional

campement   outlying farming settlement

carnet   health record book

chapalo   traditional millet beer

collège   equivalent of junior high

complet   traditional West African dress, made of three tailored pagnes

deh   exclamation used for emphasis in Dioula and Niarafolo, as both languages are tonal

Dioula   ethnicity that populates northern Côte d'Ivoire; second most widely spoken language in the country after French

folie   craziness

fonctionnaire   civil servant, i.e. nurse, teacher, agriculturalist

fou   crazy person, or to be crazy

foutou   common dish made of mashed roots, usually manioc, plantains, or African yams

grand type   bigwig, important figure

harmattan   dry season from November to March in which Saharan dust blows down into the savanna

jeune   youth; young

kabato   corn pap made by pounding kernels into flour and boiling until solid; staple in north Côte d'Ivoire

maquis   outdoor bar/restaurant, usually a shack with a few tables set up along a street where only one or two dishes are served.

maternité   maternity clinic

moulin   mill

mouso   woman

Nafuochengué   market day in Nambonkaha

Niarafolo   ethnic group of about 50,000 in northern Côte d'Ivoire; their language

pagne   two meters of printed fabric; a sarong

palabre   fight, argument

patron   boss

Peul/Fulani   nomadic tribe that populates the Sahel, and trickles into northern Côte d'Ivoire

poro   sacred forest where animist initiations take place

préfet   governor

sapé   well dressed, stylish

sans façon   without pretense, humble

tantie   "auntie," usually a heavy, loud, matronly married woman

toubabou   white person, in Dioula

vieille   old woman

vieux   old man

villageois   villager; also used as an adjective to mean redneck

ACKNOWLEDGMENTS

The patriarch of Nambonkaha slept in the bush on my last night so he could ask the ancestors to guarantee my good fortune. But my good fortune came earlier—and more arbitrarily—when I was matched with Nambonkaha. The stories of the village are derived from my journals and my letters home, and almost all of the dialogue is true to what was spoken. Political volatility has forced me to change the names of several key players and places in this book, but those who took me in know who they are. I have to thank them first: my friends and family in the village of Nambonkaha, who challenged me, believed in me, angered me, taught me, moved me. They put this story into my fingertips, and remembering them brought it galloping out. *Koro tchelé weh shön.*

There are several people whose generosity has been humbling and whose enthusiasm has been unflinching throughout the creation of this book. I would like to thank Ken and Vickie Wilson, for three pristine months in the Montana wilderness that softened my culture shock and allowed me the solitude to turn these two years into words. To Janet Fesler, who offered me an apartment and an article that kept me going; thank you for the respite I needed to refocus. Kate Simpson and Stuart Grossman convinced me that I could write in the first place and provided me with perspicacious advice along the way. To my brother, Matt—you made them dance! Thank you for thoughtful critiques and for being made of only good stuff.

To Peter Hessler, thank you for the insight, the encouragement, and, of course, the coattails. My agent, William Clark, took up this manuscript with welcome zeal and certainty, and George Hodgman, my editor at Holt, worked tirelessly to make it sing. Your candor and collaboration are much appreciated.

To the Peace Corps volunteers of Côte d'Ivoire who crossed my path from 1998 to 2000: there is nothing like it, is there? You are a tall Bock at Pierre's after transport. You are sleep on the hostel porch when the birds start up at dawn. You are peace, creativity, dedication, hope—and I am a better person for you. Thanks especially to Clare Bastable, Brett Gleitsman, Mirabai Rose, Jordan Dunyasha, John Drace, Becca Ashley, Phil Shen, Taylor Kay, Michele Daly, Garrett Watkins, Dale Miller, Mark Shahinian, Betsy Arner and Jason Knoch.

And finally, I am forever indebted to my parents, Dick and Sibyl Erdman, who threw open the doors to the whole world, guided me for a ways, and then stood back to let me find my footing myself. Thank you for your edits, for your dedication, for your wisdom, for your faith in me, and for the keen example you've set experiencing the world yourselves: with passion, humility, and grace. *Mashallah!*

ABOUT THE AUTHOR

Sarah Erdman, a graduate of Middlebury College in Vermont, still works for the Peace Corps in Washington, D.C. The daughter of parents who have spent their careers in the Foreign Service, she has lived in eight countries. *Nine Hills to Nambonkaha* is her first book.